THEATRE
in Britain

THEATRE in Britain
A Playgoer's Guide

PETER ROBERTS
With Research by
ANNE TAYLER

Pitman Publishing

First published 1973

SIR ISAAC PITMAN AND SONS LTD
Pitman House, Parker Street, Kingsway, London WC2B 5PB
PO Box 46038, Portal Street, Nairobi, Kenya

SIR ISAAC PITMAN (AUST.) PTY LTD
Pitman House, 158 Bouverie Street, Carlton, Victoria 3053, Australia

PITMAN PUBLISHING CORPORATION
6 East 43rd Street, New York, NY 10017, USA

SIR ISAAC PITMAN (CANADA) LTD
495 Wellington Street West, Toronto 135, Canada

THE COPP CLARK PUBLISHING COMPANY
517 Wellington Street West, Toronto 135, Canada

ISBN: 0 273 00221 X

Text set in IBM Universe by Print Origination, Bootle, Lancs,
printed by photolighography, and bound in Great Britian
by Unwin Brothers Limited, The Gresham Press, Old
Woking, Surrey.
G3536: 13

Contents

Introduction

And what is worth seeing in the theatre right now?' This is the sort of question to which a reviewer like myself has long been supposed capable of giving an instant reply. But in the ten years that I edited the monthly theatre magazine, **Plays and Players**, the shortlists required seemed increasingly harder to prepare. For what is deemed worth seeing' must ultimately depend on the tastes and judgment of the questioner—invariably somebody just encountered. Moreover it is rare for a theatre to offer entertainment generally thought 'worth seeing' in all departments. A mediocre play or musical may be redeemed by a brilliant central performance. Unremarkable acting may be considered unimportant in the light of the originality of the direction and design of a production. It depends on your point of view.

Fortunately, in a book too much time elapses between its completion and its publication for lists of 'Best Shows in Britain' to be considered. Even so, the notes in the twelve chapters that follow have been drawn up in the hope of providing guidelines—for the visitor to Britain in particular. Such guidelines, though, have been assembled so that the reader may have rapid access to the background to what the British theatre has to offer. And by glancing at this background, it is hoped that the reader may make his way more quickly to what **he** thinks he should see rather than what I judge as indispensable.

The formation of my own tastes and judgment must owe something to some 2,000 productions I saw in the course of preparing a decade's **Plays and Players**. The notes here could not have been prepared without that experience nor indeed without the insights provided by contributors to the magazine, whether as reviewers or interviewers. I am as grateful to them as I am to those who talked to me specifically in connection with writing **Theatre in Britain**.

The reference sections of this book, compiled by Anne Tayler, are of course concerned with the practicalities of visiting the theatre and its offshoots. They are there to help in the business of booking, travelling to a theatre and making the most of its facilities. If all three parts of **Theatre in Britain** combine to make the book's title something to be remembered with pleasure, what more can we ask?

April 1973

Peter Roberts

Acknowledgements

Grateful acknowledgement is made to all those who kindly supplied photographs for this book, and in particular to the following photographers:
Alex Agor (p. 103), Godfrey Argent (p. 61), Anthony Buckley (p. 21), John Bulmer (p. 39), Nobby Clark (pp. 93, 108), Anthony Crickmay (pp. 52, 58), Zoe Dominic (pp. 27, 70), David Farrell (p. 47), John Haynes (p. 29), Allan Hurst (p. 81), Angus McBean (p. 49), Michael Peto (p. 34), Stuart Robinson (p. 76), David Sim (p. 37), Ian Stone (p. 82) and John Timbers (pp. 15, 17).

The co-operation of the Information Officers of the Arts Council of Great Britain as well as that of theatre directors, managers and press officers of playhouses throughout the country is gratefully acknowledged. So also is advice and encouragement given by Michael Anderson, Peter Ansorge, Laurie Blackmore, Michael Croft, Denny Dayviss, Noel Goodwin, Frank Granville Barker, Frances Kelly, Chris Prins and Peter Saunders. Thanks are due also to the many specialist theatre writers consulted in the course of research, in particular to articles by Michael Billington, John Russell Taylor and Robert Waterhouse.

For Nuria and Armando

Part 1

Theatre in Britain

PANORAMA

Why Theatre in Britain? That is a most appropriate question to cast in the direction of a book such as this, intended especially for those wishing to explore, or perhaps re-explore, the English theatre and its heritage.

At the beginning of the 1970s no less well-informed a body than the British Travel Authority let it be known that two million of the visitors that came to Great Britain each year were in fact theatregoers. And, in 1972, Mr Donald Albery—the only British theatre manager to belong to a family having a theatre named after it—revealed that eighty per cent of the public attending his productions in late summer were from overseas. So what is it about British theatre that leads to increasing confidence in its ability to appeal both to a home-grown public and to one from far beyond its shores?

Twenty Questions is a parlour game aimed at arriving by a process of elimination at the truth in a given person's mind. Let us see if, by posing Ten Questions, we may come across valid reasons for British theatre's exercising a world-wide appeal. The first and basic question must of course be—**how much live theatre is in fact available**? Well, in round figures, the national dailies list some 40 mainstream theatres in central London alone. And that is without taking into account those theatres that operate at basement or rooftop level with experimental work and are hence dubbed 'fringe'. Nor does it take into account those more traditional playhouses which are beyond the half mile of Shaftesbury Avenue and hence do not have bestowed upon them those magic words 'West End'.

Out of London there are a further three major Festival Theatres and some 50 repertory companies. Some of the latter occasionally premiere new work but most of them offer the visitor an opportunity of seeing a mixture of recent new writing and revivals from Britain's treasure-trove of classical drama.

Many of these regional theatres—most of which now operate with a new production running for a period of three weeks—close for a summer period of about two months. But the mildness of the English climate, for all that it is an international joke, at least means that London theatres can remain open for all twelve months of the year. No other European capital has so much theatre to offer throughout the year.

The only truly seasonal theatres are in fact the festival theatres, which are the special preserve of the holidaymaker. Thus the visitor who wishes to go beyond London's cornucopia has a choice of the Royal Shakespeare Company's Shakespeare season at Stratford-upon-Avon from April to December, the Chichester Festival Theatre's four star-studded productions staged between May and September and the Pitlochry Festival Theatre's April to September season where eight productions are on view in the heart of the Scottish countryside. One could add other minor festival celebrations but it is probably more important now to pass on to Question Number Two.

How accessible are the offerings of so many theatres? If this question is first considered from a linguistic point of view it gives a very relevant pointer to British theatre's appeal overseas: anybody coming from Australasia, North America and the many other countries formerly comprising part of the British Empire will at least have no need of a simultaneous translation service. And the fact that English is becoming increasingly an international language, not only well spoken in places like Scandinavia but also more and more studied by the Latin nations (not to mention the developing nations), does mean that the visitor has more or less an equal chance with the locals to take on even the more obscure texts of the country's most experimental writers. Answered geographically, another pointer to overseas popularity is arrived at. The concentration of West End theatres in Shaftesbury Avenue and its immediate environs is certainly a useful time-saver for the visitor in a central London hotel on a rushed stay. And the fact that Britain as a whole is such a tiny country for anybody calling in from Australia, America and Canada must make the festival and regional theatres outside London seem easy to reach. It helps here to find that Britain has retained a good public transport system in the age of the private car.

Given the quantity and accessibility of Britain's theatres, question number three must be—**how many actually offer the famous works that are studied as part of the country's dramatic literature?**

Apart from the Medieval Mystery Plays (such as the York Cycle, periodically revived in that ancient city) very little of pre-Shakespearean dramatic literature can be seen in performance. Standard examination texts—usually studied under a heading like 'Popular Beginnings'—still have to find a company and a public to make them readily available in performances other than those given on the BBC's Radio Three. Thus **Gammer Gurton's Needle** (printed in 1575), **Ralph Roister Doister** (printed 1556) and **Gorboduc**, Thomas Norton and Thomas Sackville's tragedy, written in 1562, are unlikely to be in repertoire for the benefit of the more academic theatregoer.

With the advent of Shakespeare (whose dates, incidentally, are 1564-1616) things immediately begin to pick up, with his plays comprising the repertoire of the Royal Shakespeare Company at Stratford and one or two of them naturally finding their way into that of the National Theatre in London. Both companies also revive Shakespeare's contemporaries and immediate successors—as do occasionally London's Mermaid and Royal Court theatres. It would be an uncharacteristically barren year if one of these companies did not include a production from the works of Christopher Marlowe (1564—1593), Ben Jonson (1572—1637), John Webster (died 1630) or Cyril Tourneur (1575—1626).

As late as the 1960s, Restoration Comedy of Manners, next step in the evolution of English dramatic literature, was still sufficiently popular for it to be presented in the West End on a commercial basis. Now it is more likely to be available in the subsidised sector. So if the visitor hopes to see an English production of one of the great comedies of Sir George Etherege (1597—1651), William Wycherley (1640—1716) and, most important of all, William Congreve (1670—1729) he would be well advised to look first at the programmes of the Royal Shakespeare Company's London home at the Aldwych, or at the National Theatre's across the river.

There is an excellent chance of a revival of Restoration comedy, too, in a festival theatre like that of Chichester. The same may be said of the next, less lewd generation of comedy writers like Richard Brinsley Sheridan (1751 – 1816) and Oliver Goldsmith (1728 – 1774), who kept the British public amused with plays like **The Rivals** and **She Stoops to Conquer** before it became engulfed in bourgeois gentility and sentimentality.

Not even many academic theatregoers will regret the absence of revivals of Victorian melodrama or the plays of lachrymose sentimentality which belonged to the same period. Instead they may hope to catch some of the 'new' writers who rescued British drama from its nineteenth century low-ebb—writers like Bernard Shaw (1856 – 1950) and John Galsworthy (1867 – 1933). Though the Victorian dramatist, Sir Arthur Wing Pinero (1855 – 1934), with **The Second Mrs Tanqueray** (1893), did essay the 'serious' drama Shaw and Galsworthy were to write in earnest, the result was rather stilted and the best hope as far as Pinero is concerned is that one of his early farces—like **The Magistrate** (1885)—will be revived.

In the postwar theatre both Shaw and Galsworthy have been revived commercially in the West End, the former quite spectacularly at the beginning of the 1960s with a rash of star-studded productions. But a West End revival of Galsworthy's **Justice** (St Martin's 1968) suggested that his particular vein of humanitarian social justice pieces now needs the attention and trimming of a good literary manager in a subsidised theatre. And though even the minor Shaw of **Captain Brassbound's Conversion** managed to achieve a run in the large Cambridge Theatre in 1971 with Ingrid Bergman as its star box-office attraction, the more considered revivals of GBS have been at subsidised theatres like the Royal Court and the National. Of this period of the drama only Oscar Wilde (1856 – 1900) seems to respond unwaveringly to star productions as the 1968 Haymarket revival of **The Importance of Being Earnest** testified. Even the lesser comedies—lesser because they are tinged by both Victorian sentiment and melodrama—have thrived on star performances in spectacular settings.

The same can be said of the plays of Somerset Maugham (1874 – 1965) Frederick Lonsdale (1881 – 1954) and of course Noël Coward (1899 – 1973).

Astonishingly enough that other great—but different—Irish dramatist Sean O'Casey (1880 – 1964) continues to be disgracefully neglected in the commercial theatre. The visitor will indeed be fortunate if he even catches a subsidised theatre revival of one of O'Casey's great Dublin tenement plays, **The Shadow of a Gunman** (1922), **Juno and the Paycock** (1924) and **The Plough and the Stars** (1926).

Question four must inevitably take in the new drama. **Given the widespread excitement accorded the plays written in the wake of John Osborne's** Look Back in Anger **in 1956, are not the West End theatre lists crammed with the latest work of those writers said to have heralded Britain's theatre renaissance?**

It is true that the first generation of these writers—John Arden, John Osborne, Harold Pinter and Arnold Wesker—have continued to produce

Sarah Miles as Mary, Queen of Scots in Robert Bolt's *Vivat! Vivat Regina!*—a Chichester production which transferred to London

new work regularly. It is also true that the first generation has been followed by a second—Christopher Hampton, David Mercer, Peter Nichols, David Storey, Tom Stoppard and E A Whitehead. It is also true that the visitor is extremely unlikely to see more than one or two works derived from both generations of new writers in the West End at any one time.

Those from outside London who have read popular studies of these new dramatists, or seen their work in translation and generally rejoiced from afar at their arrival will naturally be amazed at the absence from Shaftesbury Avenue of these new voices. They will perhaps also begin to wonder if the new movement has not perhaps been critically oversold.

The truth is that with rare exceptions—like Harold Pinter's **The Caretaker** and Peter Nichols' **Forget-Me-Not Lane,** to take one example from each generation—the plays that have been avidly snapped up for presentation in translation all over Europe have in fact had very limited showings in Britain. Many have had, at best, three weeks at a small theatre like the Royal Court or else have played in repertoire at the Aldwych or Old Vic theatres—sometimes only for the minimum number of performances to enable the management presenting them to participate in the subsequent film rights. Although regional revivals of their works are useful, not surprisingly the new dramatists in Britain are very dependent on their overseas royalties, particularly those from Germany. The moral, for the visitor, is that they should not believe some of the taller stories of the new writers having destroyed the conventional theatre of entertainment in the West End. The truth is that though plays by Osborne, Mercer, Nichols and Hampton sometimes achieve very respectable runs in Shaftesbury Avenue, the older sort of non-controversial comedies and farces are still doing very nicely indeed.

Which brings us to the fifth question—posed on behalf of the great majority of visitors who are not here on a crash course of English dramatic literature (whether it be ancient or modern) but are simply looking forward to an agreeable evening out. **How good and how varied is the theatrical entertainment offered with no pretensions to great literature or art?**

The simple variety in the size of London playhouses (with Drury Lane seating 2,283 and the neighbouring Fortune a mere 424) in itself ensures an essential element of variety in the attractions on view. Thus at the big theatres of the Drury Lane size you will naturally look for spectacular musicals. And it will be surprising if there are not at least eight to choose from. Of the eight, six will probably be London productions of Broadway musicals which American visitors may think worth seeing a little more cheaply whilst they are in Britain. British musicals do not have the history of slick professionalism that distinguishes the American, so that although British plays now make up a regular and sizeable contribution to Broadway's season this cultural export does not extend to the musical field. Still, certain long-running home-grown musicals like **Canterbury Tales** have offered a musical's eye view of old, merry, lewd England that evidently has visitor-appeal.

Eileen Atkins as Elizabeth I in *Vivat! Vivat Regina!*, a performance that made her name with the general theatre-going public

18 Panorama

The smallest of the London theatres usually offer a sample of a much-loved genre, the thriller. Though there are rarely more than three of these available at any given time, the fact that Agatha Christie's **The Mousetrap** has survived 21 years demonstrates the loyalty of addicts to this particular English recipe for suspense. Its traditional country-house setting has been neatly parodied by Anthony Shaffer in **Sleuth**, which managed to dovetail the essential ingenuity of plot-twisting with a parody of the way such matters have to be contrived for the whodunit.

British sex farces also lack something of the slickness achieved by the best American practitioners like Neil Simon. That probably accounts for the fact that a company like Brian Rix's, which has been operating in theatres close to Trafalgar Square since 1950, has never surfaced in New York. Still the visitor who wants to catch something of the healthy English vulgarity that once characterised its buoyant music hall in the Victorian and Edwardian epochs can catch something of it in the blunt double-entendres of Brian Rix or similar farces.

The smaller theatres also used to house intimate revue until what must surely have been the most intelligent of them, **Beyond the Fringe**, at the Fortune from 1961, killed off the genre. It made the older sort of intimate revue, which satirised society people rather than society as a whole, seem curiously old-fashioned. Attempts to revive revue by hitching it to mime (**Chaganog**, Vaudeville 1964) or drag (**Hulla Baloo**, Criterion 1972) did not prove successful. It has been left to two members of the **Beyond the Fringe** team, Peter Cook and Dudley Moore in **Behind the Fridge** (Cambridge 1972) to keep revue from expiring altogether. In so large a theatre (seating capacity 1,275) they showed that you can successfully plant a two-man show in anything but intimate surroundings so long as the two and their material have a good enough following. The light entertainment field is completed on the one hand by variety shows, almost always at the Palladium Theatre (seating capacity 2,317) and, on the other by the nude shows like **The Dirtiest Show in Town** and **Oh ! Calcutta !**. The Palladium usually offers a summer and a winter show headed by pop singers at the top of the hit parade, with a programme leaded out with fairly crude comedy routines and the obligatory conjuror. It is all a very long way indeed from the British music-hall which can still be seen intact at the tiny Players Theatre between Charing Cross and the Thames Embankment.

Finally the entertainment picture is completed by costume dramas, especially royal ones like **Vivat ! Vivat Regina !** and **Crown Matrimonial** which have enabled actresses of the calibre of Eileen Atkins in the former and Wendy Hiller in the latter to give the sort of award-winning performances that collectors of great acting will not want to miss.

The last two paragraphs plunge us into the sixth question, which concerns censorship and the classification of entertainment that might ensure one's elderly aunt not booking for a traditional evening of nostalgic costume drama and finding herself confronted with the nude revue's assorted genitalia and friendly winks. **What, in fact, is the current situation with regard to censorship in the British theatre?**

The absence of theatre censorship is probably an important factor in explaining British theatre's popularity with overseas visitors, particularly those coming from countries that take a more conservative view of public discussion of sex and politics. Not that this has been the case

Oh! Calcutta! transferred from the Round House to the Royalty Theatre after the disappearance of censorship in Britain

here for long. An exceedingly antiquated form of theatre censorship, administered by a member of the Royal Household, the Lord Chamberlain, was abolished as late as 1968. Edward Bond, whose plays **Saved** (1965) and **Early Morning** (1968) the Lord Chamberlain attempted, respectively, to cut strenuously and ban outright, has the distinction of being the last of the post-war dramatists whose struggles with His Lordship's office became a cause célèbre and certainly hastened his belated withdrawal from the theatrical scene.

Theatre managements once took the view that they were glad to put up with the Lord Chamberlain because once he had licensed a play it could be performed anywhere in Great Britain without coming up against the strictures of pettifogging local Watch Committees. However, his departure has not in fact led to widespread local authority censorship. So in Britain you can see the Establishment from the Queen and the Prime Minister downwards satirised on stage live without the entire constitutional democracy to which they belong collapsing in consequence. Similarly, adults may decide for themselves whether nude shows like Paul Raymond's **Pyjama Tops** are in fact as feeble as many intelligent people think them to be. And dramatists in the 1970s may write compassionately about themes like homosexuality which, even in the early postwar theatre, had to be referred to with an almost crossword puzzle-like obliquity.

There is no classification of theatre entertainment like the X, AA and U system applied to films in Britain but advice from ticket agencies, theatre reviews, front-of-house pictures, not to mention the titles of shows themselves, ensure that the right horses find themselves on the right courses.

A more practical question now, as the seventh. **How conveniently does theatregoing fit into the general timetable of London life?** Not altogether satisfactorily, must be the answer from the visitor's point of view, since theatre timetables have to be geared to the fact that public transport to all intents and purposes seizes up by 11.30 pm. Early starts—7.30 and 8 pm for most entertainments—are the order of the day, with London Transport in 1972 introducing the Star Bus, hopefully rounding up theatregoers and dropping them off at the big car parks and the main train terminuses. It was a welcome streamlining approach. But the real answer would seem to lie in better general late-night and indeed all-night bus, underground and railway services. Probably many theatregoers who have had to become clock-watchers at uncut versions of **Hamlet** would welcome paying a little extra to be able to get home later.

How comfortable and well run are London theatres? Another practical enquiry to make an eighth question.

Most London theatres are old buildings with things like pillars that give rise to unsatisfactory sight lines from a (very limited) number of seats. But the fact that the buildings are old and long since paid for is a major influence in keeping London theatre prices down. Moreover they are, in general, extremely well run. By European standards performances start promptly and (Europeans please note!) people like usherettes do not have to be tipped. Programmes are not free but the National and Royal Shakespeare Company make no charge for cast lists. It's advisable if possible to place orders for interval drinks **before**

Crown Matrimonial put members of the British Royal Family on stage. Wendy Hiller as Queen Mary with Andrew Ray as the Duke of York

the performance begins. The introduction of air-conditioning and the do-it-yourself Paraloks for leaving coats help to give the older buildings a combination of historic charm and some twentieth century efficiency.

But you have to go to the modern regional and festival theatres for the convenient all-in-one package of adjoining car park, theatre restaurant, coffee bars and theatre bookstall. However the new New London Theatre (opened January 1973) offers Londoners such a deal as no doubt will the National Theatre when it opens on the South Bank in 1975 and the RSC's Barbican two years later. Meantime the Mermaid (opened 1959) with its restaurant, bars and spacious art-gallery foyer with bookstall is probably the most welcoming of London's theatres.

How expensive is theatregoing in London and what means are there of cutting down on costs whilst still having a reasonable seat? The reference section of this book does not give the price charged at each individual theatre because with the sharp increase in prices generally and the effect of Value Added Tax (introduced in 1973) in particular, the figures would almost certainly be out of date by the time the book is in the reader's hands. For the record, however, here are the range of charges for a London musical, a West End comedy and a revue in January 1973. At the Theatre Royal, Drury Lane, for the musical version of **Gone with the Wind**, bookable charges were, at the top end, £2.50 in the stalls and dress circle and, at the other, £1.80 in the upper circle. At the Savoy, where you could see Ralph Richardson and Celia Johnson in **Lloyd George Knew My Father** the range was £2.00 in the stalls and dress circle to 70 pence in the back of the upper circle. For the thriller, **Suddenly at Home** the range at the Fortune Theatre was £2.00 for stalls and dress circle seats to 70 pence for upper circle seats.

Telephoning theatre box-offices can be a time-consuming business and personal booking at them even more so. In such cases, the visitor may find it well worth using one of the theatre agencies listed in the reference section of this book which, at the beginning of 1973, were charging 45p. for their services on the upper range of theatre tickets.

If, on the other hand, saving a little money is of prime importance, it is worth bearing in mind that most theatres offer a mid-week matinee and an early performance on a Saturday at reduced prices. Most theatres offer reduced prices for party bookings, the best example of this being the National Theatre's reducing seats priced at £2.10 to £1.25 for parties of 20 or more.

The final, tenth question must concern the breakaway theatres of the lunch-time circuit. **How much is their members-only policy a bar to the visitor?** In many cases membership is effected immediately (for about 25 pence), at worst it takes a day. Criticism has been made of these fringe groups in that they have not so far had West End transfers, nor thrown up new writers and artists who have since been taken up by the general public at large. This sort of thinking is to make the fringe simply an adjunct to the commercial theatre, an alternative theatre that gets eaten up by the monster it is attempting to break away from. The way in which off-Broadway has become part of the Broadway scene should point a lesson. So should the way in which Joan Littlewood found she had to quit her Theatre Workshop in the mid-1960s because the West End was feeding off her Stratford East productions, with the result that it was certainly not the people's theatre Miss Littlewood intended. The English motto 'if you can't beat 'em, join 'em' is not one to be taken to heart in this particular instance.

NEW WRITING

Few titles have proved so potentially misleading as the one given to a play premiered by the English Stage Company at the Royal Court Theatre in London on May 8, 1956. If John Osborne's **Look Back In Anger** had not become such a watershed in English dramatic writing then the implications of its name would no doubt be unimportant. But so many new writers have been given a hearing in the wake of its success that, nearly twenty years later, it is still credited with having caused a revolution and given birth to something called The New Drama.

What is misleading about combinations of words like 'Anger', 'Revolution' and 'New Drama' is that it suggests a coherent group of embattled writers using the British stage as a rallying ground for an assault on all that is wrong with life in the second half of the twentieth century. Visitors to Britain who see revivals of the early plays of the New Drama (not to mention premieres of its latest manifestations) ought perhaps first to ask themselves three questions. To begin with, is not 'despair' rather than 'anger' the keynote to the new writing? Secondly, if it is true that this has in fact brought about a revolution, is not such a revolution within rather than outside the theatre? And, thirdly, is not the single heading 'New Drama' open to misinterpretation in as far as it seeks to bestow the status of a single movement to a number of dramatists who actually have little or nothing in common, either from the point of view of technique or from that of thematic content?

John Osborne (born 1929) certainly gave Jimmy Porter, the lead role in **Look Back in Anger**, a monopolistic gift for invective that helped to silence his two sexual partners in the play. And it is true that in his subsequent major plays it has become characteristic of Osborne's theatre for there to be a dominant central role running verbal circles round a subjugated entourage. No doubt that helps to explain why Osborne has been able to attract star actors for his plays—Laurence Olivier for **The Entertainer** (1957), Albert Finney for **Luther** (1961), Nicol Williamson for **Inadmissible Evidence** (1964), Maximilian Schell for **A Patriot for Me** (1965), Paul Scofield for **The Hotel In Amsterdam** (1968) and Ralph Richardson for **West of Suez** (1971). But, in retrospect, does not the journalistic tag, Angry Young Man, now look a little threadbare of meaning—even when modified to Angry Middle-Aged or Angry Old Man? For there is more despair than anger in Jimmy Porter's most celebrated remark, that there aren't any good brave causes left to fight for. And even more devoid of hope is the comment of the ageing Archie Rice in **The Entertainer** that, although he is the worst and unfunniest of music-hall comedians in the world, it does not matter because he's dead behind the eyes—as dead as his inert, shoddy audience.

So although Osborne has attempted to borrow something of the technique of Brecht's theatre—in **The Entertainer** especially—it would be an unwise student of the drama who tried to write up the anger in his writing as the battle-cry of a political activist. The thesis-writer, it seems, would be better advised to examine his plays for what they offer as a chronicle of the disintegration of British society following the breakup of its Empire and the breakdown of its acutely-felt class system.

An equally paralysing sense of despair rather than the invigorating impact of righteous anger is the curiously overall impression of the New Drama's most consciously political writers—David Mercer (born 1928) and Arnold Wesker (born 1932). Mercer, formerly a schoolmaster, has described himself as 'a Communist without a party'. And it is strange how the personal commitment coupled with the sense of individual isolation in this phrase reverberates around all his stage plays. For they concern men of vitality whose attempts to assert their personal identities are destroyed by the institutions to which they belong. It's a theme that can be followed from the one-act **The Governor's Lady**, staged in 1965, through **Belcher's Luck** (1966) to **Flint** (1970). In the early play, **Ride A Cock Horse** (1965) the destruction takes the form of the hero's withdrawal through madness to a state of infantilism. In **After Haggerty** (1970) the drama critic hero deals with the political catastrophes that beset him on his European lecture tours by asserting his attitude of total detachment and uninvolvement with life. Once again the student of the drama would have a hard time convincing an examiner that this oeuvre is, for all its concern with man as a political animal, revolutionary dynamite.

Arnold Wesker certainly began boldly both inside and outside the theatre. When they were staged together at the Royal Court in 1960 as The Wesker Trilogy, his three plays, **Chicken Soup with Barley** (1958), **Roots** (1959) and **I'm Talking About Jerusalem** (1960) attempted nothing less than an analysis of contemporary working-class malaise in a framework spanning a quarter of a century. And soon afterwards Wesker attempted to bring culture to the workers through his Centre 42, with its base at the Roundhouse in north London. But after an idealistic if impractical start the venture folded, with the Roundhouse becoming an international touring date for productions with an eye on the West End. Similarly, in the three plays that chronicle the family experiences of an East End Jewish family, the Kahns, the idealism of the first play gives way to lethargy and disappointment in the later two. It is true that in **Roots** Ronnie Kahn is able to inspire his girlfriend, Beatie, to think for herself. But he himself has grown so disillusioned he has to be reminded by his mother, Sarah, that if he does not care, he'll die.

Though the dynamism of John Dexter's productions of Wesker's **The Kitchen** (1961) and **Chips with Everything** (1962) brought out their vitality and social criticism of the English way of life, Wesker showed himself impatient with the sense of authenticity that was most admired in their strong direction. Thus in 1964, with **The Four Seasons** he experimented with a neutral esperanto-like dialogue whilst in 1970 he himself directed **The Friends**. Neither venture was particularly successful, so that when he and Dexter renewed their collaboration with **The Old Ones** at the Royal Court in 1972 the return to Wesker's own childhood background of East End London seemed at the time a good augury for his dramatic future—even though the play's concern with impending senility was necessarily valedictory in tone.

The response of John Arden (born 1930) to an event in the British military involvement in postwar Cyprus which fired him to write **Serjeant Musgrave's Dance** (1959) is probably the sort of creative anger that would-be admirers of the New Drama hope to find in it. By transposing his concern at the multiplication of slaughter in modern war to a town in the North of England in the 1880s he achieved what is generally held to be his finest play and is certainly proving more enduring than an agit-prop piece written specifically apropos the Cyprus confrontations. And when he has turned to other social themes, Arden's objectivity in not presenting his public with simple villains and heroes has proved his strongest suit. Thus, in **Live Like Pigs** (1958) neither the gypsy family (the Sawneys) who are forced to live in a housing estate nor the conventional family next door (the Jacksons) are characterised as wholly good or wholly bad. Similarly in his treatment of geriatrics in his play-with-masks, **The Happy Haven** (1961), the elderly in their confrontation with nursing staff are certainly not presented in any sentimental light. Since the excitement of his debut in the 1950s, Arden has kept up a steady output with **The Workhouse Donkey** (1963) and **Armstrong's Last Goodnight** (1964) and **Left Handed Liberty** (1965). But it is sad that his musical on the life of Nelson, **The Hero Rises Up**, produced in the late 1960s at the Roundhouse, and his **The Island of the Mighty** (1973) produced by the Royal Shakespeare Company have both been the cause of public quarrels with the presenting management.

One would prefer to see a writer of Arden's stature concentrate his anger on an issue like the Ulster situation, of which he has so far shown an intimate polemical knowledge. The objective standing-back and the technical assurance with which he used interpolated songs and dances (as well as the juxtaposition of verse and prose) in his early plays would seem to be the sine qua non of a great play on the tragedy of Northern Ireland.

With this thought let us leave the apparent nature of the 'anger' in the New Drama and consider whether a dramatist like Harold Pinter (born 1930) can really be lumped together with the other writers in the hope that they will conveniently be considered as a group. In as far as his early plays—**The Birthday Party** (1958) and two one act works—are comedies of menace they have attracted the epithet Kafkaesque. And productions of these plays in Eastern Europe—where situations like that depicted by Kafka in **The Trial** are a living reality—have certainly given the plays a political reverberation. But, as John Russell Taylor has pointed out in his excellent analysis of Pinter's work, the turning point came in 1960 with **The Caretaker,** where the menace switched from a fear of something outside to a terror his characters have in communicating with one another and of being totally known in their intimate relationships. Thus, in **The Caretaker,** much of the audience's attention is directed on the efforts of Davies, the tramp, to avoid being identified by the brothers Mick and Aston into whose household he attempts to intrude. Since then, Pinter's career might be baldly (though not entirely inaccurately) summarised as a refinement of his characters' desire to evade the curiosity their past in particular excites in those seemingly closest to them. With **The Homecoming** (1965), **Old Times** (1971) and the one-act plays **Landscape** (1968) and **Silence** (1969) one notes also that Pinter has moved up the social ladder into settings that are immensely more elegant than those which provided the background to

26 New Writing

the confrontations of **The Caretaker** and the one-act plays, **The Dumb Waiter** and **The Room** of 1960. The most important development of all, however, has been his skill in achieving the maximum dramatic effect with the minimum of words. So, in **Old Times**, a character has only to reach for a cigarette or uncross his legs to pack as much theatrical punch as an Osborne character in full self-hating tirade.

But what really disposes of any efforts to pass off the New Drama as a coherent movement is to look at some of the writers side by side. Take, for example, two who have been presented by the National Theatre—Tom Stoppard (born 1937) and Peter Nichols (born 1927). To start with, neither can even be called a National Theatre writer. For though the presentation of Stoppard's **Rosencrantz and Guildenstern Are Dead** at the Old Vic established him in 1966 and was followed with a National Theatre production of **Jumpers** in 1972, the rest of his work has been seen elsewhere. **Enter A Free Man** (1966) and **The Real Inspector Hound** (1968) surfaced in the West End whilst the one act **After Magritte** made its appearance at a lunch-hour theatre. And though Peter Nichols is to follow his Old Vic play, **The National Health**, with **George Orwell's England** for the National Theatre, the play that established him, **A Day in the Death of Joe Egg**, opened in Scotland and transferred in 1967 to the West End of London, where his **Forget-Me-Not Lane** also ran in 1971.

But beyond keeping a foot in the subsidised and the commercial theatre, these authors have little else in common. Thus what has been most admired in Stoppard's work is his crossword-puzzle-like wit and the sheer abstract technical skill with which all the seeming irrelevancies in his dialogue are in the end slotted into a perfect and seemingly inevitable pattern. Perhaps, in this respect, he is at his most masterly in **The Real Inspector Hound** where his satire on the vanity of two drama critics and his parody of an Agatha Christie-type thriller are brilliantly dovetailed. The National Theatre's public have found Stoppard's **Jumpers** equally ingenious and witty, though the fact that one of the characters is undergoing a nervous breakdown leaves them totally unmoved. And this is no doubt as it should be. For Stoppard is at his strongest when he manipulates his characters with the same disregard for them as real human beings that the Court of Denmark show for Rosencrantz and Guildenstern in Shakespeare's **Hamlet**.

You cannot say that Peter Nichols, on the other hand, lacks dexterity in the handling of his characters. In all three of his major plays there is direct address to the audience—a device used particularly well in **Forget-Me-Not Lane,** where the teacher hero is seen as both an adolescent and a divorced husband in a play that switches with stunning ease backwards and forwards in time. But where in Stoppard what most impresses is the brilliance of the wit and the technical adroitness of the plot construction, in Nichols it is above all the uncloying compassion that the author has for his creations which leaves the most lasting impression. And this no doubt accounts for his success in being able to introduce an impression of real-life humour to subjects that were hitherto thought of as fit only for funeral parlour—type solemnity. Thus one is able to laugh in the face of a human catastrophe like the child

Paul Scofield in John Osborne's *The Hotel in Amsterdam*—one of the many stars Osborne's plays have attracted

that is nothing more than a vegetable in **A Day in The Death of Joe Egg** without calling into question the good taste of author or audience.

Another pair cheerfully grouped under the New Drama heading but really having nothing whatsoever in common apart from their year of birth are David Storey (born 1933) and Joe Orton (1933 — 1967). Like Stoppard later, Orton had a keen sense of parody, so that in **Loot** (1965) he satirised detective fiction just as in **What The Butler Saw** (1969) he constructed a farce on the artifices of the farce convention. But the essential Orton quality, running throughout his work, is the inappropriateness of the artificiality of his dialogue to the extraordinary violence of his stage action. Thus in the play that made his name, **Entertaining Mr Sloane** (1964), a young lodger kicks his landlady's father to death whilst her reaction is to be absorbed in the niceties of her language.

What is extraordinary about Orton is that he should have been so widely imitated on the basis of so small a quantity of finished work. Apart from his first play, the one-act **The Ruffian on the Stair** which was coupled with **The Erpingham Camp** at the Royal Court in 1967 under the heading 'Crimes of Passion', no other play by him for the stage survives. And though there was so much violence in these two one-act plays (the first is an intricately plotted revenge play; the second a holiday camp depicted as a concentration camp) they hardly equal the crime of passion which ended Orton's own life at the hands of his jealous friend and flatmate.

The novelist David Storey had his first stage play, **The Restoration of Arnold Middleton**, produced at the Royal Court in the year in which Orton was murdered—1967. Since then he has collaborated with the director, Lindsay Anderson, in what appears to have been an ideal partnership since **In Celebration** and **The Contractor** (1969), **Home** (1970) and **The Changing Room** (1972), all premiered at the Royal Court, are being followed at the same theatre with **The Farm** and **Cromwell**. And it's difficult to think of a better dramatist than Orton to throw this body of work into contrasting relief. For where Storey's characters adopt a spare and often regional naturalism, Orton's speak with a cultivated primness that is as elaborately artificial as the epigrams Oscar Wilde bestowed on his aristocrats. And where Orton's work marks a crescendo of action and violence, Storey's offers a diminuendo of both. So whereas in 1967 Storey actually showed his schoolteacher hero going mad on stage in **The Restoration of Arnold Middleton**, by 1970 he had sufficiently refined his technique to take his public into a mental home (ironically entitled **Home**) without the public being aware of the location until well into the play. Instead of the histrionics of **Snake-Pit** confrontation, he offered a glimpse of the patients' suffering rather by what they failed to say and do. The violence both in time and place was offered at a second or third remove. Similarly, instead of the busy action of the first play, in **The Contractor** and **The Changing Room** he offered plotless evenings in the conventional sense. But just as it would be foolish to dismiss **Three Sisters** as a play about three girls who never went to Moscow, so it would be short-sighted to describe **The Contractor** merely as the putting up and taking down of a wedding marquee tent or **The**

Ralph Richardson and John Gielgud in David Storey's *Home*, first produced at the Royal Court

Changing Room as the preparation for and the recovery from a game of rugby league football.

Perhaps it may now be conceded that though the new writers may have brought about a revolution in British drama they belong to no single movement. Just what that revolution amounted to might best be gauged by glancing at the work of Edward Bond (born 1935) since, more than those of any other dramatists, his plays helped to topple the censorship of stage plays as exercised until 1968 by a member of the British Royal Household, the Lord Chamberlain. In the censor's declining years, dramatists already managed to write openly about taboo subjects such as lesbianism, which was the subject of Frank Marcus' popular **The Killing of Sister George** (1965). But this was at the cost of gentlemanly wrangling with characteristically English compromise being arrived at by the substitution of one swear word for another, one gesture for no gesture at all.

When Bond arrived in 1965 with **Saved**, in which a child was stoned to death in its pram by a gang of boys and smothered in its own faeces, a head-on confrontation with the Lord Chamberlain was arrived at. And this could only be temporarily smothered over by turning the Royal Court into a club theatre which was therefore technically not subject to censorship. But by 1968, when Bond had moved on from the realism of **Saved** to the surrealism of **Early Morning** in which the Queen's forebear, Queen Victoria, was depicted as having an affair with the nurse, Florence Nightingale, the Lord Chamberlain issued an outright ban on the play and a point of no return had been reached. With his version of **Lear** (1970), Bond was to depict an even greater measure of cruelty. But by then the new dramatists had won the right and the respect to treat whatever subject they liked in whatever manner they felt most appropriate, with the public given the credit for having the intelligence to decide for itself what it did not want to see.

Another dramatist whose head-on clash with the Lord Chamberlain helped to force the jettisoning of the old system of compromise was Charles Wood, particularly with his original and unromantic view of the military way of life. In **Dingo** (seen at the Royal Court in 1967) he effectively demolished the false heroics of the second world war just as in **H, or Monologues at Front of Burning Cities** at the Old Vic in 1969, he got to the core of the strange patriotism that made General Havelock and his costly relief of Lucknow a Victorian hero cult. It's doubtful whether anybody had the remotest idea before Wood wrote these plays (and his one-act works staged in the early 1960s) that the clichés of the military argot could have been mined to produce such fascinatingly complex and hard-hitting pieces of stagecraft. What is more to the point is that, without the decline and fall of the stage censor, it's doubtful whether such works would ever have been staged. And even if after much wrangling and cuts they had been deemed fit for public viewing, the economics of the British theatre until the mid-fifties were such that their actual presentation would be in grave doubt. The works of Wood—and still less those of Bond—were hardly in the taste of the then all-powerful management, H M Tennent.

So this is where the true revolution in the New Drama seems in fact to lie. First, the most militant and uncompromising of its writers won the right to deal honestly with aspects of life that a Lord Chamberlain would have preferred to keep from the English theatre public. And secondly, by producing works that the whole world wished to see in translation, they totally upset the economics of conservative theatrical management by proving that there was actually money to be made from promoting new and unheard young dramatists. One of the many ironies of this situation, however, is that the writers of promise who now have Arts Council support in their fledgling days more often than not end up making a living as screenplay writers—rather than from their stage plays—no matter how prestigious these may be considered.

As the 1970s get under way, the latest arrivals to the New Drama go off in as many directions as their predecessors. Christopher Hampton (born 1946), for example, in a play like **The Philanthropist** (1970), opts for a two-act comedy of manners in a realistic setting. Howard Brenton (born 1942), the most solid talent to emerge from the lunch-hour theatre scene, on the other hand, has uncompromisingly made his name with short strip-cartoon playlets such as **Christie in Love** (1969). In investigating hitherto taboo subjects like necrophilia, Brenton has boldly dispensed with the conventional dramatist's trappings of psychological pointers carefully planted in a plot's exposition and development in favour of a dialogue and a succession of visual images that is the theatrical equivalent of the strip cartoon and its speech bubbles.

With such a variety of material and technique to hand, the student of post-war British theatre attempting to impose some sort of academic pattern on the field must necessarily command sympathy on account of the sheer waywardness of his subject. Even so, there are a number of possibly useful lines of enquiry. There have, for example, been a number of remarkable author/director collaborations that might reward investigation—Peter Terson (born 1932) is a case very much in point, since he has elaborated one sort of play with Michael Croft and the National Youth Theatre—**Zigger Zagger** (1967), **The Apprentices** (1968) and **Fuzz** (1969)—and quite another, more intimate style with Peter Cheeseman, who first discovered his talent and staged his early plays at the Victoria Theatre, Stoke-on-Trent—**A Night to Make the Angels Weep** (1964) and **I'm In Charge of These Ruins** (1966). John Dexter's collaboration with Arnold Wesker, Michael Blakemore with Peter Nichols and Lindsay Anderson with David Storey suggest that the New Drama owes much to authors who have found the right directors to premiere their work.

An even more promising line of enquiry would seem to be the New Drama's assassination of the character of the British family. At the working class level Edward Bond in **Saved** has shown that there is another side to the cockney chirpiness that the Joan Littlewood musicals like **Sparrers Can't Sing** have brought out in East London households. At the suburban middle-class level Peter Nichols in **Forget-Me-Not Lane** throws a particularly bright light on the destructiveness of parent/child relationships. And Peter Barnes (born 1931) at the aristocratic level of **The Ruling Class** (1968) suggests that family relationships in the peerage are far from being cosy. The contrast of any one of these plays with the picture of British family life drawn in Dodie Smith's **Dear Octopus** (1938) gives a vivid impression of what differentiates the Old Drama from the New.

It would be neat to be able to suggest that another means of organising the dramatic material is through the theatres which have promoted individual dramatists. And in so far as the Royal Court have championed John Arden and Edward Bond and the Royal Shakespeare Company David Mercer, it would seem to be a valid system. But it breaks down all too quickly in some cases. For instance it seemed inconceivable that when Brendan Behan (1923-1964) had his first successes with Joan Littlewood's productions of **The Quare Fellow** (1956) and **The Hostage** (1958) any other director could turn his wayward Irish talent into effective theatre. But when his third play, **Richard's Cork Leg** came to be produced posthumously in Dublin and London in 1972 it was pieced together by other hands.

Finally, the biggest question of all must be why so few of the works of the New Drama have been written by women. At the outset Shelagh Delaney (born 1939) with **A Taste of Honey** (1959) and Ann Jellicoe (born 1927) with **The Knack** (1961) especially had suggested that this was to be an area where women would be as liberated as men. But by the 1970s no women of the stature and with the consolidated output of Arden, Osborne, Pinter or Storey had emerged—despite some lively championship on the part of the National Theatre in an experimental season at the Jeannetta Cochrane Theatre in the late 1960s. Maybe the next revolution in the New Drama is for it to become as much a woman's preserve as the British novel already is.

ACTING

Would you put your daughter (or son) on the stage? If you see her as a budding Maggie Smith (or him as a Laurence Olivier in the making) your application for a place at the Royal Academy of Dramatic Art, or its handiest equivalent, is undoubtedly already in hand.

Although the stage-struck are rarely susceptible to reason, you might be wiser first to get in touch with Equity, the actor's Trade Union in Britain. Founded in 1929, its offices and consulting rooms are set amongst the most exclusive in England—in the doctors' street, Harley Street, London W1.

The sobering news from Equity's General Secretary is that although the actor began the early seventies with some modest minimum pay rises (£18.00 a week minimum in the regions; £30.00 in the West End) the actor's lot is not a happy one and is likely to become unhappier. The aspirant to stardom should reflect—at least for as long as it takes to assimilate Equity's depressing figures.

The total membership of the Union is reckoned to be 20,000 and growing at the rate of one thousand a year. But many of these are singers, dancers, comics and the like who, in the days before it became amalgamated with Equity, would have belonged to the Variety Artistes' Federation. It is calculated in fact that of the total number, 13,000 are what is known as straight actors.

What is really most striking, however, is not the size of the profession but its average earning power. Equity's researches claim to show that at any one time 75 per cent of its members are out of work—or 'resting' as the theatrical euphemism has it. Further enquiries reveal that at the beginning of the seventies the average annual income for an actor was £800 whilst that for an actress was £450. In mid-1972 the official government sources revealed that the average male earnings for manual and service workers were, in round figures, £1,600 per annum and the average female earnings £830 per annum. Now would you put your daughter (or son) on the stage?

Clearly in such an overcrowded profession, its members are not in a strong position to negotiate for the basic working conditions that operate in a country like, say, Hungary, where their calling is both better regulated and more respected. The idea of a London actor, like his counterpart in Budapest, having both paid summer holidays and retirement pensions is at present certainly not on. In Britain actors may be regarded as less glamorously remote creatures than they used to be but too many people still look upon their calling as a soft option to real work.

The actor's name in lights outside a West End theatre—or alongside a major role in a subsidised national ensemble—makes him appear king of the castle. In fact almost always the reverse is true. First of all, in postwar Britain, the actor is in the hands of his agent. The old days, when an actor landed a part by answering an advertisement in the profession's weekly newspaper, **The Stage**, and negotiated directly with

the management, now seem quaintly old-fashioned. A director casting an important role will invariably consult **Spotlight**, a fascinating publication carrying photographs of the profession's most venerated and most humble members. That will give the director a lead for auditions which, if successful, will result in negotiation between management and agent. The problem from the actor's point of view can sometimes be that an agent wishes the artist on his books (from whom he is going to make his ten per cent) to be employed as remuneratively as possible. In other words he may push a young actor into television, films or advertising when his formative years should be in repertory and the live theatre. In so under-employed a profession, however, it would be foolish to pretend that an actor is going to quarrel with an agent who can keep him in work.

There are other aspects of the actor's life that the would-be star should bear in mind. In postwar Britain the role of the director, particularly in the subsidised field, has become an increasingly powerful one. In such a setup actors sometimes receive critical reviews for a performance that is in fact a faithful carrying out of a director's instructions. The stage-struck should also be aware of the actor's constant need to prove himself. At auditions, which can be cruel exposure sessions, he must again convince the powers that be of his talent, no matter how many glowing notices he may already have in his cuttings-book.

In such conditions it goes without saying that the actor needs good health and a highly developed sense of humour. He belongs to a profession where competition is cut-throat and where a reputation, once made, has to be jealously guarded and fought for—especially when, as often happens, a particular style or part which happens to be an actor's strong suit may be out of fashion. The old idea of the actor being some sort of exotic flower could hardly be further from the truth.

In some ways of course things have improved. The coming of subsidy to the theatre in Britain has meant that the few actors belonging to the major subsidised ensembles do have a measure of security without the feeling—like, say, members of the Moscow Art Theatre—of having signed their careers away to one particular company. And the advent of television to Britain has offered the actor an important secondary outlet to offset the difficulties which have arisen through the economic problems of the film industry and the consequent falling off of work in this area. The coming of commercial radio, on the other hand, has so far provided a bonanza for the disc jockey rather than for the actor. But the postwar advent of tourism in Britain has meant increasingly long seasons in the festival theatres and greater prosperity in London. Overseas visitors are keeping shows running through the former slack periods, like the summer holidays and the beginning of the year, when native theatregoers are getting over the expense of Christmas and consequently tend to neglect live theatre.

When people, not concerned with the aforementioned harsh realities of the actor's life, talk instead of the great tradition of English acting they usually mean that embodied by the leading actor knights and dames whose names have been made in the classical field—Gielgud,

Ian McKellen as *Richard II*. One of the new generation of British actors, he came to the fore without going to drama school

Olivier and Richardson, Peggy Ashcroft, Edith Evans and Sybil Thorndike. And if these same people are asked to define the English 'style' which they also talk about, the explanation usually centres on the voice.

Since Shakespeare is the touchstone by which most leading actors are eventually measured perhaps it is not surprising that the English actor's skill in verse-speaking is so admired. The English actor is thought of as being stiffer and less inclined to gesticulate than American and Latin actors. There may be an historical explanation for this. In the nineteenth century the vaudeville tradition of the music-hall went in one direction and the straight actor, whose desperate efforts to achieve professional status and respectability for his calling culminated in the bestowal of a knighthood on Henry Irving in 1895, went in another. So the acrobatic tradition was thought of as something belonging to low comedy and the variety hall, whilst great acting came to be thought of in terms of rhetorical magnificence even if, with the passing of time, it became more naturalistic.

But however much historical truth there may be at the root of this, there is a certain futility in trying to define an 'English style' of acting. For the theatre is a place extremely susceptible to fashion and change. At the end of the 19th century the actor managers were predominant. And, against elaborately naturalistic settings, their performances were nothing if not grandiose. An actor like Henry Irving would take a melodrama like **The Bells** and reshape it to fit his own style and personality. But the coming of new writers as different as Lonsdale, Maugham, Shaw and Galsworthy called for different styles.

How elusive is the term 'English style' if we think of the plays that constitute some of the major departures this century. The histrionic panorama is bewildering in its variety. On the one hand we have the late Noël Coward's clipped, nervous-seeming manner which was first widely recognized in his own play, **The Vortex** in 1924. At the other extreme, as late as the 1940s we have the late Donald Wolfit giving an outsize performance in the old actor-manager vein as a wartime **King Lear**. Nothing is more indicative of the theatre's susceptibility to the smell of its particular time than a glance at old magazine photographs of long-vanished productions or recordings of voices now old or silent. A glance at production pictures of, say, Laurence Olivier and Peggy Ashcroft as Romeo and Juliet in 1935 and Judi Dench and John Stride in the same parts in Zeffirelli's famous Old Vic production in 1960 shows how even period productions carry something also of the period in which they were produced. But to really gauge the difference in acting styles over half a century it's best to listen to a recording like that of the Chichester Festival Theatre **Uncle Vanya** (1963) and compare it with recordings made late in life by artists like Ellen Terry long before Chekhov was ever produced in Britain

When Laurence Olivier held an opening press conference for the National Theatre he was asked if the National Theatre would adopt some specific acting style. The questioner obviously had something identifiable in mind as that adopted by Comedie Francaise or the Moscow Art Theatre. Olivier's reply was that each production would be played in the style appropriate for it.

Somebody once said that there were as many acting styles as there were actors. And style is a very dangerous word to apply to acting, for it conjures up a certain mannered way of speaking and moving which is

Vanessa Redgrave in the title role of *The Prime of Miss Jean Brodie*

not a characteristic feature of English performers. One could venture certain broad lines of classification only. Most easily recognizable, of course, is the 'personality' player. An actor like Kenneth Williams or Robert Morley, to cite two very different types of actor, gives very much the same sort of performance in whatever play he appears in. The public know what to expect and would be disappointed, not to say astonished, if Robert Morley started being funny in the way that Kenneth Williams is—or vice versa.

Historically the safest classification one can make is between the matinee idol type of male role—much in favour between the wars—and the rougher diamonds that Jimmy Porter in **Look Back in Anger** offered the actor in the British theatre after 1956.

The theatre that came before **Look Back in Anger** has been dubbed 'french window' drawing room comedy and the theatre that came after as 'kitchen sink' drama. Both terms are foolish, pejorative simplifications thrown about by theatregoers whose tastes are for very different kinds of theatre. Here, however, they are useful in so far as they point to contrasting schools of acting. Elegance, good looks, the ability to wear attractive clothes and move effortlessly in magnificent settings are qualities that a public looks for in an actor, or more likely an actress, in a comedy with french windows to it. Isabel Jeans and Evelyn Laye are actresses who have been particularly successful in exuding the glamour of this form of entertainment. Jack Buchanan and Ivor Novello were actors who spelt a certain sort of theatrical magic for its matinee audiences in particular.

Now let us take a look at four major artists who have emerged since 1956—Tom Courtenay, Albert Finney, Joan Plowright and Vanessa Redgrave. Neither of the men is conventionally good-looking in the old matinee idol sense. Neither of the ladies is a chic mannequin sort of actress. With the exception of Vanessa Redgrave, all have a residual regional flavour to their way of speaking English which is an essential part of their acting personality. Formerly to be accepted in the classics—in Shakespeare in particular—this would have had to be eliminated to achieve the accent neutrality of the standard BBC announcer. In 1969 Nicol Williamson was playing a dynamic Hamlet at the Roundhouse and though the performance varied enormously from night to night no attempt was made to smother the actor's personality by eliminating his accent. The packed houses attested to the fact that young people were too excited by the actor's jagged personality to worry that the Prince of Denmark did not have the aristocratic manner a brilliant interpreter of the role like John Gielgud had endowed him with over a period of 15 years.

Gielgud's career in the 1950s is in fact very relevant to the changing theatre to which the British actor had to adjust. As a Shakespeare actor, particularly in the roles of Hamlet and Richard II, Gielgud had embodied a sensitive and aristocratic tradition. As a director of the West End producing management, H M Tennent, who were a particularly powerful organisation in the immediate postwar theatre, he had appeared in literate sensitive plays like those of N C Hunter (**A Day By The Sea**, Haymarket, 1953). But there was a growing dissatisfaction with the failure of these plays to come to grips with the problems of contemporary Britain and the controversy over Lee Strasberg's The Method, culled from Stanislavksi's teachings, channelled a good deal of criticism at the stiffness and hauteur of the English West End school of acting.

The upshot of all this was that when the new British writers who followed in the wake of Osborne had their first successes, Gielgud took refuge in the world of the one-man show, with his Shakespearean recital **The Ages of Man**. The absurdist dramatists, like Beckett and Ionesco, who were much played at the time, had nothing to offer an actor such as Gielgud. Donald Pleasence in Harold Pinter's **The Caretaker** at the Duchess in 1960 or Peter Bull in Beckett's **Waiting for Godot** at the Criterion in 1955 represented a very different sort of theatre from the Shakespeare, Chekhov or H M Tennent West End production that had nurtured an artist like Gielgud. Olivier, on the other hand, with his appearances in Osborne's **The Entertainer** (1957) and as Berenger in Ionesco's **Rhinoceros** (1960), successfully channelled his career to take in the new drama both in the British mould of social criticism and in that of the absurdist dramatist. Gielgud's (and Ralph Richardson's) turn had to wait until a second generation of new writers, notably David Storey with his play, **Home** (1970), provided these two actor-knights

Nicol Williamson in Tony Richardson's production of *Hamlet* at the Round House

with parts and a seat in the dressing room of the theatre most closely associated with the new movement, the Royal Court.

More important for the health of the British theatre, of course, is the appearance of a new generation of lead players, rather than the successful adaptation of senior players to changing trends in writing. Of the two major national ensembles, the National Theatre Company and the Royal Shakespeare Company, the latter have perhaps had the edge in bringing new talent to notice. David Warner, Ian Richardson and Ian Holm were all three players who moved from spear-carrying ranks at Stratford-upon-Avon to major Shakespeare roles and thence to modern work produced by the company in its London home at the Aldwych. And at the National Derek Jacobi and Ronald Pickup made similar company progress. At the Chichester Festival Theatre, Eileen Atkins consolidated the reputation she had achieved as Childie in Frank Marcus' **The Killing of Sister George** (1965) with her performance as Celia Coplestone in the 1968 revival of Eliot's **The Cocktail Party** and, in 1970, as Elizabeth I in Robert Bolt's **Vivat ! Vivat Regina !** The Royal Court, 'the writer's theatre', showed an able eye too for spotting those who make exciting 'actor's theatre' notably with Victor Henry (in Christopher Hampton's **Total Eclipse**, 1968) Richard O'Callaghan (in Donald Howarth's **Three Months Gone**, 1970) and Judy Parfitt in Peter Gill's revival of D H Lawrence's coalmining plays (such as **The Daughter-in-Law** 1968). And in the West End Julia Foster, an actress who got her first breakthrough with the Nottingham Playhouse revival of Wedekind's **Lulu**, went on to establish herself firmly in the front rank with **Notes on a Love Affair** (1972) and **The Day After the Fair** (1972). In the regions, the Prospect Touring Company's presentation of **Edward II** by Marlowe and Shakespeare's **Richard II**, with Ian McKellen in the name parts, consolidated with the general theatregoing public the reputation this actor had made as a National Theatre player.

How else to consider English actors except in the light of the style they may have, the way they cope with different and successive schools of writing? Well of course their lives, looked at historically since they first began to be known as individuals and have parts written for them in Shakespeare's times, forms an essential point of perspective. And the best way to begin to encompass a field that includes so many colourful names is to seize upon those who represent a part of Britain's celebrated theatrical dynasties.

Today the best-known theatrical family is certainly that fathered by Sir Michael Redgrave (born 1908) a former schoolmaster and the really genuine intellectual amongst our major senior actors. At the end of 1972 Sir Michael himself had made a belated return to the West End in John Mortimer's **A Voyage Round My Father** after an unhappy association with the National Theatre in its opening phase had led to his doing more film than stage work. Redgrave's wife, Rachel Kempson, was appearing in John Osborne's latest play, **A Sense of Detachment**, at the Royal Court, in which play it was her duty to read straight passages of pornographic literature that were received in stunned silence. Redgrave's son, Corin, had concluded a successful season with the Royal Shakespeare Company at Stratford-upon-Avon having made his first professional appearances at the Royal Court in Shakespeare and Wesker at the beginning of the 1960s. Of the sisters Vanessa and Lynn, the latter had proved herself the comedienne of the family particularly with the National Theatre in its productions of Peter Shaffer's **Black Comedy** and a revival of Coward's **Hay Fever**. In the West End she achieved something of a tour de force playing six different parts with the farceur Richard Briers in Michael Frayn's **The Two of Us** at the Garrick in 1970. Vanessa had become more involved in films after a brilliant stay with the Royal Shakespeare Company in 1961, when she played Rosalind in **As You Like It** and Katharine in **The Taming of the Shrew,** and a great West End success with the name part in **The Prime of Miss Jean Brodie** at Wyndham's in 1966. Without doubt a prodigiously talented family.

Going back a generation or so one is tempted to recall the union of the Thorndikes and the Cassons when Sybil Thorndike married Lewis Casson in 1908. Their partnership, which spanned 60 years, must be classified as the most distinguished, varied and challenging of the husband and wife teams. Those like the Lunts in America and John Clements and Kay Hammond, Michael Denison and Dulcie Gray in Britain have tended to be more successful in the field of light entertainment than the Cassons who, though they had their share of this, made vital contributions to classical theatre from the Greeks to Shaw to Chekhov.

Going back a little in the mist of theatrical time the three most important theatrical families to emerge are the Keans, the Kembles and the Terrys. Edmund Kean (1787 — 1833) was the arch exponent of villainy whose Shylock, Richard Crookback and Iago were acclaimed as the work of a genius—albeit a fitful one who did not have the range to play the romantic or the patrician roles. His son Charles Kean (1811 — 1868), though Eton-educated and destined for 'better' things, followed his father on to the stage and even appeared with a dying Edmund Kean at Drury Lane in **Othello** in 1833. With his wife Ellen Tree (1806 — 1880), Charles went into management at the Princess' Theatre (1851 — 1859) where, along with his contemporary, Charles Kemble, he pioneered attempts to produce costume plays with the beginnings of historical accuracy.

There were several generations of the Kemble family and far too many gifted members to mention here. By far the most famous of Roger Kemble's twelve children, however, was Sarah Siddons (1755 — 1831) the English tragedienne par excellence and probably the most famous Lady Macbeth of all time. Roger's eldest son John Philip Kemble (1757 — 1823) and his youngest Charles (1775 — 1854) were not quite eclipsed by their sister's career, however. John Philip, though thought to be rather on the formal side, was a successful Hamlet, Brutus and Coriolanus whilst Charles, after a poor start, cornered the lighter roles of Mercutio, Mirabell, Orlando and Romeo and, in his 25 years on the stage, did more than anybody else to educate his audience into an accurate appreciation of period.

So extraordinarily colourful were the lives of the Keans and the Kembles it is surprising that a biographical backstage account of them has not met with the success of a backstage play like Pinero's **Trelawny of the Wells.**

The same could be said of the Terry family who were the nineteenth century equivalent of the Kembles. They, too, are in such numbers as to be beyond the scope of a detailed account in a book like this. But no self-respecting theatregoer can be ignorant of the great Ellen Terry (1847 — 1928), Irving's leading lady at the Lyceum in its late Victorian heyday, or of her son Edward Gordon Craig (1872 — 1966) whose nine years as an actor with Irving's company were followed, improbably, by his later distinction as an advocate of a totally alien theatre in which design predominated and the actor was a mere puppet.

Readers with time on their hands to explore the ramifications of the great theatrical families of the Keans, Kembles and the Terrys will find not only stories that are stranger than fiction but will also receive the assurance that whatever else they may have been such actors were never merely puppets.

DIRECTION

Nothing is quite so revealing as the name the public chooses to attach to a new production. At the beginning of the 1970s the two most widely discussed revivals in Britain were almost certainly **A Midsummer Night's Dream** in the repertoire of the Royal Shakespeare Company and **Long Day's Journey into Night** in the National Theatre's programme. Why should the first, colloquially referred to as Brook's **Dream**, carry the label of its director, Peter Brook? And why should the second, often referred to as Olivier's **Long Day's Journey**, bear the cachet of its lead actor, Laurence Olivier?

Both Peter Brook with Shakespeare's play and Laurence Olivier with O'Neill's were of course interpretative artists. So in settling to denote a particular revival of a comedy by the Bard as Brook's **Dream**, what evidently most fired the public's enthusiasm was the excitement and originality of the overall direction of the production—however good its cast. And if O'Neill's play came to be thought of as Olivier's then, despite the quality of Michael Blakemore's direction, what clearly most caught the playgoer's imagination was the chance·it gave to see a theatre actor of genius at the height of his powers.

Few, at any rate, disagreed that the first was a good example of what has become known as Director's Theatre, whilst it can be argued that the second was the apotheosis of Actor's Theatre. But how many admirers of both realised that the phenomenon of director-as-star in the British theatre goes back barely 40 years whilst that of the actor-as-star began soon after the building of Britain's first playhouse almost 400 years ago in 1576?

A glimpse of the set-up of the British theatre a hundred years ago is instructive. We read that star actors from London were in the habit of joining a local stock company to play a lead Shakespeare role without so much as a rehearsal. The company just altered traditional moves and 'business' to accommodate his performance. We read of would-be actors, with the right letters of introduction to the right managers, being pitchforked straight into a professional performance with only the know-how of seasoned colleagues to carry them through the ordeal. In such working conditions, the idea of a play being filtered through the vision of a sensitive, university-educated director, working in anxious collaboration with his designer and lighting designer, was, to say the least, impractical.

It follows that any guidelines here to the work of leading British directors in the 1970s have to be prefaced by some notes on the reforms that have brought about their existence. And such notes must necessarily take us briefly to Russia, Germany and France through the thickets of realism, anti-realism, symbolism and, most important, audience alienation. Stanislavski's work in Russia, that of Reinhardt, Piscator and Brecht in Germany, the theatres founded in Paris by Antoine and Copeau must all be borne in mind by any playgoer wishing to see in perspective the careers of directors in the contemporary British theatre.

44 Direction

There is more than a touch of romance attached to the name of the man the history books usually credit with being both the first internationally recognized director and the artist who first introduced realism to the theatre. George II, Duke of Saxe-Meiningen (1826 – 1914) married an actress, Ellen Franz, when such a calling was far too disreputable for a Duchess. Ellen Franz was in fact never given this title, but she did have the distinction of forming with her husband a company that successfully pioneered realistic staging, first in the Duke's own Court theatre and, from 1874 onwards, on tour in Europe. So Stanislavski, who was to be the great exponent of realism in Russia, saw the troupe on its second visit to Moscow in 1890. And Antoine, whose Théâtre Libre was to introduce realism to Paris in 1887, caught up with the company in Brussels on one of its increasingly frequent tours outside Germany.

English theatre historians acknowledge the good Duke's reforms when, both as a production's director and designer, he insisted on historical accuracy in sets and costumes and in the treatment of crowds like those in **Julius Caesar** which were presented as a collection of individuals rather than the conventional group of rhubarbing extras. The same historians, however, feel that the Duke's wealth, and consequent ability to undertake international tours with his company, enabled him to steal some of the thunder rightly belonging to the first reformers, who introduced realism to the London stage and the British theatre long before the Meininger Company was spreading the movement via Stanislavski and Antoine to the rest of Europe.

Don't forget Charles Kemble (1775 – 1854), they patriotically ask. It was he after all who was the first to attempt to bring historical accuracy in costumes and settings to his Shakespeare repertoire. Spare a thought, they go on, for the formidable Madame Vestris (1797 – 1856), whose authoritarian management of the Olympic Theatre brought about the introduction in 1832 of the box set with its real ceiling, real doors and real windows to replace the old painted backdrops. And what about Sir Squire and Lady Bancroft, whose twenty years in actor management (1865 – 1885) elaborated the box set even further in the cause of establishing drawing room comedy with the plays of Tom Robertson? Although his plays now make particularly feeble reading compared to those of Chekhov (with which Stanislavski was to establish naturalistic direction at the Moscow Art Theatre), Robertson's work has to be seen in the prevailing London context of crude melodrama and burlesque. Indeed all the avant-garde writers and directors in the British theatre of the 1950s and 1960s who have tried to liberate the British theatre from its middle-class addiction to the elegant fatuities of the drawing room comedy ought to remember the Bancrofts who brought it about. They, in their time, were pioneers and reformers too.

So much has been written about the best-known director of them all, Konstantin Stanislavski (1863 – 1938), his founding of the Moscow Art Theatre in 1898, his development beyond the Meiningen-inspired realism into the psychological naturalism of his direction for that company of Chekhov's **The Seagull** (1898), **Uncle Vanya** (1899), **Three Sisters** (1901) and **The Cherry Orchard** (1904) that it is tempting to recall here only the ungrateful author's reaction to his director's elaborate symphony of naturalistic sound effects. After **Uncle Vanya** Chekhov swore his next play would be set 'in a land which has neither mosquitoes nor crickets nor any other insect which hinders conversation between human beings.'

The extraordinarily detailed naturalism of these Chekhov productions has endured well over half a century, as was seen when the Moscow Art Theatre appeared in London in 1958 and 1963. So perhaps it is not surprising that some write off Russian twentieth century theatre as merely a beautifully preserved museum, pausing only to advise the would-be naturalistic actor to devour Stanislavski's books—**My Life in Art** (1924) and **An Actor Prepares** (1926) in particular.

In fact Stanislavski hardly deserves to be stuck with the naturalistic label since his later teachings contradicted his earlier experiments and above all because he gave a hefty heave up the ladder to the arch-enemy of naturalistic acting, Vsevold Meyerhold (1874 – 1943). The Russian public never saw what Meyerhold actually achieved in 1905 when Stanislavski put him in charge of the Moscow Art Theatre Studio. But when, the following year, Meyerhold went on to direct at another and bigger theatre it was clear that far from preserving the theatre of detailed illusion, he reduced the actors to marionettes. This was a fate prescribed for them by the Englishman, Edward Gordon Craig (1872 – 1966), Stanislavksi's collaborator on **Hamlet** at the Moscow Art Theatre in 1912.

A similar, if not quite so violent see-saw in attitude to direction can be seen in Paris with André Antoine (1958 – 1943) and his Théâtre Libre and Jacques Copeau (1878 – 1949) and his Vieux Colombier Theatre. Antoine had already experimented with realistic settings by the time he saw the Meininger Company in 1887, when he was inspired to match the decor with the naturalistic acting pioneered by the Duke's company. This made possible French productions of naturalistic plays like those of Ibsen, Tolstoy, Strindberg and Turgenev, as well as recruiting French novelists of the naturalistic school for the stage. But when Copeau founded his Vieux Colombier in 1913 he embarked on such a process of simplification both in acting style and decor that it eventually approached symbolism.

A useful link emerges with Copeau's retirement to Burgundy in 1924 to found a group of actors known as 'les Copiaus' for some of these formed part of the famous Compagnie des Quinze directed by Copeau's nephew, Michel Saint-Denis (1897 – 1971). Saint-Denis was to become a key figure in the history of the rise of the director in England with his founding of the London Theatre School before the Second World War and his work after it in the short-lived Old Vic School, not to mention the still flourishing Royal Shakespeare Company.

Meanwhile in Germany the once all-important role of the actor was being dwarfed by the appearance of the new star-directors. For who really cared who was playing what parts in the ultra-lavish if somewhat vulgar spectacles staged by Max Reinhardt (1873 – 1943)? Their declared intention was to free the theatre from the grip of literature so that the lavish new technical resources of staging could be spectacularly unleashed on the public, who were visually bedazzled by Reinhardt's massive crowd effects. Erwin Piscator (1893 – 1966) was just as ruthless about the text of the plays he directed and was one of the first to use film and animated cartoons to reinforce a directorial point.

Bertolt Brecht (1898 – 1956), who worked with Piscator at the beginning of his career, was to move in an entirely opposite direction. For where Reinhardt had wanted to overwhelm his public with the

46 Direction

sheer scale of his productions and where Piscator had sought to excite them in evolving epic theatre through expressionistic techniques, Brecht wanted his audience above all to reflect on what they saw. His theory of audience alienation, about which there has been so much controversy, is basically that the audience, instead of losing itself completely in the naturalism of the theatre of illusion or being overwhelmed by the extravagancies of the theatre of technical effects, should instead stand aside, aware of the traps of both illusion and spectacle, so that the content (especially the social content) of the play should be considered dispassionately in performance.

Brecht's influence in Britain was to be posthumous. It followed the first visit of his Berliner Ensemble to the Palace Theatre in 1956, shortly after his death. Before taking up the impact Brecht was to have on the new directors coming to the fore in the British theatre in the 1950s it would be as well to look back on the rise in Britain of the director whose beginnings we left a few paragraphs back with Charles Kemble, Madame Vestris and the Bancrofts.

When much of the glory for the innovations of these three had been taken over by the Meininger Company, British theatre settled down to allowing the director's role gradually to increase in importance, with none of the really spectacular see-saw movements that characterised his advent in Russia, Germany and France. The most avant-garde of British director-cum-designers, Edward Gordon Craig, in fact retired to Florence in 1908 after a nine-year stint with Irving's company as an actor, thereby allowing progress from the actor-manager theatre Irving epitomised to be made under the guidance of more pragmatic hands than Craig's.

The key figures in the transition from the presentation of Shakespeare in the lavish but long-winded manner favoured by the actor-managers like Irving at · the Lyceum Theatre and Sir Herbert Beerbohm Tree (1853 – 1917) at His Majesty's were William Poel (1852 – 1934) and Harley Granville-Barker (1877 – 1946). Poel's Elizabethan Stage Society (1894 – 1905) toured Shakespeare in Poel's idea of the Elizabethan stage, shorn of all the sumptuous trappings favoured by the school of Irving and Tree. The society was praised by Shaw and engaged Granville-Barker as one of its actors before he went on to the Royal Court Theatre where, in partnership (1904 – 1907) with J E Vedrenne, he made it as much an avant-garde theatre as it is today with productions of Shaw, Galsworthy and Ibsen. Granville-Barker's later productions of Shakespeare at the Savoy Theatre (**The Winter's Tale, Twelfth Night, A Midsummer Night's Dream**) were considered so epoch-making that the theatrical world was astonished when, after their presentation was concluded (between 1912 and 1914), Granville-Barker remarried and retired from the practical business of direction to become a translator and scholar, which resulted in his famous **Prefaces to Shakespeare**.

Although Peter Brook (born 1925) is probably the best-known internationally of contemporary British directors, the major director from a visitor's point of view is the founder of the Royal Shakespeare Company and the director, from November 1973, of the National Theatre, Peter Hall (born 1930). When he took over the Shakespeare Memorial Theatre at Stratford-upon-Avon in 1960, Hall found a public used to seeing a summer season of miscellaneous Shakespeare revivals led by visiting stars performing with a company .that was re-formed

Alan Howard as Oberon and John Kane as Puck in Peter Brook's brilliant revival of *A Midsummer Night's Dream.*

each year. By the time he handed on his job to Trevor Nunn (born 1940) eight years later in 1968, a permanent company, the Royal Shakespeare Company, had been formed, with a London home at the Aldwych where Royal Shakespeare actors could be seen in modern works.

In those years Shakespeare's 400th birthday had been celebrated with the presentation of his History plays under the heading of **The Wars of the Roses**. The collaboration of the Cambridge don turned director John Barton (born 1928) was of vital importance to this cycle, especially his skill in editing the texts. Hall's policy of presenting Shakespeare's plays as an integrated package has been carried on by Trevor Nunn, who with his associate director, Terry Hands (born 1941), has presented seasons of the Late Romances (1968) and the Roman plays (1972) at Stratford.

Peter Brook's association with the RSC has spanned both the Hall and the Nunn regimes. His work there has emerged as great directorial explosions that have carried the company's name throughout the world.

48 Direction

In 1962 it was his Beckett-inspired treatment of **King Lear** that was premiered at Stratford and went on to tour Europe and North America; in 1970 it was his innovatory treatment of **A Midsummer Night's Dream** that was to do the same. Meantime productions of **The Marat/Sade** (1964) (inspired by Artaud's Theatre of Cruelty) and **US** (1966) on the Vietnam War and Seneca's **Oedipus** (for the National Theatre in 1968) ensured that theatre avant-gardists continued to refer to Brook with an awe and veneration no other English director has commanded—internationally at least.

Directing at the Royal Shakespeare Company's Stratford and London homes has always been marked by a strong overall company approach to the question of design. Whether in the Hall era, when John Bury was the RSC's Head of Design, or in the current Nunn epoch with Christopher Morley in John Bury's shoes, an habitué of the company would know at a glance he was attending one of its performances even if led into the theatre blindfolded. Sets are simple, often to the point of austerity, with a stage sloping into the auditorium and with breaks between scenes marked by blackouts and not the old-fashioned drop of the curtain. All RSC directors, whether it be Peter Hall directing Harold Pinter at the Aldwych or Trevor Nunn reviving Tourneur at Stratford-upon-Avon, work within the company's design format.

Austerity in the design department was also a hallmark of William Gaskill's (born 1930) artistic direction of the Royal Court Theatre which he assumed on the death of the English Stage Company's founder director, George Devine, in 1965. By the time he gave up the post in 1972, Gaskill had emerged as the most deeply influenced of British directors by the Berliner Ensemble's London visit in 1956 and the most prolific director of Brecht in Britain. He championed the plays of Edward Bond against an initially hostile press, himself directing **Saved** (1965), **Early Morning** (1968) and the Bond **Lear** (1972). In case this makes Gaskill sound capable of directing only severe or didactic work, it should be added that two productions he undertook for the National Theatre, of which he was an Associate Director in its opening years (1963 – 1965) were of Farquhar comedies—**The Recruiting Officer** (1963) and **The Beaux' Stratagem** (1970), both with the French designer, René Allio.

Another director to make his name at the Royal Court and then move on for a period to the National Theatre is John Dexter. At the Royal Court his association was principally with Wesker's plays—**Chicken Soup with Barley, Roots** and **I'm Talking About Jerusalem,** (staged as the Wesker trilogy), **The Kitchen, Chips with Everything,** and **The Old Ones.** Like Gaskill's, his initial stay as Associate Director of the National was short (1963 – 1966) but he returned in 1971. When the National Theatre still used the Chichester Festival Theatre for its summer seasons there was a fascinating collaboration between Dexter and Gaskill on John Arden's play, **Armstrong's Last Goodnight** (1965),—fascinating because Dexter's methods were those of an extrovert authoritarian director whilst Gaskill's reputation rested on the quieter approach of the teacher par excellence, the studio exercise and improvisations man.

Laurence Olivier as Othello in John Dexter's production at the Old Vic, one of the National's first and greatest successes

50 Direction

Joan Littlewood, director of Theatre Workshop at the Theatre Royal, Stratford E15, has also been well known for favouring group improvisations in her productions and the stories are legion of writers who have left her rehearsals in their early stages only to return for the opening night and find a text they claim barely to recognize. Joan Littlewood, though in the theatre since the 1930s, first came to the notice of the general public in the late 1950s when her Stratford East productions began to transfer one after the other to the West End—**The Quare Fellow** (1956) and **The Hostage** (1958) by Brendan Behan, Shelagh Delaney's **A Taste of Honey** (1958) and the Cockney musicals—**Fings Ain't Wot They Used T'Be** (1959), **Sparrers Can't Sing** (1960) and, most famous of all, her attack on the futility of World War One, **Oh! What a Lovely War** (1963).

The problem for Joan Littlewood was that she was having the wrong sort of success. Her ideal in setting up Theatre Workshop was to found a People's Theatre in East London, which was why her shows were replete with folksy cockney humour rather than with overt, grim didactic moralising on capitalist society. Disappointed with having become instead part of the West End works, Joan Littlewood left Stratford East in 1964 with dreams of starting up a people's Fun Palace—but in practice to work abroad. In 1967 she was back at her Theatre Royal and at the beginning of the 1970s was providing visitors with a fascinating contrast with that other internationally revered British director, Peter Brook. Whilst Brook's rehearsals were conducted in the hushed atmosphere of a high church ritual and were increasingly concerned with esoteric matters like that of finding a new theatrical language, Littlewood's preparations were made in the matey spirit of a public house sing-song with the over-riding aim of communicating with the people rather than with the intellectuals.

In as far as the public now goes to see a production by Peter Brook or Joan Littlewood on the strength of their reputation rather than that of the writer or the cast leads, these two such dissimilar artists can be advanced as practitioners of Director's Theatre as mentioned at the beginning of this chapter. Actor's Theatre such as Olivier's Othello—where the draw is above all the magnetism of a central performance—helps to throw into relief what is meant by director's theatre. But in this connection it must be remembered that Olivier is himself a director of the first rank, as he showed at Chichester with **Uncle Vanya** (1963) and Miller's **The Crucible** (1965) and at the Old Vic with O'Casey's **Juno and the Paycock** (1966) for the National Theatre. Younger actors, too, like Peter McEnery (born 1940) and Ian McKellen have shown themselves anxious to be directors as well as actors. Indeed in 1972 McKellen helped form an Actor's Company, the whole point of which was that the cast should be collaboratively responsible for a production rather than allowing the actors to be considered as modelling material for a Brook or a Littlewood. Inevitably any theatre company presents a power structure in which at different times different elements of the team predominate. Though the struggles behind the scenes may sometimes be fierce, all that the public is concerned about is what most fires its imagination and satisfies its theatregoing instinct—the end product.

Because one knows that battles are often fought to make the result a success, it's pleasant to conclude this chapter with some notes on collaborations that have survived the pressures of theatremaking over a number of years. Reference has already been made both to the Peter Hall/Harold Pinter and the Arnold Wesker/John Dexter author/director partnerships. These have been followed by a partnership at the Royal Court between a novelist turned dramatist and a film director turned theatre director. Lindsay Anderson (born 1923) did not in fact direct **The Restoration of Arnold Middleton** (1967), the first of David Storey's plays to be presented at the Royal Court. But **In Celebration** (1969), **The Contractor** (1969) **Home** (1970) and **The Changing Room** (1972) were all successful Storey/Anderson collaborations and 1973 began with the promise of two more from the same team.

Another and equally fruitful author/director partnership has been that of Peter Nichols (born 1927) and the National Theatre's Associate Director, Michael Blakemore (born 1928). The collaboration began on **A Day in the Death of Joe Egg** (1967) which came to the West End from Scotland, continuing with **The National Health** (1969) which was presented by the National Theatre at the Old Vic, and **Forget-Me-Not Lane** (1971) which transferred to the West End from the Greenwich Theatre.

It is interesting to note that all the directors mentioned are at work in the subsidised theatre. No doubt Harley Granville-Barker, the first British director of importance, would have approved. It was as a result of trying to run avant-garde theatre at the Royal Court on commercial lines that he took up the cause of subsidised theatre and, as far back as 1907, published the first manifesto for a National Theatre in Britain. Maybe if both subsidy and a National Theatre had not had to wait until after his death in 1946, Granville-Barker would not have given up directorship for scholarship. At least, no matter how honourable, that does not seem to be a fate in store for the directors who, either through the sheer virtuosity of their approach or through their sensitive promotion of new writing, are making the British theatre the exciting place it now so often is.

DESIGN

'It's the sort of musical that you come out of whistling the sets' somebody remarked after the first night in London of **Blitz !** back in 1962. Is it strange that some ten years later this comment is remembered as a criticism both of Lionel Bart's music and of Sean Kenny's spectacularly designed recreation of the World War Two bombing of London? The designer's pyrotechnics had, after all, evidently excited the spectator.

Perhaps an answer ought to be sought within the overall context of post-war British theatre design. If this is taken to span the 25 years from 1945 to 1970, it probably seems an absurdly wide context in which to seek an answer to any one question. Yet, as it happens, there are two good reasons why **Blitz!** is relevant to the overall picture. One is that Sean Kenny's career has itself played a major part in the design revolution which has taken place in that quarter of a century. And the other is that the revolution concerns nothing so much as the relationship of the set to the rest of the production. Oversimplifying, you could say that it marks a swing of the pendulum from a painterly flamboyance at the beginning of the period to a sculptured austerity at the end.

Since one of the most striking features of the West End in the 1970s is the sight of musicals buoyed up with sets as applause—invoking as those of **Blitz !**, this swing-of-the-pendulum guideline may at first seem unconvincing. The sight of Scarlett O'Hara fleeing home to Tara in **Gone with the Wind** at Drury Lane (1972) hardly marked the triumph of sculptured austerity. And how does one explain the appearance of a seemingly real river steamer in the Adelphi revival of **Show Boat** except as a swing in the opposite direction of the design pendulum? The best answer is to point out that the design revolution happened outside the West End at Joan Littlewood's Theatre Workshop, at the Royal Court and the Royal Shakespeare theatres. From them the commercial theatre has taken something of the old and something of the new—just as and when it suits its purpose. In passing, however, it should be said that the West End manager Michael Codron (born 1930) has shown as shrewd an eye for the new writers as he has for the new designer—a talent that was perhaps seen at its happiest in 1964 when he premiered Joe Orton's **Entertaining Mr Sloane** in a setting by Timothy O'Brien.

It suits this chapter's purpose to suggest that what the new designers in the subsidised or experimental theatre were reacting against was the sort of design epitomised by the work of Oliver Messel (born 1905), Cecil Beaton (born 1904) and Leslie Hurry (born 1909). The first thing that has to be said about all three of them is that their creations had such a highly personal style that a regular theatregoer could put a name to their sets and costumes as soon as the curtain went up. And to the

Ralph Koltai designed *Back to Methuselah* for the National Theatre—Derek Jacobi and Louise Purnell as Adam and Eve immediate postwar generation, in a Britain of rationing and utility wear, no more glamorous escape could be envisaged than Messel's designs for productions like **The Sleeping Beauty** at Covent Garden in 1946 or **Ring Round the Moon** in the West End in 1950.

Similarly Cecil Beaton's sets and costumes for the revival of Pinero's **The Second Mrs Tanqueray** in 1950 and his costumes for **My Fair Lady** in 1956 conjured up a vanished world of romantic elegance light years from Britain in full mid-twentieth century. And the swirling, brooding intensity of the sets that Leslie Hurry bestowed on Shakespeare revivals at the Old Vic whisked the public along a path where a painter-designer provided magnificent decoration for the stage production in hand.

The same year that **My Fair Lady** opened in London—1956—Brecht's Berliner Ensemble came to the Palace Theatre with **Mother Courage** and **The Caucasian Chalk Circle**. As an astonished and excited public was struck by the impact of the asceticism of the Ensemble's productions, it became clear that designers other than those of the school of Messel, Beaton and Hurry would have to appear before Brecht could make his belated appearance on the British stage. And as the same year saw the start of the arrival of the new generation of writers like Arden, Beckett, Pinter and Wesker, such designers were even more in demand if the right design solution were to be found on the necessary shoestring budget for a drama far removed from the world of Tchaikovsky's ballet, the escapist musical or the Victorian drawing-room melodrama. So it was just as well that Joan Littlewood, down at her East End Theatre Workshop, was quietly introducing Britain to the long-established continental system of appointing a resident company designer—even if this was in rather an unorthodox way.

John Bury (born 1925) joined Theatre Workshop in 1954 as an actor who was prepared to help out with lighting the shows. Though he did little painting and less drawing, he found that by the time he left Littlewood's company in 1964 to be Head of Design for Peter Hall's new Royal Shakespeare Company at Stratford-upon-Avon, he had chalked up over 20 productions at Littlewood's Stratford East home. And they included productions as famous as **A Taste of Honey, Fings Ain't Wot They Used T'Be** and **Oh! What a Lovely War**.

Bury exemplifies the theory that necessity is the mother of invention. Where the old school of designers had used a paint brush he busied himself with a camera. And where their models had been in balsa wood, he worked from the texture of the real materials that came to hand. Lack of money meant that sets were built from things like corrugated iron or left-over wood. The result was that when Bury moved on to Stratford-upon-Avon he designed from the company's workshops rather than from a drawing board. And he therefore needed to know hitherto unconventional things like what sound a material makes when you hit it.

The highpoint of Peter Hall and John Bury's early collaboration at Stratford was reached in the mid 1960s when a major unifying factor in the staging of all Shakespeare's history plays under the umbrella title of **The Wars of the Roses** was Bury's set. It was made of expanded metal with textures created by swilling the metal down with acids and copper solutions. And what the actors in this context wore were not the old embroidered costumes but clothes which were treated with the new plastics, rubber and latex to suggest richness. Above all Bury's entrée into the design world as an electrician for Joan Littlewood productions showed in the new directional lighting that was used. Instead of repeating the shadowless stage of the old painter's theatre, directional lighting emphasised the texture of the new materials adopted. Moreover it meant that the actor no longer had to make-up with black triangles to his cheeks in order to give back to his cheeks the hollows that they had in ordinary life.

The Hall/Bury partnership continued outside the Royal Shakespeare Company when Hall handed over the company's artistic direction to Trevor Nunn in 1968. Both, however, returned from time to time to collaborate at the RSC's London home on productions of a rather different scale such as Pinter's one-act plays, **Landscape** and **Silence** (1969). They will continue to work together at the National Theatre. Meantime Hall and Bury's concept of examining Shakespeare's plays in related groups with a director/designer collaboration spanning a number of productions bore fruit. Under Trevor Nunn's regime, sequences like Shakespeare's Late Romances and his Roman Plays were staged. And Christopher Morley, the company's new Head of Design and Nunn's principal production partner, explored basic ways and means of finding a coherent answer to the problem of designing for the Bard into which the company's modern work could also be accommodated. Examples of this were seen in the black and the white 'box' seasons of 1969 and 1970 in which settings, always on a forward-tilting stage, were reduced to a chamber-like enclosed space in which costumes were designed in a colour that was of as much significance as the few carefully-chosen props.

Apart from director/designer partnerships like the Nunn/Morley collaboration (especially notable for the 1966 **Revenger's Tragedy** and the 1969 **The Winter's Tale**), the RSC also gained strength in the Hall epoch from the work of Clifford Williams and Ralph Koltai (their 1964 **The Jew of Malta** being especially remarkable) and later from Terry Hands and Timothy O'Brien—with **The Merry Wives of Windsor** (1968) and **The Man of Mode** (1971) standing out.

What the Royal Shakespeare Company have in fact done is to fill in the period till their modern Barbican Theatre in London is ready by evolving a company solution to the problem of designing Shakespeare for a proscenium stage from which the old-fashioned curtain has been banished, whilst the maximum use has been made of the technical developments in modern stage lighting.

Within this framework each of the director/designer partnerships has been free to find its own solution to the problems raised by individual productions. Thus a basically 'outside' team like that of the director Robin Phillips and the designer Daphne Dare was able to make an impressive contribution within the prevailing house-style with their **Two Gentlemen of Verona** at Stratford in 1972.

Finally, it must be said that an important feature of the company's work in the early 1970s has been the use of costumes that are neither arbitrarily pegged to a certain period nor arbitrarily modern. They were designed to give simultaneously a hint of the play's period and a hint of relevant contemporary styles. The result has been that a young audience has not been made to feel they ought to be experts on period trimmings to get a revival's full flavour whilst, at the same time, they were given a visual opportunity to sample references to the world about them and so to receive the play both in terms of its period and in terms of the time of its revival.

56 Design

What John Bury did for the Royal Shakespeare Company, Jocelyn Herbert (born 1917) achieved for the Royal Court Theatre. Her first designs there—for Ionesco's cluttered play, **The Chairs** (1957)—were to be deeply untypical of the paring-down-to-essentials that marked her collaboration with the directors John Dexter, William Gaskill and Lindsay Anderson. The most thoroughgoing of these partnerships was with Dexter and involved the London premiere of Wesker's more important plays—the **Trilogy** and **Chips with Everything** (1962). She cleared the Royal Court's tiny stage to its back wall, so that it seemed to take on the proportions of a far larger acting area, and used it with a searching selectivity that was perhaps at its most impressively severe in Lindsay Anderson's production of **Home** by David Storey in 1970.

Since William Gaskill, the most Brecht-influenced of British directors, was artistic director of the Court during the greater part of this period, Jocelyn Herbert's 'less is more' approach fitted the theatre's general outlook extraordinarily well. As with the Royal Shakespeare Company, a number of good director/designer partnerships were formed within the prevailing design outlook. The most notable of these was probably that of Peter Gill and John Gunter. Both revived D H Lawrence's coalmining plays after a period of painstaking research into their author's background. If one had to sum up the most lasting impression of the Royal Court's overall approach to design it would have to be in the selective naturalism of these three plays—**The Daughter-in-Law, The Widowing of Mrs Holroyd** and **A Collier's Friday Night**. With the back wall and the stage lights on view no accusation could be levelled to the effect that the director or designer were going in for old-fashioned Moscow Art Theatre naturalism. Yet their extraordinarily accurate choice of a few props and the correct use of them conveyed a sense of reality that mountains of naturalistic scenery could hardly have achieved.

It was a sign of the times that none of the designers who formed the partnership that undertook the Royal Court and Royal Shakespeare productions of the 1960s could talk of the future without talking also of the design of theatres themselves. And this brings us back to Sean Kenny (born 1932), who trained as an architect before making his name as a designer at the Royal Court and Mermaid theatres. More than anybody else he championed the cause of harnessing theatre set design to the design of the buildings they occupied. Because sets of his like **Blitz !** dwarfed productions with his own signature as unmistakably as any of the work of the Messels, the Beatons and the Hurrys, he has seemed sometimes to be moving in the opposite direction to the designers who have scrupulously sought to interpret Shakespeare and the new writers with a near-anonymous simplicity of means. Yet Kenny, more vociferously than any other designer, has made theatre managements, both commercial and subsidised, aware of the need to make every use of modern technology in the theatre.

His most bitter complaint has been that theatres have been designed from the outside inwards by architects who did not really understand theatrecraft. They ought, he claimed, to be designing from the stage outwards. Though his polemical attitude has upset some, even they have to admit that Kenny has at least practised what he preached. When his sets for **Gulliver's Travels** at the Mermaid in 1968 became the raison d'être of the evening he was sensible enough to direct it himself. And after complaining of the restrictions of the West End proscenium arch theatres, he went ahead and designed the open spaces that constitute the theatres of the Gardner Centre in Sussex University.

A frequent source of attack on Kenny's part was the British theatre's slowness in using the latest lighting equipment. As this has little by little been installed, so the postwar period has seen the rise of a new member in the production team—the lighting designer. Gradually theatregoers have come to recognize names like Michael Northen (born 1921), Robert Ornbo (born 1931) and Richard Pilbrow (born 1933) alongside the famous directors and designers. Their work used to be undertaken (in Britain) by the director and (in America) by the designer. But the increasing sophistication of lighting resources has brought forth the specialist who in turn has done much to revolutionise staging—particularly in the effective use of the apron-stage and in-the-round theatre. And the pioneering work done by the Czech designer, Josef Svoboda, with his polyecran screen in introducing Britain to the full resources of projected sets in productions at Covent Garden and at the National Theatre suggests that the potential for the lighting designer in the 1970s is by no means exhausted with the introduction of computerised lighting controls.

The fact that Svoboda made his theatre debut in Britain designing for the National Theatre is an indication of the catholicism of its approach to design since Sean Kenny remodelled its Old Vic stage and designed its opening production (**Hamlet**) in 1963. It has dipped into the world of international design with baroque sets and costumes by the Italian, Piero Gherardi for the 1969 revival of **The White Devil** on the one hand and, on the other, with the bare open stage and near-nude actors in the work of the director/designer, Victor Garcia, for **The Architect and the Emperor of Assyria** (1971). Between these two extremes, every conceivable style has been essayed in work ranging from the painstakingly detailed reconstruction of nineteenth century Venice in Julia Trevelyan Oman's sets and costumes for the 1970 **The Merchant of Venice** to the abstractions of Ralph Koltai's designs for **Back to Methuselah** in 1969. The National, therefore, has certainly not failed to take design along every possible path—within the restrictions laid down by its use of the Old Vic proscenium, with which it has to live until the completion of its own building, which is to include apron and arena staging as well as a proscenium.

So, whilst the National's tenancy of the Old Vic has been excitingly exploratory from a design point of view, it cannot be claimed that the company has adhered to a policy that would fit neatly into any thesis of the 25-year post-war period representing progress from decorative flamboyance in the painterly manner to an austere use of the acting area with a sculptor's sensitive appreciation of texture and the choice of significant form.

The regional scene, which used to be thought of as an abbatoir of design talent in the days of weekly and fortnightly repertory, is now happily in a healthier position. This is partly due to the new theatres which accommodate companies with facilities to design for runs of three weeks or to present a repertoire system. And, apart from a general subsidy to Regional Theatre, the Arts Council has helped in the design field by running a scheme whereby selected design graduates are seconded to the better regional theatres for a one-year period on a trainee basis. During that period the design trainee, as well as gaining general practical experience, is responsible for the overall design of one

Another scene showing Ralph Koltai's designs for *Back to Methuselah*

production. Though it is true young design students are easily exploited, there is no wish in Britain to form a closed shop such as exists in the United States. There, even the most eminent designers who wish to work in the theatre are subjected to a three-day examination and it is reported that on average only three of every hundred applicants get through. In Britain this is not thought to have brought about a better standard of design in America. Artists, however, are concerned at the ease with which they can be overworked and to protect the more vulnerable of younger designers moves have been made to set up a designer's association.

Unfortunately, like actors, their position is not a strong one since too many design students are chasing too few jobs. Some feel local authorities should spend more money on improving courses instead of taking on responsibility for so many students. More practical experience of theatre during training is always being advocated by students who have found that playing with models at school ill fits them to deal with the crises of shortage of time, shortage of money and shortage of patience on the part of directors and actors in the theatre itself.

Television certainly takes up a large number of design graduates, and theatre designers of the calibre of Timothy O'Brien have acknowledged the value of television work. But the box-like naturalism that pervades nearly all television drama is not every student's idea of an exciting career. Most, however, take a pragmatic and practical attitude to their situation, so it is perhaps not surprising that the names of the great design theorists—like Appia and Craig—are seldom bandied about either backstage or in the television studios. One student aptly summed up a characteristically British attitude to the abstractions of the purely intellectual approach with the remark, 'Design theory is for the over-fifties.'

ECONOMICS

Just as it used not to be the done thing to ask a lady her age, so no British theatre manager was ever expected to disclose the financial statistics behind a presentation with which he hoped to seduce the public. The essential 'magic of the theatre' was thought to be imperilled if the actual cost of laying on its charms were ungallantly catalogued. So if a London impresario of the old school had opened his accounts book to the press, it would have been as much a matter of astonishment as if a mature actress had confided to an interviewer the amount of dye that went into her hair, the quantity of caps that concealed her blackening teeth or the number of face-lifts that enabled her to perpetuate a youthful spell.

When Richard Findlater published his book, **The Unholy Trade**, in 1952 the long silence was for the first time effectively broken. And the book's historical breakdown of the finances and abuses of Shaftesbury Avenue conveniently anticipated the arrival of a new generation of theatregoers who were no longer prepared to be fobbed off with accounts of the romantic aspects of life amongst the stars—fascinating though these continued to be. The new anti-illusionist staging inspired by the approach of Brecht's Berliner Ensemble, coupled with the appearance of a new breed of dramatists anxious to confront the public with the hard facts of life about them, combined to create a suitable climate for the emergence of a more questioning playgoer. Where one generation had loved to rhapsodise over the matinee tea-tray at the sheer glamour of the theatre, a new one trained a beadily speculative eye on the economics of the venture.

Of course in New York, the Broadway tradition had been rather different and was keenly reflected in the relevant trade papers. Whereas New York's **Variety** (in its highly colourful vernacular) had always spelt out the finances of American theatre, the London **Stage** had a long weekly tradition of discretion on this front. Not only did **Variety** tell you what everything was grossing but its theatre criticisms were also strictly angled from an investor's point of view. **The Stage**, on the other hand, managed even in the early 1970s to go no further in this respect than to report that a smash hit 'had broken all box-office records.'

Not surprisingly, therefore, it was the Americans who were first off the mark in the 1960s with a number of books revealing who had paid for what—and how—by the time a show's first night bouquets helped to cover the business deals with floral tributes. Publications like **The Season, The Producers** and **From Option to First Night** openly chronicled the day-to-day dealings of Broadway and off-Broadway's hit-or-flop economics. In Britain the follow-up to Findlater's **The Unholy Trade** was less spectacular. The figures that were most consistently put before the public concerned the amount of money the Arts Council of Great Britain was given by the Government each year. This had begun in the financial year ending in 1946 with a total grant-in-aid of £235,000 but had risen by 1971/1972 to practically twelve million pounds.

60 Economics

During that period Britain acquired its first Minister of the Arts (1964 – 1970) in Miss Jennie Lee. Her successor, Lord Eccles, was able to announce early in 1973 that the Arts Council's grant for the financial year 1973/1974 was to be increased by three and a half million pounds to bring the figure up to a grand total of £17,388,000. The annual publication of figures of this kind and the often much-publicised scramble by competing organisations to get their fair slice of the subsidy cake have all helped to make the intelligent British theatregoer aware of the importance of the economics of the theatre. In particular these figures helped them to realise how government subsidy prevented the post-war collapse of British regional theatre.

On the commercial front, a West End manager at last came round to giving the public an insight into the financial workings of the postwar British theatre when Peter Saunders published **The Mousetrap Man** in 1972. The book was so called because Mr Saunders was the manager responsible for breaking all records by presenting the Agatha Christie thriller, **The Mousetrap**, at the Ambassadors' Theatre where, in 1972, it entered the twenty-first year of a widely-expected quarter of a century's run. Even Mr Saunders, however, did not depart from the English managerial tradition of reticence to say precisely how much **The Mousetrap** cost to run and what its casts were paid. Since Peter Saunders has acquired the freehold of the Vaudeville Theatre, and long leases on the Ambassadors and the adjoining St Martin's during the presentation of **The Mousetrap** it seems safe to assume the long run has not been achieved at a loss.

At the close of his book, Peter Saunders gives some notes on 17 of a total of some 40 British theatre managers. The most striking overall feature about them is the lack of flamboyance of the sort that William Cody (1846 – 1917), better known as Buffalo Bill, has made almost traditional amongst succeeding American theatre managers from Florenz Ziegfeld (1867 – 1932) to David Merrick today. Apart from C B Cochran (1872 – 1951), the great promoter of musical comedy and lavish revue in London, the British managers have been more reserved business men than public personalities.

Should any theatregoer be so fascinated by their production as to think of joining their ranks, what are the elementary facts he should bear in mind? The first is that despite escalating costs, the newcomer has a better chance of gaining a managerial foothold in the 1970s than he would have had in the 1950s. This is because up to that time a single management, H M Tennent Ltd, held what amounted to a monopolistic position in the post-war theatre. This came about because this management, headed by Hugh 'Binkie' Beaumont (1908 – 1973) brilliantly and quite legally made the most of a government dispensation with regard to exemption from the payment of entertainment tax, first imposed in 1916. By forming a non-profit distributing subsidiary company for the production of plays that were partly educational or cultural, both this and the parent company were allowed to forego the payment of entertainment tax. The idea was that the parent company should subsidise its uncommercial and cultural subsidiary by being given every government encouragement to survive. The result, from the point of view of other aspiring managements, was that H M Tennent had first

The Mousetrap: this is how Agatha Christie's marathon-running play looked at the Ambassadors theatre in 1969

call on the best stars, the best West End theatres and the best touring date theatres. Nobody in the business wanted to fall foul of an organisation on whose goodwill their career depended and the public and critics were too impressed by the exceedingly high standard of Tennent presentations to question the system that brought this about. Of course the smaller managements were highly dissatisfied with the arrangement and their voices were eventually heard through a Member of Parliament, Woodrow Wyatt, who sought to introduce a bill to clear up the anomalies in the tax-exemption system. Although in the course of the debate Mr. Wyatt revealed that the Tennent subsidiary, Tennent Productions Ltd, was registered as a charitable trust and therefore paid neither income tax nor entertainment tax, the necessary support was not forthcoming for his bill to go through. But this notwithstanding, the position of the smaller companies thereafter began to improve and the situation was finally resolved in 1957 with the abolition of entertainment tax altogether.

In 1973 the managements' worry lay with the introduction of Value Added Tax, a new tax likely to make theatregoing even more expensive in Britain than it had come to be. So anybody wanting to go into management in the 1970s has to concern himself with the problem of inflationary costs, which bring London increasingly into line with New York's switchback economics. Some indication of the way costs have in fact spiralled since Tennents' set up in management in the immediate pre-war years is indicated by the production budgets of two of their presentations. In 1938 the company staged **Spring Meeting** by M J Farrell and John Perry which starred Margaret Rutherford and Joyce Carey. It cost £800 to put on. In 1961 the same management produced a sequel by the same stars, and with the same number of supporting actors in the same setting. The cost then was £6,000. Eleven years later, in 1973, a one set play with half a dozen characters of this kind had come to cost between £15,000 and £20,000 to bring to Shaftesbury Avenue. And if any would-be manager finds this figure daunting he should bear in mind that a full-scale West End musical of the early 1970s needs an investment of between £150,000 and £200,000.

If the would-be manager remains undismayed by these facts and figures, what other elementary information should he take into account? The first, obviously, is that the costs are so great that he cannot enter the commercial arena with any of the idealistic motives that fired George Devine when he set up the Royal Court's English Stage Company, with the motto that the new writers to be promoted 'had the right to fail.' With a spiralling capital investment at stake, the commercial pressures are more than ever to find formula comedies, farces and thrillers, preferably as vehicles for stars whose popularity rests either on their repeating a much-loved style of performance (like Kenneth Williams) or on their being capable of generating a strong nostalgic appeal such as the big names of the 1930s and 1940s are now able to muster (Marlene Dietrich, Anna Neagle and Ginger Rogers are good examples).

Occasionally a young theatre manager like Michael White (born 1936) has the breadth of taste and canniness to produce money-spinners like **Oh! Calcutta!** and **Sleuth** on the one hand and, on the other, to risk translated cultural imports like his London productions of Brecht's **The Resistible Rise of Arturo Ui** and Romain Weingarten's **Summer**. But it is worrying that a new generation of young theatre managers is hard to spot on the horizon. Just how important they can be is illustrated by the happy coincidence of the arrival on the managerial scene of Michael Codron (born 1930) at the time of the breakthrough of new dramatic writing in the mid-1950s. Codron's record of bringing new writing talent into the orbit of the West End is an impressive one. Highlights from the list read: Harold Pinter's **The Caretaker** (1960), Joe Orton's **Entertaining Mr Sloane** (1964), David Mercer's **Ride A Cock Horse** (1965), Christopher Hampton's **When Did You Last See My Mother?** (1966), Charles Wood's **Fill the Stage with Happy Hours** (1967), Tom Stoppard's **The Real Inspector Hound** (1968), David Storey's **The Contractor** (1970) and Christopher Hampton's **The Philanthropist** (1970). So long as there is the financial bait of an example like **Oliver!**, the £15,000 musical that made over a million, the West End ought not to fail to attract fortune seekers. But where are those with the know-how both to make money and sustain new acting, design and writing talent within the West End farmework?

Perhaps the failure of a new generation of Michael Codrons or Michael Whites to materialise owes something to the uncertainty of West End theatre buildings themselves. From an economic point of view, the advantage of their age is that the actual cost of building them has long since been paid off. But they occupy central sites in London which in real estate terms give a poor return on their potential value. British Actors Equity, sensing the threat to the very heart of British theatre, launched a campaign in 1973 to preserve the theatres it felt to be most threatened by the developers. It is to be hoped that their campaign is successful, since the history of newly-built postwar theatres in the West End has not been a happy one. The vast Stoll Theatre was developed as an office block with the cinema-like Royalty, built at basement level and reached by a side street, being the only survivor of a once all-entertainment site. The Prince Charles Theatre, opened in 1962 as the first new West End theatre in 37 years, soon became a cinema after a very brief and inglorious career as a theatre proper. It would be a sad day to witness sites like those occupied by Wyndham's or the Garrick theatres reduced to office blocks with basement cinema-like theatres thrown in as a sop to bygone times.

Even assuming the West End remains more or less intact, any would-be manager will find the business of taking his place amongst the 40 existing West End producers a major test of nerves. One of the main reasons why barely twenty managers at the beginning of 1973 were in fact fully operational is that very few of them are both theatre owners and production company managers. So if a would-be manager has the necessary £2,000 to have taken a year's option on a play and secured the agreement of the necessary stars to appear in it, he still has a very long haul ahead of him, even assuming he has had the satisfaction of making the best preliminary choice available to him of casting, direction and design. And in the discovering of a script and the marrying it up with a production team that will make it a profitable enterprise probably lies the sense of power and managerial creativity that is the attraction of the job of being a producer. But if the stars, directors and even designers are big enough names they too enter into the gamble of play production by being contracted on the basis of receiving a percentage of the box office takings as well as being employed by the manager for an agreed period. In that case they share his next biggest anxiety to an even greater extent for—even assuming he can find backers—he still has to find a theatre.

It is impossible, therefore, to ignore the business of owning a theatre in the context of producing a play. Large organisations like the Stoll Theatre Group, which owns or leases the Queen's, the Globe, the Lyric and the Apollo on Shaftesbury Avenue as well as theatres like the Theatre Royal, Drury Lane and Her Majesty's, have such enormous resources of their own that they hardly fit into the normal West End production pattern. Should they decide on a production, they have their own theatres and they are in a position to raise the capital for production from their own resources.

Other managements, however, operate in other ways. A large production company which mounts spectacular musicals will be interested only in investors who have sums like £10,000 to gamble on a new show. This is the sort of money you need to participate in the launching of a musical like **Half a Sixpence** or **Gone with the Wind**, staged by the most flamboyant of British theatre managers, Harold Fielding. The smaller groups tend to deal in sums like £250, though one manager, Charles Ross, has advertised for units as small as £25. At this level productions are financed by people who enjoy gambling in the theatre as much as they do on the race track. In the business they are called 'angels' and managers who use them tend to stick by backers who have remained faithful through thick and thin. If a manager thinks he has a winner on his hands, clearly he is going to give first opportunity of investing in it to those who may have lost on a previous venture which perhaps succeeded on tour but failed to find a London theatre.

And this is where production companies which are not also theatre owning companies are at a severe disadvantage. They have to get a show on the road in the hope that a theatre will fall free at the right moment. In the 1950s, before the high incidence of tourist theatre-going, London theatres used to be easier to find in the summer but almost impossible to obtain in the autumn and winter months. Now it is a round-the-year scramble to get the right theatre.

Once a manager has optioned a play and cast, paid for the most expensive item on his budget (the sets and costumes), found the backers to get it on the road and then found a suitable theatre, he may discover his greatest worry is getting the play withdrawn. For if it is not a success, the standard contract may require him to give the play a run of five to six weeks. Hardly any London theatre can now be hired at a fixed rental. And the contract stipulates that the management owning the theatre should participate somewhere between twenty and twenty-two per cent of the weekly gross takings.

If the show is a flop the production management may still have to keep the theatre open for a good month. If, on the other hand, the takings slip below an agreed figure—the 'getout'—the theatre-owning management can exercise its right to cause the producing management to withdraw the play, so that something more potentially rewarding can be brought in in its place.

One of the curious anomalies in this system is that the production management pays the wages of the theatre staff employed by the theatre owners, such as the stage door-keeper, the usherettes and the box-office staff. One production manager, who had had a particularly tough time in raising the capital to finance a production that had a dodgy opening, was appalled to go into the theatre he had hired and find that the box office manageress had taken the phones off the hook and was getting on with her knitting! Fortunately, in this case, he was able to persuade the owning management to make a replacement. It is interesting to speculate how the lady concerned might have handled the situation if her employer had insisted on her staying.

Opera and Ballet

For those hoping to take an informed interest in British opera and ballet, particularly overseas visitors, two useful points promptly emerge. One is that the history of both is so short that it takes far less time to bone up on these two fields than it does on the country's drama. The other is that, however shaky the visitor's knowledge of English either just as a language or—for the more sophisticated—as a reflector of class and regional nuances, an evening of pleasure can still be had. Not a word of the language has to be known even if, in extreme cases, a friendly translator of the programme's plot synopsis and general background notes is rather important.

The best way of substantiating the claim that the history of British ballet and opera is brief is to put forward the likeliest date for celebrating their first 50 years. In the case of ballet a good time would be in 1980. And for opera it could be as far off as 1996.

Why 1980 for ballet's first half century? Well, by then, it will be exactly 50 years since the founding of the Camargo Society in London, which happened to coincide with the first London season in 1930 of Ballet Rambert, known in those days as the Ballet Club.

Of course there are all manner of excuses for bringing forward the date. You could, for example, write off the importance of the Camargo Society by pointing out that its evenings of subscription-audience performances were to last only three years before the organisation was amalgamated with the Vic-Wells Ballet—about which more anon as the forerunner of the current and all-important Royal Ballet. Instead, you could claim that the founding, in 1920, of the Royal Academy of Dancing which is still in existence, was a much more fundamental milestone. But the setting up of this school, as well as the many others that came into being in the 'twenties, marked the gestation rather than the birth of British ballet. Without the schools there certainly would not have been the dancers to form the British companies that were set up in the 1930s. But these schools, important though they were, had more to do with what is best described as British ballet's incubation than with its birth. So, since we celebrate our birthdays from the day we give our first independent whelp in the world and not from the moment of our conception, thus let it be with ballet.

When you remember that the home of the Russian Imperial Ballet was at the Bolshoi from 1783 and when you recall, even more amazingly, that the beginnings of the Danish Royal Ballet are dated from 1726, it's remarkable that the British companies, led by the Royal Ballet at Covent Garden, should now rank amongst the world's other major ensembles which are so much longer in the tooth.

Dame Margot Fonteyn, partnered by David Blair, as Princess Aurora in *The Sleeping Beauty* at the Royal Opera House, Covent Garden. Dame Margot is an artist whose career epitomises the whole history of ballet in Britain

68 Opera and Ballet

This miracle would certainly never have been performed but for two exceptional women—one born in Poland and one in Ireland. Dame Marie Rambert (born, as Marie Ramberg, in Warsaw, 1888) and the Irish Ninette de Valois (born, as Edris Stannus, in 1898) jointly mothered ballet in Britain. So any visitor genuinely thrilled by their offspring will want to remember how the arch talent-spotter, Rambert, turned her Ballet Club into its current nimble Ballet Rambert. Equally, they should welcome some recollection of how Ninette de Valois willed the hopeful Vic-Wells Ballet of the 1930s into today's history-filled Royal Ballet. But before chronicling the country's indebtedness to these two Dames—both have been honoured with damehood for their labours—it might be as well at this point to sidestep briskly into the origins of British opera to search for parallel beginnings in that field.

What with Purcell and Handel having written operas in and for London (in the seventeenth and eighteenth centuries respectively) and what with Gilbert and Sullivan having produced an immensely popular and quintessentially English version of operetta in the nineteenth, it probably seems perverse even to attempt to date British opera from 1946. But the triumph that year of the world premiere of Benjamin Britten's **Peter Grimes** at Sadler's Wells put English opera on the world map with a momentum that no earlier attempts managed. It led, for example, to the founding in 1947 of the English Opera Group (under Britten, John Piper and Eric Crozier) which spawned both the Aldeburgh Festival in Suffolk and the Opera School, subsequently the London Opera Centre. Thus, at one blow, we have the operatic equivalent of the ballet schools of the 1920s and, with the Aldeburgh Festival in June, where much of Britten's work has been premiered or revived, an operatic festival that is as authentically English as the Shakespeare festivities at Stratford-upon-Avon.

Aldeburgh may seem a modest event on which to base a claim that Britain, through Britten, can at last claim the beginnings of a truly English indigenous opera. But consider how modest was what came before. For, however much we admire Purcell's **Dido and Aeneas** (1689), the Italianate operas Handel wrote for London by the time he became a British citizen in 1726, Gay's **The Beggar's Opera** (1728), or Balfe's 29 operas capped by **The Bohemian Girl** (1843), we find ourselves into the twentieth century with embarrassingly little. Where, amongst such a motley collection, is the British equivalent of Wagner's Ring Cycle that keeps the Bayreuth Festival afloat? Where is a British parallel to the Italian tradition of Rossini, Bellini, Donizetti, Verdi and Puccini which provides an opera house like Milan's La Scala with its so-replete native opera seasons?

Of course it had been noted long before 1946 that the British operatic cupboard was on the bare side. In fact as early as 1922 a British National Opera Company was founded to consolidate the pioneering work done by Sir Thomas Beecham's Opera Company, founded in 1915 and liquidated in 1920. Before the British National Opera Company itself was also wound up in 1929 it had premiered a number of English operas including Holst's **The Perfect Fool** and Vaughan Williams' **Hugh the Drover**. And the Sadler's Wells Opera, long before it premiered Britten's **Peter Grimes** in 1946, had done sterling work in premiering English operas including Vaughan Williams' **Sir John in Love**. Indeed the fact that Sadler's Wells Opera Company was founded by Lilian Baylis (as the operatic wing of her three companies operating at the Old Vic and Sadler's Wells Theatres) at the beginning of the 1930s means it has an excellent claim to be the begetter of a continuing operatic tradition in England. Even today Sadler's Wells, now firmly established in central London at the Coliseum, maintains Lilian Baylis' original policy of presenting opera in English with the intention that English audiences should understand what singers are expressing as well as listening to the way they set about it. In 1972 Sadler's Wells Opera made its first bid to be called the National Opera Company and, if it is eventually successful in this, its pioneering work will be justly rewarded.

But much of that work is in having introduced Britain to the international operatic repertoire in English with English singers rather than in establishing an internationally recognized school of English operatic composers. And without in any way wishing to detract from Sadler's Wells, it must not be forgotten that the Carl Rosa Opera Company, which was founded by Carl Rosa in 1873 in Manchester, had built up, by the time it folded in 1960, an exceedingly honourable tradition of touring opera in Britain and introduced the country as a whole to works like Bizet's **Carmen**. And in doing so profitably years before such things as Arts Council subsidy existed, the Company had proved that the British had a real love of opera even if in those days the country could not produce a school of opera composers on the scale of those coming from Italy, Germany and Russia.

In the wake of Britten's success things have looked up considerably. The Carl Rosa tradition of touring international opera has fallen, improbably, to the Glyndebourne Touring Opera which it does with Arts Council subsidy. One says 'improbably' because Glyndebourne's summer season of opera, founded in his Sussex country estate in 1934 by John Christie, can claim to have been amongst the world's most exclusive and elitist opera gatherings. Even today the tradition of dinner jackets for gentlemen and evening dresses for the ladies persists and the visitor can still see such smartly-attired people incongruously gathered at Victoria Station on mid-summer afternoons en route to Glyndebourne. Although Glyndebourne has staged Nicholas Maw's **The Rising of the Moon**, its achievements have not been with the promotion of British operatic writing but rather with maintaining a high standard of small-scale productions from the international repertoire. Its Mozart productions have been particularly distinguished.

Perhaps 1946 was a decisive year in establishing that Britain was coming of age operatically. Until then the Royal Opera at Covent Garden had, since 1858, run seasons of international opera except for breaks during the First and Second World Wars. But in 1946 it formed its first permanent company and, as though to prove that Britten's **Peter Grimes** was no postwar flash in the operatic pan, a whole succession of operas by British composers have followed. They include Britten's **Billy Budd** (1951) and **Gloriana** (1953), Walton's **Troilus and Cressida** (1962), Tippett's **The Midsummer Marriage** (1955), **King Priam** (1962) and **The Knot Garden** (1970), Humphrey Searle's **Hamlet** (1969), Richard Rodney Bennett's **Victory** (1970) and Peter Maxwell Davies' **Taverner** (1972). This last was even given Promenade Performances—an idea borrowed from the BBC's Promenade Concerts at the Albert Hall in which standing room in the centre of the Hall is available cheaply for the young. At Covent Garden it proved rather to be squatting room—but was nonetheless an extremely welcome sign that

Covent Garden could abandon the diamond horseshoe image better suited to the era of carriage and horses, not to mention canary fanciers.

As always in Britain, one has to be cautious about advancing claims for the nation based on what happens in London. As the 1970s get under way, however, the most encouraging signs have been the growth of strong National Opera Companies in Wales and Scotland.

Neither the Welsh National Opera nor the Scottish National have yet opera houses of their own. Each works from a temporary base much as the National Theatre has worked at the Old Vic pending the completion of its own new home on the South Bank. Of the two, the Welsh National was set up first, in 1946, with the Scottish being formed as recently as 1962. In its early years the Welsh National depended on an amateur chorus to give up their holidays in support of an operatic season which at that time had no permanent orchestra. Even so, it managed to revive Verdi operas then virtually unknown in Britain like **Nabucco, I Lombardi** and **I Vespri Siciliani**. Under Michael Geliot's artistic direction, it now has its own orchestra, the Welsh Philharmonic; its chorus is professional and its repertoire ranges from Beethoven (**Fidelio**) to Strauss (**Die Fledermaus**) and from Mussorgsky (**Boris Godunov**) to Berg (**Lulu**). The next step is for the company to move from Cardiff's New Theatre, where its triumphs have so far been celebrated, into its own Opera House in the same city.

Scottish Opera's progress has been similarly meteoric. Under Alexander Gibson's artistic direction it began in 1962 with a total budget of £6,000 and three performances apiece of **Madam Butterfly** and **Pelléas and Mélisande**. Ten years later the budget had risen to £550,000 with a correspondingly increased output and with the result that it also urgently needed a permanent operatic home. At the beginning of the 1970s its base was still the King's Theatre, Glasgow, where it staged works as spectacular and demanding as Berlioz's **The Trojans**. Its involvement with Edinburgh has largely been at the time of the Edinburgh Festival, to which it has contributed productions ranging from Stravinsky's **The Rake's Progress** to Britten's **Peter Grimes** and Wagner's **Die Walküre**. It publishes its own opera magazine, adopts a pragmatic policy towards opera in English (generally comic operas are given in English with weightier works like **The Ring** being performed in their original language). It also runs Scottish Opera for All, a mini-opera company taking opera in small-scale productions to outlying districts where facilities are lacking for visits of full-scale productions.

Having thus glanced at the principal strands of the infant British opera, we must now return to the more senior British ballet, which we dropped a few paragraphs back just as Dames Ninette de Valois and Marie Rambert were poised to do nothing less than will British ballet out of little more than thin air.

Ninette de Valois was a soloist with Diaghilev's Ballet Russe in the early twenties and then returned to London to found her own dancing school, rather quaintly called the Academy of Choreographic Art. When Lilian Baylis asked her to devise the dance sequences for her Shakespeare productions at the Old Vic and to use her own pupils for this work an historic friendship was set up. For when Lilian Baylis was

Benjamin Britten in rehearsal. Britten's *Peter Grimes,* premiered at Sadler's Wells in 1946, got British opera off the ground in what was to prove a prolific post-war era ambitious enough to open the Sadler's Wells theatre as a companion theatre to the Old Vic north of the river, she appointed Ninette de Valois to head and run the newly-formed company, known first as the Vic-Wells ballet (when the company alternated at both theatres) and then as the Sadler's Wells Ballet when it settled at that theatre. She had already choreographed **Job** with music by Vaughan Williams for the Camargo Society and for her own Sadler's Wells Ballet she produced more works including **The Rake's Progress** (based on Hogarth's paint-ings). And in **The Haunted Ballroom**, which de Valois choreographed in 1934, a then unknown member of the corps de ballet was given her first solo role. She was Margot Fonteyn, destined to become the company's prima ballerina, taking over roles like Giselle from Alicia Markova, who had led the newly-formed troupe in its opening seasons. By the 1970s the company had moved to Covent Garden and, since 1956, had been renamed the Royal Ballet. But Fonteyn was still dancing with the company. By then into her fifties, she no longer had the speed of her youth. Even so her appearances were always sellouts, since for both young and old she embodied the entire history of British Ballet. It was as though at the Bolshoi in Moscow you could still see the Russian ballerinas who created the lead roles in Tchaikovsky ballets such as **Swan Lake** or **Sleeping Beauty**—in both of which, incidentally, Fonteyn excelled in British productions.

Alicia Markova, the first-ever British ballerina, had been a member of Diaghilev's Ballets Russes. When the great man who had revitalised Russian ballet in London and Paris died in 1929 and his company was disbanded, it was only natural that Markova should be Sadler's Wells' first ballerina. Later, with her partner, Anton Dolin, she left to form her own company. Much later, in one of several Markova/Dolin partnerships, a company known as Festival Ballet was to emerge in 1950. Unlike the Royal Ballet this has no home and its two principals have both long since retired. But it has survived, having undertaken world tours and returning to give regular London seasons at the Festival Hall, the New Victoria Theatre and at the London Coliseum where its programmes of the Tchaikowsky ballets make good family entertain-ment. It was a sign of just how far British ballet had developed when Festival Ballet appointed a new artistic director in 1970. For the newcomer to that post was Beryl Grey, formerly one of the Royal Ballet's ballerinas, who emerged after the company had moved to Covent Garden in 1946.

A much smaller company, comprising 20 soloists, no corps de ballet, much less a ballerina, embodies as much British ballet history as the Royal and Festival Ballets. For Ballet Rambert is such a group and its founder, Marie Rambert, can rightly claim to have done as much as Ninette de Valois, Margot Fonteyn and Alicia Markova have achieved in their different fields to get British ballet accepted internationally.

To say that Ballet Rambert is the oldest British company is accurate but unfortunate in as far as it makes it sound institutionalised. On the contrary, it is today a small and sprightly company—appropriately, for it began operations in a tiny converted Church Hall—the Mercury—which Marie Rambert's husband, the playwright Ashley Dukes, had bought. Marie Rambert had come to Britain in 1914 and married in 1918 after studying with Jaques Dalcroze in Geneva and then working with Diaghilev's Ballet Russe—at one point as a coach to the great Nijinsky.

Retrospectively, it is interesting that six years after opening her own school of dancing in 1920, Marie Rambert encouraged a young man to produce a short ballet for one of Nigel Playfair's revues, **Riverside Nights**, at the Lyric Theatre in Hammersmith. The ballet was called **A Tragedy of Fashion** and the choreographer Frederick Ashton—the future leading British choreographer, dancer and eventually artistic director of the Royal Ballet at Covent Garden.

When Marie Rambert got her Ballet Club operating at the Mercury Theatre, Ashton was given plenty of scope for developing his choreographic talents, as were other major British choreographers like Antony Tudor and Andree Howard. In the intervening years Ballet Rambert has become internationally recognized, toured Europe and Australia and survived more than one financial catastrophe.

For the visitor coming across the company for the first time in the 1970s, the year to bear in mind is 1966. That year Marie Rambert appointed as her associate director Norman Morrice, who helped to remodel the company on its current small—scale lines. So this is not the troupe to go to for the big three-act works and the conventional Dying Swans and wilting Sylphides. It's the ensemble to watch for an integrated group of soloists executing work which is contemporary in its feeling, unfussy in its decor and wide-ranging in its music. Though the company still uses the Mercury as a base, its London seasons are usually at the Jeannetta Cochrane Theatre in Holborn, the Young Vic across Waterloo Bridge or at Sadler's Wells in Islington.

Though itself so compact, Ballet Rambert has now evolved an even smaller unit, the Rambert Dance Unit, with four dancers and two directors, to take ballet where space and technical facilities are so limited that the Company itself cannot appear.

For visitors wishing to get even further away from the mainstream world of white tutus and points, The Place in Euston makes essential visiting. There, under its founder Robin Howard and under the artistic direction of Robert Cohan, the London Contemporary Dance Theatre has its home. Robin Howard, a devotee of Martha Graham, had been responsible for bringing her company to London in 1964 and wished to follow this up by setting up a school for British dancers to explore and train in the area of contemporary dance that Martha Graham had pioneered. The school now operates at The Place, and in the seasons that have followed its establishment there in 1969 British dancers have given the lie to the previously held assumption that contemporary dance was the exclusive preserve of American dance groups like those of Merce Cunningham, Alvin Ailey and Paul Taylor.

Despite the availability of small groups like the Royal Ballet's touring offshoot, Ballet for All, Rambert's Dance Unit and other small groups, the health of ballet in Britain as a whole would not look so good were it not for the founding of regional groups which help to parallel the appearance in the operatic field of the Welsh National and Scottish Opera. The Scottish Arts Council began deliberating on the setting up of a Scottish Ballet Company in 1966. The lengthy task of finding and training the necessary personnel was solved when the already existing Western Theatre Ballet, under Peter Darrell's artistic direction, agreed to be renamed the Scottish Theatre Ballet and move north. The transformation took place through the Scottish Opera, in that the Western Theatre Ballet first started being the Scottish Theatre Ballet by providing the dance sequences in Scottish Opera's production of **The**

Trojans. In an odd way one is reminded of Ninette de Valois providing the dance sequences to Lilian Baylis's Shakespeare productions at the Old Vic in the late twenties before setting up the fully fledged Vic-Wells Ballet.

Though closely associated with modern dance and modern composers like Bartok, Hindemith and Messiaen, Scottish Theatre Ballet has been anxious also to produce a classical repertoire. With a company of 26 dancers, it has not yet the facilities to stage a **Swan Lake** or a **Sleeping Beauty**. But Peter Darrell's medieval version of **Giselle**, premiered at the Edinburgh King's Theatre in April 1971, showed that the company was ready to make as much of a reputation in the classical repertoire as it already held in the modern dance field.

Wales still has no ballet company to match its National Opera. However in Manchester a company has grown up to give encouragement to those looking for regional companies beyond Scotland. The Northern Dance Theatre, founded and directed by Laverne Meyer, had its trial run at the University Theatre in Manchester in March 1969. By 1972 this theatre had become its base, for the troupe had adopted a policy of developing in a way that would be regional in character but international in outlook. It now has a repertoire of 15 ballets to music ranging from Benjamin Britten to Brahms and from Schubert to Messiaen and gives London seasons of these. And its dancers are trained in both classical technique and the modern methods of the London School of Contemporary Dance

True balletomanes will not wish to miss the regional work of the Scottish Theatre Ballet or the Northern Dance Theatre, for the experiments of companies such as these represent in the 1970s the sort of pioneering work the Dames Marie Rambert and Ninette de Valois were undertaking in the 1930s. As long as what they created continues to renew itself and to be stimulated by the arrival of new, ambitious ensembles of the sort they sprang from, ballet in Britian will continue both to flourish and excite.

REGIONAL THEATRE

For most people British theatre is London theatre. If they do put the West End behind them, it is for certain out-of-town festival theatres which are somehow not thought of as being 'regional'. They will go to see Shakespeare performed at his birthplace in Stratford-upon-Avon. They will go to the Chichester Festival Theatre's summer season of star-studded revivals. They will venture as far afield as Scotland to forage amongst the unpredictable offerings of Edinburgh's August Festival or to relax in the Perthshire hills in the mixed repertoire available at the Pitlochry Festival Theatre. Such opportunities to get away from the wear and tear of metropolitan theatregoing are certainly not to be overlooked when they can be coupled with the sightseeing of some of the best the British countryside has to offer.

In so far as these festival theatres, which have grown up with the post-war development of British tourism, have in fact contributed to the decentralisation of theatre in Britain they provide the key to the understanding of the regional scene. For it is an area that has always been bedevilled by the irresistible power exercised by London. Indeed were it not for the work of two important philanthropists the history of regional theatre in the twentieth century, at least up to the post-war advent of subsidised theatre, could well be written purely in terms of an artistic assembly line for London, or else a place for disposing profitably of its entertainment effluent. Not for nothing were the regions patronisingly referred to as 'the provinces'.

Before recalling regional theatre's indebtedness to its two private patrons, it might be as well to look at the overall structure against which they operated. In particular it is useful to contrast what the public was offered in the twenties and thirties with what is available today. The contrast between the picture then and the picture now helps to soften the disappointment those currently dedicated to the development of theatre out of London may feel about its new lease of life in the post-war era of subsidised drama.

If you were a regular theatregoer in the inter-war years, living outside London and unwilling to be satisfied merely with variety shows offered at the local music-hall, you had two choices open to you. Either you went to your local repertory company or else, if you lived in one of the bigger towns, you visited one of the large touring date theatres.

The trouble was that the repertory company was almost certainly a weekly repertory, operating with quite inadequate financial resources. The direction and design were, therefore, at most of rudimentary competence and the sort of plays presented were run-of-the mill material most likely to make quick money at the box office. The cast often had to double up as scene shifters and scene painters, as well as learning a new part each week.

The system has been defended as an excellent training ground. For it was maintained that the would-be actor could learn all aspects of his craft in conditions that were far more practical than the more leisurely,

finishing-school atmosphere of the drama schools of the period.

The touring system has been defended on the same grounds. One of the century's most distinguished British actors, Sir Ralph Richardson, has described how in his early days his job was to give as close an imitation as possible of the West End stars whose parts he played on tour. Gradually, he explained, he learned his craft and found his own style, by copying the London actors he most admired.

Besides these conditions, the current system of three-weekly repertory in a newly-built municipal playhouse, with Arts Council and local authority subsidy enabling the artistic director to tackle worthwhile plays that are not sure-fire box office successes, must seem at first a paradise. For however valid the pre-war attitude of using the regions as a training ground for the profession, it does not reflect very flatteringly on an out-of-London public. The regional audience was treated like a preview audience today, who pay reduced prices to see what are frankly presented as rehearsals held in public of the eventual finished production. And one famous inter-war manager, Henry Sherek, has said that in the twenties and thirties touring was so much cheaper than after 1946 that he could often recoup the cost of a production before it even opened for its lucrative West End run. Later, once London had had its fill of a particular entertainment, one, or perhaps a number of post-West End tours would be embarked upon. But very rarely in such cases did the London cast, that is to say the big-name cast, accompany the touring versions.

With so little prestige and a correspondingly lower salary level attached to them, it is not surprising that the regions remained a training ground for the true centre of British theatre—London. In the circumstances those who got out of regional theatre cannot be blamed. If once they were stuck in weekly repertory—or summer seasons of seaside farce—artists had to develop mechanical tricks for covering up their inability in the time to give considered in-depth performances. It was a sad day when an actor had to accept that he would never be anything more than a rep actor.

Thanks to the grocery business the regional picture was not entirely black. Annie Horniman (1860 – 1937) owed her fortune to Horniman's tea and the Gaiety Theatre in Manchester owed its theatrical renaissance (1908 – 1917) to Miss Horniman. Similarly, Sir Barry Jackson (1879 – 1961) owed his wealth to Maypole Dairies and Birmingham owed its Repertory Theatre to Sir Barry.

After accomplishing nothing less than giving Dublin its National Theatre by building the Abbey, Miss Horniman moved from Ireland to Manchester, where she bought an already existing theatre—the Gaiety— and refurbished it. In her company's ten-year occupation of the building, from 1908, it is estimated she staged 200 plays. Some of these had so authentic a regional flavour that they became known as the work of the Manchester school of dramatists, whose most distinguished exponents were Brighouse, Houghton and Monkhouse. So in those early days Miss Horniman premiered a play like Brighouse's **Hobson's Choice** which, when Britain finally had a National Theatre in the 1960s, was quickly incorporated in its repertoire. Not only did the Horniman company appear in London but it also toured Canada and the United

The Yvonne Arnaud Theatre in Guildford. One of the most attractive of the theatres to be constructed in the 1960's building boom

78 Regional Theatre

States. Having also staged the works of important contemporary dramatists like Shaw and Galsworthy, it seems in retrospect odd that Miss Horniman should decide in 1917 that she had had enough of running her own company. By 1921 the Gaiety had become a cinema and until her death in 1937 Miss Horniman took no further active interest in the drama. She had certainly earned her retirement.

Sir Barry Jackson, on the other hand, stayed the course more or less to the end of the road. He began by building the Birmingham Repertory Theatre in 1913 and, in the following 22 years, provided an extremely catholic selection of plays, the highpoint of which was perhaps the staging of Shaw's mammoth **Back to Methuselah**. In recent times it has needed all the subsidised resources of the National Theatre to mount a project of that order.

As a director, Barry Jackson is remembered as the man who livened up the rather hidebound traditions of Shakespeare production by reviving the Bard's works in modern dress. At first treated as a fashionable novelty, they soon proved a means of looking at familiar texts with a fresh eye.

To Sir Barry also belongs the honour of initiating the British in the habit of summer festival theatregoing. He set up the Malvern Festival in 1929, mainly as a base for championing Shaw with the production of his new works. After 1937 Sir Barry withdrew from Malvern, though it continued to function till the Second World War. Later attempts to reopen it have not proved successful. In some ways its place has been taken by the Pitlochry Festival Theatre whose founder was in fact inspired to start in Scotland by what he had seen in Malvern. Barry Jackson himself moved on to become a post-war director of the Shakespeare Memorial Theatre, known today as the Royal Shakespeare Theatre.

Although the Liverpool Playhouse, opened as the Liverpool Repertory Theatre in 1911, did not have the patronage of an Annie Horniman or a Barry Jackson, it was the third beacon of light in the dismal pre-war regional theatre scene. It has the honour of being the oldest surviving British repertory theatre and some of the country's most distinguished actors (Sir Michael Redgrave is one) began their careers on its stage.

Some indication of the momentum regional theatre has gained in the sixties after the accelerating decay, in the late forties and the fifties, of the old weekly repertory system and the breakdown of the pre-war touring network can be seen by reading **The First 25 Years**. This is a publication put out by the Arts Council of Great Britain to celebrate its first quarter century. The Arts Council itself grew up out of an improvised body, the wartime Council for the Encouragement of Music and the Arts (CEMA) which was responsible for allocating government funds to keep Britain culturally alive during the bleak years of the war Thus, ironically enough, the long-established German system of subsidising the arts came to Britain through fighting a war with Germany.

It is just as well that it made its belated appearance here. For not only did it enable the country that gave Shakespeare to the world to have its own National Theatre. It also meant that the chronic centralisation of theatre in London did not grow even worse by the time the new drama made its appearance in 1956.

Two factors were at play that brought about the collapse of the old regional structure. The first was a question of economics. The large old touring theatres were run-down and in urgent need of expensive maintenance. But they occupied valuable sites in the centre of cities that could be more profitably exploited as shop and office accommodation. And the mounting cost of touring, with the consequent cutting back of tours, meant no businessman was going to invest in a system that had clearly come to the end of its days.

The other factor that struck more at weekly repertory than the tour was the arrival of television in Britain and its establishment throughout the whole country by the beginning of the fifties. On television, which at that time had a certain novelty value, regional audiences were offered the same standard of entertainment available to those in the capital. When the rival bid for their attention comprised a run-down weekly repertory company with novice actors, or old ones ground down by the system, it was not surprising that regional audiences began to limit their theatregoing to the traditional and relatively spectacular Christmas pantomime only.

It is fortunate that subsidy came to the rescue at this point, though it is very doubtful if regional theatre could have been saved by municipal subsidy alone. In 1946 Parliament passed a bill authorising local authorities to use six old pence (2½p) in every pound levied from the rates for the subsidy of the arts. Very few indeed availed themselves of this opportunity, and were not municipal subsidy spurred into activity by the impetus of joint ventures with Arts Council-administered subsidy from central government the philistinism in the British town halls would certainly have been more pronounced than it is.

But not all local authorities believed that their duties lay no further than important areas like sanitation and local welfare services. In **The First 25 Years** we read of the building of the first civic theatre—the Belgrade in Coventry in 1958. Since then the momentum has gathered to the extent that whereas the Arts Council publication lists only this one theatre for 1958, by 1971 the annual rate of building had mounted to 13 with a further 23 projects in the pipeline. Superficially, therefore, it looks as though a combination of economics and television destroyed all that was bad in the old regional system and that the arrival of subsidy produced a shining row of subsidised new theatres, where work of a much higher quality could successfully be attempted. Alas, the story is neither as simple nor quite as rosy as that.

The first point that has to be made is that new theatre buildings do not in themselves make exciting new theatre. There has to be a long term collaboration between the management of an old theatre that is to go on to occupy the new one and the civic authority responsible for the change. Above all, the new theatre needs to be designed by an architect who has a real practical knowledge of theatre and its working priorities if a mere monumental façade to civic pride, coupled with civic ignorance of theatre, is not to result.

The best example of how these things can miscarry is to recall the Pembroke Theatre on London's doorstep in Surrey. The Pembroke had been a disused Church Hall converted into a small in-the-round theatre. At the beginning of the 1960s it gave the British premieres of plays like J P Donleavy's **Fairy Tales of New York** and Thomas Wolfe's **Look Homeward, Angel**, both of which transferred to the West End of London. Naturally, it attracted London critics and name artists like Margaret Rutherford, Fay Compton and Susan Hampshire. Then came a new theatre, the Ashcroft, part of a cultural complex called the

Fairfield Halls in which Croydon Corporation incorporated a concert hall and art gallery with the theatre. But the latter was not built with close consultation with the Pemroke's management, whose in-the-round staging could not be carried out in the new theatre. The result was that the Pembroke closed its doors whilst the Ashcroft never achieved the identity of a permanent company. The critics and the name artists stopped coming and the Ashcroft became just another touring date with occasional summer seasons of farces.

The new theatres that have followed in the wake of the Ashcroft and the Coventry Belgrade have fitted into three categories. The first, and perhaps the best, are those built simply as theatres—like the Nottingham Playhouse which opened in 1963. Like most new theatres it has a restaurant, bookstall and facilities for displaying exhibitions of paintings. It therefore belongs firmly to the postwar concept of the theatre as a place that is open to the public all day long and not just during the evening show and perhaps for the occasional matinee. Secondly, there are the theatres that belong to part of a cultural complex, like the Ashcroft in Croydon which opened in 1962, or to a sports complex, like the Billingham Forum Theatre, built in 1968 as part of a centre that incorporated things like an ice rink and a gymnasium. And thirdly, there have been the campus theatres, like the Northcott Theatre built as a part of Exeter University in 1968, or the Gardner Centre built the following year as part of the new Sussex University near Brighton.

In theory, new theatres which are part of a larger centre should attract a new theatre audience—either of people primarily interested in sport or else of undergraduates who find a theatre on their doorstep. In fact these projects can misfire. The Billingham theatre, for example, had a strong smell of swimming baths about it in its early days and it has not proved to be one of the major regional theatres with a strong individual artistic direction or a famous permanent company. And the campus theatres have an unhappy record of not belonging quite to town or gown. They don't belong to the undergraduates because the theatre has no function as a showcase for a department of drama and they do not feel part of the town because they are situated well out of its centre. This may account for the chequered career of the Brighton Gardner Centre, though it has to be admitted that the Northcott in Exeter has performed a formidable task in using its base to provide tours for the whole of the South West.

A look at some of the better designed theatres like the Mercury Theatre in Colchester, designed by a theatre designer, Christopher Morley, in full co-operation with the artistic director who was to move in, fill one with hope. Others, like the Adeline Genée Theatre in East Grinstead, invoke instead despair. The Adeline Genée, built in 1967, has had a succession of artistic directors who have reopened this new theatre with impressive-sounding manifestos and have had to abandon their plans all too soon. It seems extraordinary that the architects and planners of the Adeline Genée did not take into account the fact that their new theatre was not only outside the centre of East Grinstead but was not even on one of the town's bus routes. How can a new theatre hope to form part of a community if its planners take so little account of the community's needs?

Regional theatre, like most structures, is a power structure that repays close study. In assessing a regional theatre's policy and reputa-

The Nottingham Playhouse, another theatre whose design reflects the new post-war concept of the theatre as a building to be used all day

tion, therefore, it is worth considering who wields the power. Is it in fact the artistic director who is the titular boss? Or is he in the hands of the board of the theatre, the dozen or so lay members representing local interests in the running of the organisation? Or is he working with one or both eyes on the Arts Council, from which a large part of his theatre's subsidy comes?

Two famous rows that came to public attention in the sixties give a good idea of the sort of fighting an artistic director must be capable of and which forms a part and parcel of theatrical life of which the general public are usually in happy ignorance. At the Nottingham Playhouse, John Neville, who was the theatre's artistic director from 1963 – 1967, put in his resignation in an attempt to get an additional grant from the Arts Council. The Board of the Nottingham Playhouse felt that John Neville had acted over their heads, so that when he subsequently withdrew his resignation they refused to allow him to do so. Here we have a power struggle between the three parties involved—an artistic director, the theatre's board and, indirectly, the Arts Council. In 1967, too, at the Victoria Theatre, Stoke-on-Trent, Peter Cheeseman, its artistic director, had a dispute with his theatre manager, Stephen Joseph; The Studio Company Ltd of which Joseph was the boss and Cheeseman the artistic director received Arts Council subsidy, so the Arts Council had every right to come down on Stephen Joseph's side with the view that it was time for Cheeseman to move on. He had been director of the theatre for five years since 1962 and the view was held that it was best both for the artistic director and for the theatre if a change were made. So Cheeseman was locked out of his theatre and the quarrel lasted from March to October, when the situation was resolved with the Studio Company being reconstituted as the Stoke and West Stafford Trust Ltd. Cheeseman's company took jobs locally until the situation was settled.

Normally it would probably be in everybody's best interests if artistic directors moved on from theatre to theatre at periods approximating to

five years. The point about Cheeseman's case, however, was that he championed the cause of a theatre belonging to the locality in which it existed. Instead of merely staging local productions of London's popular or prestige successes, Cheeseman pioneered the musical documentary with six drawn from local sources. The best-known of these, **The Knotty**, traced the birth, life and death of a local railway company bearing that nickname. The aim of a theatre undertaking work of this kind is to be indigenous without being parochial.

One of the main bones of contention in regional theatre is the presentation of experimental, avant-garde material. A play or style of production which is accepted in a large metropolis like London may be found to be deeply shocking by a regional audience whose taste and outlook is different. One solution that is increasingly adopted is to stage more conventional material in a regional theatre's main bill theatre and to present the more provocative productions in a studio theatre, or, if this is lacking, in special late-night shows for younger audiences who might be expected to be more on the wavelength of such work. The alternative is often for an artistic director to embark on a policy of confrontation with his public who, he feels, should 'get with it' and who in turn complain to the theatre's Board—who in their turn haul the offending director up for trial.

But it would be a mistake to conclude on an entirely discordant note.

It is true that a number of post-war British theatres have been unsatisfactorily designed from the point of view of the company occupying them. It is true that all is not sweetness and light between regional directors, their boards and the subsidy-givers. On the other hand there are very many positive aspects of the regional theatre which, when all is said and done, is in much better shape than it was in the old inter-war years. The Arts Council, for example, subsidise young writers, designers and technical staff to work with companies, many of them regional, for year-long periods, which must mean the regions will continue to be a training ground in the best sense. And as long as there are directors committed to their theatres and prepared to fight for their rights whether they win, like Peter Cheeseman at Stoke-on-Trent, or lose like John Neville in Nottingham, the regional theatre will thrive. It is the absentee artistic director, the middle-of-the-road man who is using his position to land eventual work elsewhere, who betrays the idealism of Annie Horniman and Barry Jackson.

The Knotty—the most famous of the six musical documentaries at the Victoria Theatre, Stoke-on-Trent. These documentaries, written by Peter Terson and directed by Peter Cheeseman, pioneered a new movement in regional theatre where productions were drawn from local sources instead of being merely reproductions of London successes

THEATRE HERITAGE

Which side you come down on in the central issue concerning theatre collections in Britain must largely depend on how much time you have to spend on them. For this issue basically concerns the pros and cons of the present distribution—and hence accessibility—of the abundant material available.

If you are on what is literally a flying visit you will have ample reason to deplore the fact that the legacies from Britain's rich theatrical past are now scattered amongst umpteen public and private collections all over the country. If, on the other hand, you are involved on a months-long research project, it may be less irksome to discover that the English have not yet got round to organising all those precious letters, prompt copies, costumes, playbills, account books and so forth into one vast supermarket of a museum in the heart of London's theatreland.

This, of course, is not because such an idea has failed to cross the minds of people involved in such matters. In fact 1956—the year of the breakthrough in the new drama—was also a year to be reckoned with in the less hectic world of theatre collections. In October of that year the British Theatre Museum Association was formed, with the ultimate aim of establishing a National Theatre Museum which one would imagine the busy visitor would find as welcome and as convenient as the centralised collections of paintings in the National Gallery and National Portrait Gallery in Trafalgar Square.

16 years after the British Theatre Museum Association's initial deliberations, campaigns were being launched in 1972 to secure a home for a central theatre collection. Some accommodation has now been promised in Somerset House, opposite the emerging National Theatre on the banks of the Thames. Speculation was of course considerable on the likelihood of a National Theatre housing a National Museum. In the meantime, though, the Association contents itself with a single certainty—its temporary home in Leighton House, W 14. There, at least, its incomparable Henry Irving Archives are safely lodged for the benefit of the public, along with a growing number of important additional bequests.

The upshot of all this, however, for the theatregoing visitor who wants to take in the past as well as the present, is inevitably time and energy-consuming visits to a varied assortment of collections, both in and out of London, many of which offer overlapping glimpses of yesterday's theatre. Here, then, is an imaginary (though probably characteristic) day in the life of a collector of the theatrical past.

'By 10 am at the Victoria and Albert Museum in South Kensington to take a first look at the Gabrielle Enthoven Collection. Didn't even attempt to sample more than a dozen of its million playbills and

Dame Ellen Terry, whose portrait by George Frederick Watts can be seen in the National Portrait Gallery, Trafalgar Square, London

programmes, though managed to look at a few of the first-night notices that span all openings since 1925. Had a look round the Harry Beard Collection of Toy Theatres and was surprised to find those on view represent only a fraction of the number bequeathed to the V & A.

'By 11 am at the British Theatre Museum for a quick look at its James Barrie letters and Harley Granville-Barker manuscripts. Time before lunch—and whilst still in West London—to visit the London Museum in search of costumes worn by Henry Irving and the Martin Harvey collection of designs and prompt books.

'Lunch in Trafalgar Square and a visit to the National Portrait Gallery to see pictures of the famous. After this, and by special arrangement with its owners, off to South London and the private collection of the Mander-Mitchenson partnership in Sydenham. A bit tired by now but, whilst south of the river, to the Dulwich College Library to look at the diary and correspondence of its founder, Elizabethan actor Edward Alleyn (1566 – 1626). On to the Dulwich College Picture Gallery to see its theatrical portraits. Enjoyed these, but wished we had the right contacts to get into the Garrick Club back in WC2, with its portraits going back from the present to Garrick's times. Tomorrow must go to Birmingham's Public Library and see the Shakespeare First Folios, not to mention the Restoration Quartos . . . .

Whether such a person is here to see the sights or for research, it's hard to believe he would not make an easy convert to the cause for centralising British collections. Which brings us to a related secondary issue—the manner of their presentation. Should they be laid out along time-honoured conventional lines? Or should they be tricked out with all the resources of special lighting effects, recorded voices and taped period music designed to nudge the onlooker's imagination into a fairground-like journey into times past?

Richard Buckle, who mounted the Diaghilev Exhibition in 1954 and the Shakespeare Quatercentenary Exhibition in 1964, introduced the British public to this dynamic use of the resources now available for the world of exhibitions. If the Utopia of a central Theatre Museum or Institute is ever realised—with all the cash resources that that implies—research students would probably be more than satisfied with the computerisation of the reference sources and similar aids to the processes of study. But the non-specialist theatregoer might revel in the interior son et lumière presentation of vanished eras, linked with historical films and old recordings, and might help to swell the ranks of those theatregoers prepared to look over their shoulders from what is being currently offered both on and off Shaftesbury Avenue.

In case all this sounds like a campaign to sack every public and private collection in the land for the benefit of some hypothetical museum marvel in the capital, it had better be pointed out that there are excellent reasons for leaving some collections exactly where they have always been. What, for example, would be the point of taking a bulldozer to the Ellen Terry Museum in Smallhythe, Kent, so that its contents could form a room in some metropolitan mausoleum? The whole point of making a train and local bus journey to Smallhythe is to see the cottage in whcih the great life-loving Victorian actress spent her last years—and to see it much as she saw it. Equally it would be foolish

David Garrick, the great 18th century actor-manager. Robert Edge Pine's portrait of him can be seen in the National Portrait Gallery

to advocate the removal of the contents of Shaw's Corner from Ayot St Lawrence. If you take the trouble to catch a train to Welwyn Garden City and then the bus for Shaw's Corner, it is precisely because you want to take a look at the Victorian rectory and garden in which GBS lived out the last 40 of his extraordinary 94 years. No—these are the collections which should be left as they are. Only a special retrospective exhibition of the life and times of Ellen Terry or Shaw could constitute grounds for the removal of the contents of these museums—and then strictly on loan only.

One important reservation remains about collections from the past, whether they remain in the homes of their long-since departed owners or are exhibited (in whatever fashion) in a public or private museum. And it is the concept that a museum and its contents belong to the deceased and are therefore quite unrelated to the current living theatre. In fact, of course, both past and present form part of a continuing tradition. The re-creation, by whatever means, of theatremaking in successive bygone generations serves its highest purpose if it sharpens our perception and enjoyment of today's playgoing. How, then, to bridge the gap between the quick and the dead?

The short answer to that one is the incorporation of relics from the past with a currently operating theatre. And it has already been thought of by the creators of post-war London and regional theatres who have provided foyers for art exhibitions to be viewed en route to the auditorium. At the Mermaid Theatre, for example, it is often possible to see exhibits relating to the play on view. And at Sam Wanamaker's Globe Theatre—on the site of Shakespeare's Globe—this process has been taken even a step further. After the Wanamaker Globe's first season, given under a tent structure, a museum was immediately opened on the nearby site of the Elizabethan bear-baiting pit. The next step, which the Globe Theatre Trust has already taken, is to put forward a plan incorporating the museum with the theatre that will eventually replace the tent used for initial seasons. In as far as Sam Wanamaker is operating in the Elizabethan equivalent of Shaftesbury Avenue, it is difficult to believe much opposition will be encountered in marrying an exhibition space for the remains of Elizabethan theatre with a building hopefully to be put up in the reign of the second Elizabeth.

Of course both the National and the Royal Shakespeare Company attempt to provide good historical sightlines in their programmes, which carry notes, photographs and engravings all sketching in the background of the production you are to see. Neither company, however, at the beginning of the 1970s, had a London home with adequate facilities to extend this work into fully-fledged foyer exhibitions. And in the commercial theatre of course it is immensely more profitable to sell the customers refreshments than expensive-to-mount cultural enlightenment. Still, there is always the hope that some advertiser in the usual 10 penny West End programme might one day think a foyer exhibition a good means of indirect self-promotion. Not many theatregoers, after all, can be happy with the mere cast-list and brief biographies that constitute most London theatre programmes.

Some theatres, however, hardly need to wheel in museum pieces, for they themselves are remarkable historical monuments. For example, the Theatre Royal, Drury Lane is the oldest West End theatre still in use. It occupies the site of the theatre given one of the two Royal Patents when Charles II was restored to the throne and the theatre began to pick itself up from the setback of Cromwell and the Puritans. And if Drury Lane, trailing clouds of glory associated with names as varied as Nell Gwynne, David Garrick, Mrs Siddons and Edmund Kean, is not enough for you, there is always the Theatre Royal in the Haymarket. The present interior of the Haymarket was rebuilt in 1904—17 years before Drury Lane's was reconstructed in 1921—so it has age as well as a succession of names like Nash (who built its Portico in 1821), Henry Fielding (who wrote its political satires) and His Grace, William, Duke of Cumberland (who started a riot) to hold your interest. And both Drury Lane and the Haymarket have their ghosts to boot.

Finally it should be remembered that London—indeed Britain as a whole—is a vast alfresco museum where those sufficiently interested can themselves take their own time-trips. In addition to providing a how-to-get-there guide to the museums, the reference section of this book also lists the helpful GLC plaques that have been put up where the theatrically eminent once lived in London. Statues to them can also be traced. And for those who want to start a do-it-yourself theatre museum to add to their souvenir programmes and recordings-of-the show, a list of shops selling books, design work, production photographs and so forth has also been provided.

Macbeth compared life to 'a poor player/that struts and frets his hour upon the stage/And then is heard no more . . . a tale told by an idiot . . . signifying nothing.' For those who take an intelligent interest in the theatrical past, not only is the poor player not forgotten but the significance of what he achieved is seen in the light of his contemporary counterpart.

YOUNG PEOPLE'S THEATRE

Once upon a time in Great Britain, people who were not yet considered old enough to rank as adolescents were called 'children.' The BBC used to broadcast a 5 pm programme for them daily called Children's Hour. And this was introduced by friendly souls known reassuringly by names like Uncle Mac and Auntie Muriel. Nowadays both adolescents and pre-adolescents are referred to as Young People. And the live entertainment provided for them appears under the heading Young People's Theatre. It is not presented by surrogate Aunts and Uncles.

What's in a name? Well, in this context, the substitution of Young People for Children denotes something of a revolution on a number of fronts. The avuncular attitudes embodied in the much-loved BBC programme have certainly had to be jettisoned because of a fundamental change in young people themselves. Self-styled aunts and uncles would find it hard to make themselves heard amongst the upheavals of the 1970s as reflected in Student Power, Infant Drug Addiction, the Generation Gap, Teenage Spending Resources and what popular psychologists call the Ever Earlier Maturing of the Young.

But the very existence of Young People's Theatre in Britain denotes a revolution of another sort. For this now flourishing branch of theatre has come about only as a result of a bitter and often fiercely competitive fight on the part of a small group of pioneers. Their battle has been for state subsidy through the Arts Council who, in the immediate post-war years, showed a remarkable reluctance to channel public funds in this direction. Not until the mid-1960s did the Arts Council make a full-scale investigation of the companies dedicated to providing junior theatre. It has been reliably reported that the delay in publishing the findings of this investigation was due to the severe criticism that had to be made of the then prevailing standards. Perhaps this situation was not surprising, as a Young People's Drama Panel in the Arts Council, to consider the allocation of public funds for this work, was not set up until 1967.

Pioneers pointed at the long tradition of subsidised theatre for the young in Eastern European countries. Though sceptics were not slow to suggest such state bounty was mindful of the potential for a measure of early political indoctrination, the English could take little pride in the well-intentioned but financially-starved efforts of the earliest workers in this field. Some idea of its attainment is afforded by recalling the work of an all-female company touring Shakespeare for student consumption. The more buxom of these ladies took on the Falstaff parts in the Bard's repertoire. With the greatest respect to the ideals that inspired this work, one wonders what insight it in fact gave to Shakespeare in performance and how many whose first encounter with the classics came about in this way were encouraged to explore them further in adult life.

Some historical perspective to the immensely improved and varied work available to young theatregoers in the 1970s is gained by reference to the Young Vic which was founded in 1946. This was an offshoot of the Old Vic Centre, the school for actors headed by Michel St Denis (1897 – 1971). Graduates of the school—and they included subsequently famous names like Keith Michell and Joan Plowright—appeared in Shakespeare (and other) productions by George Devine (1910 – 1966) and Glen Byam Shaw (born 1904). Productions were seen in the regions and at matinees at the Old Vic Theatre in London. The company also toured Europe. But in 1951 the organisation perished for lack of funds, although it could hardly have had three more distinguished names at the helm. St Denis left to superintend regional drama in France. Devine went on to become grandfather of the New Wave drama by founding the English Stage Company in 1956 at the Royal Court. And Glen Byam Shaw was to move on to Stratford-upon-Avon immediately before the Peter Hall era and then to oversee Sadler's Wells Opera in the exciting period of its move from Sadler's Wells Theatre to the Coliseum. It was an accurate forecast of the troubles ahead that three such great men of the theatre should fail to get the backing they needed to consolidate their work in young people's theatre.

When, five years later, in 1956, Michael Croft created the National Youth Theatre he found himself in charge of an organisation that was both an asset and a stumbling block in the renewed fight-for-subsidy stakes. The asset was the vitality of the young company drawn from schools all over the country. The stumbling block proved to be the Youth Theatre's amateur status.

Initially, during summer holiday after summer holiday, the NYT's reputation was based on its Shakespeare productions. They were judged good enough to be both televised and presented in the West End. Croft's modern-dress production of **Julius Caesar**, directed as a political thriller and eagerly performed by its youthful cast as such at the Queen's Theatre in 1960, was a good example of this early work. Later the company was to attract the collaboration of one of the new British dramatists—Peter Terson. He worked closely with Croft and the large number of available actors to evolve, successively, **Zigger Zagger** (1967), **The Apprentices** (1968) and **Fuzz** (1969)

These plays—all given in summer seasons at the Jeannetta Cochrane Theatre—made an interesting contrast with standard West End fare. For the economics of the commercial theatre forced West End managers to seek small-cast plays that would make lively escapist entertainment for a still predominantly middle-aged and middle-class audience. The hordes of eager young actors of the National Youth Theatre enabled Terson, on the contrary, to deploy casts of Shakespearean dimensions. And of course the themes of the plays had to be concerned with the problems of contemporary Britain from a young person's point of view. With shrewdness and humour the Terson plays took London theatre-goers through unfamiliar territory like that of soccer hero worship (**Zigger Zagger**), adolescent growing pains at the factory bench (**The Apprentices**) and the world of student demonstrations (**Fuzz**). Without a grant to build it, Croft commissioned the designer of the Mermaid Theatre, Elidir Davies, to design a permanent home for the National Youth Theatre where it could fulfil his ambition to set up a professional wing. But the group's amateur status was put forward as creating a dangerous precedent for subsidy. If one amateur company was given a grant then the floodgates would open. This was a strange argument, as the National Youth Orchestra, which received Arts Council backing, was similarly non-professional.

But the controversies of this period now make boring reading, since the company's future was saved at the eleventh hour. The London Borough of Camden offered the National Youth Theatre its Shaw Theatre at a peppercorn rent and an annual grant of £15,000 from the Arts Council enabled Croft to set up his professional wing—the Dolphin Theatre Company—once he was installed in 1971. As well as its regular London seasons at the Shaw and other theatres, the National Youth Theatre now has branches in the north of England. Meantime the professional wing aims to present six productions a year ranging from the classics to new modern work. Names like Mia Farrow, Vanessa Redgrave and Simon Ward at the Shaw Theatre have helped to put this theatre (between Euston and King's Cross stations) on the map for the general theatregoing public.

Another pioneer, Caryl Jenner (1917 – 1973) did almost as much campaigning as touring in this field. Like Croft, she made a bid to put the theatrical cart before the subsidy horse by announcing her intention of setting up a permanent London home under canvas after years of touring. This proved to be unnecessary when, in the mid-1960s, she was given a six-year lease on the Arts Theatre in central London and set up the Unicorn Theatre which has staged plays for all age groups. The fastest worker of all, however, has probably been Frank Dunlop. Before joining the National Theatre to become Laurence Olivier's associate director, Dunlop had founded Pop Theatre, which first flourished at the 1966 Edinburgh Festival. As its name implies, the company had sought to revive Shakespeare in a broad contemporary idiom that would appeal to large popular audiences. Once at the National, Dunlop set about reviving the Young Vic cause which Devine, St Denis and Byam Shaw had so honourably lost at the time when Dunlop himself was a student of the Old Vic School.

Nineteen years after the first Young Vic had disbanded, Dunlop got a second off the ground in August 1970. The Greater London Council had given the venture its blessing with a five years' lease at a token rent on a site practically opposite the Old Vic Theatre, where the National Company plays until its own theatre is completed in 1975. Thanks to £30,000 from the National Theatre's own resources and £30,000 from the Arts Council, Dunlop was able to get a theatre built to his own specification instead of moving in on a complete project as Croft and Jenner had done. It seats 450 on red-stained benches arranged round a long thrust stage. The most important feature of the design and finish is the theatre's informality and the openness of the actor/audience relationship. The aim is to avoid the formality of West End theatregoing with its dinner-jacketed front of house manager, plush seats and cherub-decorated boxes. If a young audience is to feel at home in a theatre then the building must have something of the free and easy atmosphere of the cinema and of the pop concert.

Since its 1970 opening the Young Vic has made its mark in two respects. It has given opportunities to younger members of the National Theatre Company to play lead roles that they would have been unlikely

A scene from the National Youth Theatre's most famous production—*Zigger Zagger*, written by Peter Terson in collaboration with the director, Michael Croft and members of the NYT

to secure at a first stab in the main-bill auditorium. And the productions—by no means exclusively cast from the National's Company—have usefully taken into account the existence of a new generation of theatregoers who have grown up since the new British and Absurdist dramatists made their initial impact in Britain in the 1950s. A good example of this policy at work was the revival at the Young Vic of John Osborne's early **Epitaph for George Dillon** and **Look Back in Anger** to coincide with the premiere at the Royal Court of Osborne's **A Sense of Detachment** late in 1972.

Experimental seasons with a pop-group like The Who in the same theatre that presents a revival of Beckett's **Waiting for Godot** show the Young Vic ready to dispense with the old cultural barriers which used to be snobbishly put up between the young intellectual on the one hand and the aficionado of popular music on the other. Apart from all this, the theatre has also proved a useful platform for experimental touring groups like Portable Theatre.

Another project, the Midlands Arts Centre in Birmingham, has also cut across long-held British prejudices. This Centre, founded by John English in 1967, dovetails theatres for young people with sports facilities. This is worth mentioning since the emphasis in British schools—particularly the Public Schools—has been on sport and the development of 'the team spirit'. From this tradition there developed a certain antagonism between the hearty and the arty—the latter having to make their interests felt extra-curricularly. Centres like Birmingham's help to dispose of this 'either-or' attitude to sports and the arts and enable young people to move freely from one world to the other.

Specialisation, on the other hand, is the feature of the Molecule Club at London's Mermaid Theatre. Set up in April 1967, it was conceived on the lines of 'science can be fun' and seemed to have proved its point by 1973 when an audience of one million had attended its morning and afternoon performances. Aimed at the 7 to 12-year-olds in particular, its documentary plays with music have sought to take science out of the school laboratory and relate it entertainingly to the modern world. A good example of the approach was **Backfire!** given at the Mermaid in the autumn of 1972. This explored the pros and cons of the car in modern Britain and in trial play format invited the young audience to judge the usefulness of private transport on the one hand against the cost in terms of air pollution and the scale of road accidents. Such plays in no way overlap with the work undertaken either by the Young Vic or the National Youth Theatre in London. Unlike either of these organisations, the Molecule Club receives no subsidy from either the Arts Council or the Ministry of Education. Its backing is from private sponsors who, at the beginning of 1973, numbered over one hundred.

At the beginning of the 1970s so much work was being done in Britain generally in the young people's field that a talk-in on the subject was held by the Council of Repertory Theatres. No greater indication that times had changed in this area could be given than one point of view that was openly put forward at the conference. It was suggested that in some cases regional theatre work for the young was being enthusiastically undertaken because it was certain to elicit a measure of subsidy. That would certainly have astonished the first pioneers in the field.

Regional work in theatre for the young is more difficult to outline than the development of the principal London companies because the approach varies from company to company. From its Stratford-upon-Avon headquarters, for example, the Royal Shakespeare Company's chief involvement in this sphere began in 1966 with the setting up of Theatregoround. This has taken productions—ranging from full-scale productions like the 1972 **Richard II** to recital programmes like **The Hollow Crown**—to schools, colleges and community centres. In a sense it is a touring edition of the company's work at Stratford and in London, designed to reach young theatregoers who live far away from either of these two centres. Most of the smaller regional theatres are involved in other ways. Probably the most common link is with a junior supporters' club aimed at encouraging young people to come to both main-bill programmes and productions specially mounted for them. The more ambitious, however, visit schools and colleges and liaise in education work through the appropriate County's Drama Adviser.

An important professional organisation that has specialised in the provision of theatre for schools is Brian Way's Theatre Centre, founded in north London in 1953. With the help of grants from the Nuffield and Gulbenkian Foundations—as well as one from the Arts Council—Theatre Centre has set up a temporary headquarters from which it has put on the road no less than seven companies taking programmes, many of them written or devised by Brian Way himself, for both primary and secondary schools. A special emphasis in Theatre Centre's programmes, which visit theatreless areas in particular, is on audience participation by young people.

These programmes range from **Let's Make a Story** (devised for village schools) to scenes from **Macbeth** and **The Tempest** (devised to give secondary school students some insight through his works to Shakespeare and his life and times). Theatre Centre claims to visit 2,500 schools in 74 different educational areas in Great Britain each year, so it is surprising that an appeal for £90,000 to build a permanent studio and research centre had not by 1973 provided this hard-working group with the up-to-date home that it deserves after 20 years service. Instead the organisation began 1973 with alarm cries for increased subsidy, without which it could not continue to operate. From what follows, its experience would seem to be more than ever needed and its economic plight hard to understand.

This is not the book in which to keep the reader over long in the classroom. But it has to be said that drama in education has undergone a revolution in Britain at least as great as that in the changed attitudes to the provision of theatre for the young. For those at school in the late 1940s, drama was something from classical literature—usually a Shakespeare play—on which study would begin at the age of 12 or 13. Often the key speeches were learnt parrot-fashion and the right answers to the eventual examination questions were inculcated so that the student had little sense of a personal discovery of the text. And if parents or teachers were worried about a pupil's manner of reading, elocution lessons were resorted to. These took the form of ironing out class or regional accents. The result, unfortunately, was a highly artificial and self-conscious manner of expression.

But by the 1970s drama in school was increasingly something that the young encountered in their very first days. From the very beginning they were invited to improvise imaginary stories and evolve group plays by the end of the term.

96 Young People's Theatre

Regional theatres can be involved in the educational use of drama in schools in different degrees. Some may merely stage a particular examination classic or listed new play which will ensure the attendance of those who have to become familiar with the work for their studies. Others may go a step further with after-the-play discussions in which the actor and the director answer young people's questions about the interpretation of the text. Others again may go into the schools either with an examination play or else to undertake work related to the new drama improvisation sessions.

Finally, it would be pleasant to report that there had been a parallel development in the commercial theatre's provision for young theatre-goers. In fact the only constant factor in this sphere is that interest has been limited to the Christmas holiday period. The only change has been the replacement of the traditional Christmas pantomime by an increasing number of matinee plays for the young.

The pantomime, as its name implies, is a bizarre anglo-saxon evolution from the commedia dell' arte. Its English development can best be traced when the Players Theatre, near London's Charing Cross, revives Victorian pantomime. It is certainly intriguing that pantomime in Britain should involve a double travesti casting so that these stage adaptations of children's nursery stories like **Cinderella** or **Jack and the Beanstalk** should result in the Principal Boy being played by a girl, with the comedy role of the mature Dame entrusted to a male comedian. Although in the most immediate post-war years there used to be six or seven revivals a season of traditional British pantomime in London, by the 1970s it had retreated to the Palladium where it was sustained with a cast headed by the stars of pop music. In fact, pantomime's only real new lease of life has been its transfer to ice in the vast arena of the Empire Pool, Wembley. Although something is lost in that the skaters' voices have to be dubbed, much is gained in the lavishness of the spectacle.

The matinee performances that have replaced traditional pantomime have drawn on stage adaptations of well-known children's books like those of Enid Blyton or A A Milne. The forerunner of these was James Barrie's **Peter Pan**, written as long ago as 1904 and revived each year with a distinguished line of famous actresses undertaking the role of the perpetual boy.

One would feel happier about the mass revival of stage adaptations of nursery classics at Christmas if there were evidence of new and good writing for the young. Nicholas Stuart Gray (born 1919) has made some notable postwar contributions with new plays and adaptations in which he has also appeared. So has David Wood (born 1944). And Robert Bolt's **The Thwarting of Baron Bolligrew**, staged by the Royal Shakespeare Company at the Aldwych in 1965, was an encouraging sign. Otherwise it has to be said that good new writing in Britain for young theatregoers is as thin on the ground as good marionette theatres. Perhaps the most promising writer in this field is Christopher Martin, whose plays staged by the Unicorn Theatre at the Arts and at the Victoria Theatre, Stoke-on-Trent, in the summer of 1973 show a dramatist wishing to take young people's theatre beyond the once-innovatory stage of audience participation.

ALTERNATIVE THEATRE

Why assemble the notes in this chapter under the heading Alternative Theatre? It could be called Underground Theatre. It could be called off-West End Theatre. It could be called Fringe Theatre. In fact the existence of these and other current names is a pointer to the sheer variety of companies and work that is often packaged as the London equivalent of New York's off-off-Broadway. But Alternative Theatre is probably the safest umbrella under which to place the exceedingly heterogeneous activities that Britain has to offer in this area. For if the groups concerned have anything in common at all it is merely that what they can provide is an alternative to mainstream commercial theatre.

If that sounds as ambiguous as the fringe, underground and off-West End labels, it is meant to be. The point is that to attempt to define Alternative Theatre, it is necessary to invoke a network of seemingly minor considerations quite apart from the dramatic goods which constitute the raison d'être of the various enterprises. These apparently minor considerations concern matters like location, timing and scale.

By location is meant that Alternative Theatre is to be found in public houses, on buses and in the street as well as in basement and attic theatres. By timing is meant the fact that this type of theatre tends to function at lunch time and late at night rather than during the conventional evening hours. By scale is meant both the size of the productions themselves and that of the premises in which they are staged. Minority theatre of this kind is most frequently characterised by short, one-act productions put on in small spaces where the relationship between the actor and the audience is necessarily a very close one.

Perhaps consideration of the content as well as the milieu of Alternative Theatre will help to convince the visitor of the wisdom of exploring it under that ambiguous heading. Two extreme cases will provide an indication of the diversity of its acitivites. For example, in the autumn of 1970 a number of passers-by in London's Sloane Square were approached by a member of a company known as The People Show. The man in the street was asked, in a whisper, if he fancied a half-minute show that was to include violence, sex and drugs—all for the price of one penny. A positive response was followed by a visit to a nearby public telephone-box where another member of The People Show recounted a brisk de Sade anecdote. The street spectator was then invited to watch a cube of sugar being injected with a red fluid and was finally given a quick cuddle by a female member of the group.

This was an experience of a rather different order from that offered at the Soho Poly, the lunch-hour theatre, during the autumn of 1972. Here a full house of 60 people watched a revival of a neglected Shaw farce, **Overruled**, staged in period and with the good professionalism that might be expected in one of the nearby Shaftesbury Avenue theatres.

Can experiences of this kind be said to belong to a single movement?

That is something that the visitor must make up his own mind about in the light of the key personalities, dates and places that eager chroniclers of this scene have already allocated to it. As far as key personalities are concerned, the foremost is without doubt Jim Haynes. Like many leaders in the Alternative Theatre he is an American who has made his reputation by coming to Britain and setting up organisations that challenge mainstream theatre. The first of these was in Edinburgh, where Haynes fathered the Traverse Theatre in 1963 in a former brothel. Although ten years later Haynes had moved on, The Traverse was not only surviving but had extended its work by setting up a Traverse Theatre Workshop. And apart from introducing Britain to important off-off-Broadway writers, The Traverse had found its own local dramatist to promote in the person of Stanley Eveling (born 1924), lecturer in philosophy at Edinburgh University and author of **The Lunatic, the Secret Sportsman and the Woman Next Door** (1968) and **Dear Janet Rosenberg, Dear Mr Kooning** (1969). These plays and other Traverse work found a London foothold in theatres like the Jeannetta Cochrane, the Open Space and the Young Vic.

It could be argued that London might never have had a flourishing Alternative Theatre to welcome the productions were it not for Haynes' next venture. This was in 1968, when he took over a former warehouse and reopened it as the Drury Lane Arts Laboratory. This proved to be an arts bazaar where visitors could wander from floor to floor all through the day and night seeing old movies and new theatre groups. Many of the groups which have since become well-known in their own right first came together at the Arts Lab.

They received further encouragement in the autumn of 1970, by which time the Drury Lane venture had been and gone. William Gaskill, then artistic director of the Royal Court, opened up both the main auditorium and the Court's tiny Theatre Upstairs to the new groups. In a twenty-day festival, called **Come Together**, the general public was given nothing less than a non-stop round-the-clock opportunity of seeing the underground groups which had first come to general attention when Haynes had opened his Arts Lab.

The two biggest successes of the **Come Together** festival helped to show what variety there was in the Alternative Theatre. One was **Ken Campbell's Roadshow**—a programme devised by Ken Campbell from shaggy dog stories and smutty songs that had for years been going the rounds of the bar rooms of British pubs. It was performed with the utmost informality in staging that sought to recreate the atmosphere of the show's pub origins. The other great success of the Royal Court's season was Heathcote Williams' play, **AC/DC**. This was a play that assaulted the ears and eyes of the public with characters so high on drugs that the audience either hailed it as the 'first authentic masterpiece of the 1970s' or abused it as 'utter rubbish.' Whether the public looked back with Ken Campbell at a culture centred on alcohol or forward with Heathcote Williams at one that maintained itself on hard hallucinatory drugs, it had to be agreed that the Royal Court's festival had established that the Alternative Theatre now looked as though it were here to stay.

Older and possibly wiser commentators of course maintained that it

The Almost Free Theatre's production of Peter Handke's *Offending the Audience*. Lunch time theatres are an important showcase for such short, experimental pieces had all happened before. They pointed to the little theatres that had begun to spring up in London late on in the 1920s. These had come to be called collectively 'The Other Theatre' in a book by Norman Marshall. Such tiny playhouses as the Boltons, Gateway, New Lindsey and Qhad, in their day, also tried to provide a platform alternative to the West End. But in the late 1940s they petered out. And it was only twenty years later that something of what they had stood for gained a fresh impetus from Broadway's Alternative Theatre—the inspiration of off-Broadway and later of off-off-Broadway.

As the 1970s get under way so much activity is apparent in the resulting experimental field that it seems wise to get one's bearings by attempting some elementary classification. And the basic classification that has to be made is between places and faces.

The buildings that house Alternative Theatre can themselves be divided into two groups. There are the lunch time theatres that run their own seasons of plays and experimental programmes. And there are a number of theatres that also offer an informal London touring circuit to itinerant companies which have no homes of their own for this purpose. The Cockpit Theatre in-the-round, off the Edgware Road, is an Inner London Education Authority theatre which holds festivals of Alternative Theatre not unlike that held at the Royal Court in 1970. The Oval House Theatre Club in South London at Kennington also holds short festivals in its two auditoriums as well as providing a touring date for the new groups. The Roundhouse in Chalk Farm often provides a stopping place for them. Other theatres that double up with their own productions as well as providing a touring date are the Royal Court's Theatre Upstairs, the Young Vic, the Hampstead Theatre Club, The Open Space Theatre and the King's Head Pub in Islington. These are the places to watch in order to see the premieres of new experimental work or to catch up with those that have already had their first showing out of London.

What continuity there is in the small lunch-hour theatres comes from their artistic direction rather than from the productions themselves or the actors that appear in them. Scattered in all parts of London and subsisting on small grants from the Arts Council and the local authority, they are in no position to engage a permanent company Nor would it suit their programme planning to do so, since their productions (usually running for two to three weeks) range from revivals of neglected short classics to the premieres of one-act plays from contemporary writers. In this respect they perform a similar service to that provided by the BBC's Radio Three which, under its former title of the Third Programme, has a proud record of giving first performances of plays by Beckett and Pinter as well as introducing modern European drama to British audiences.

The lunch hour theatres that are accommodated in pubs (like the Play Room in central London and the Bush Theatre in Shepherd's Bush) are clearly well placed to give their public a chance to toast a success or drink away the memory of a failure. But this side of the Alternative Theatre is much more satisfactorily integrated when the artistic directors of the theatre also manage to run the pub too. At the beginning of 1973 this ideal had been achieved only by Dan and Joan Crawford at the King's Head in Islington. Their success in creating a pleasantly informal environment out of a derelict Victorian pub could well encourage others to take on this double function. At Islington it has meant that the pub proper has been a meeting place for folk singers and artists, whilst a back room, seating 60 for lunch or supper, has enabled Londoners (who like to eat where they do their playgoing) to see premieres of new works by important writers like David Mercer (**Let's Murder Vivaldi**) and Tom Gallacher (**Revival!**)

It has been suggested that another possible improvement in lunch-hour theatres would be the exchange of productions, with resulting longer and more remunerative runs. Certainly there would be little overlapping as far as local audiences are concerned since the concentration of a few theatres in central London (such as the Little and the Soho Poly) is offset by thriving theatres in Richmond (The Orange Tree), Brixton (The Dark and Light) and the East End (the Half Moon).

Because the inspiration for all this activity in London pubs and basement theatres is to be found in off-off-Broadway, it has been remarked (with a measure of peevish chauvinism) that London's Alternative Theatre is dominated by expatriate Americans. Apart from the charismatic figure of Jim Haynes, three other Americans have indeed extended and enlivened the British theatrical scene. Without Ed Berman, Charles Marowitz and Nancy Meckler it would certainly have been a less controversial place.

In establishing their respective ventures both Berman and Marowitz have shown a remarkable gift for fund-raising and for arousing provocative publicity. Berman's lunch hour venture—the Almost Free—is what it says it is. You pay what you can afford but you cannot get in for nothing. Apart from being a pioneer in the London lunch-hour field, with one-act plays by Tom Stoppard, Peter Nichols and David Rudkin to his credit, Berman has experimented in several other directions. His Interaction Company, which moves into the Almost Free in the evenings, presents folk and poetry festivals. Berman has also organised a roving group that takes its work into schools, mental hospitals and remand homes. And in the summer Interaction has its own bus, brightly got up as a Fun Bus, where young people can enjoy an improvised street theatre show.

Charles Marowitz (born 1934) comes into this chapter as the founder of the Open Space which opened in a Tottenham Court Road basement in 1968 with a prison soap opera that transferred to the West End. But any initial fears that this theatre was to be merely a satellite for Shaftesbury Avenue were quickly dispelled when the theatre got into its first few years, with lunch-hour shows by important new writers like Howard Brenton, as well as the evening presentation of Marowitz' own collage Shakespeare—**Hamlet, Macbeth** and **An Othello**. These Shakespeare programmes—a legacy from Marowitz' collaboration with Peter Brook on his Theatre of Cruelty season at the LAMDA Theatre in 1964—have proved popular at international avant-garde festivals. Like most alternative theatres, the Open Space has been unable to keep a permanent company over an extended period but its hospitality to visiting companies like the Edinburgh Traverse (with Stanley Eveling plays) has helped to make it an interestingly unpredictable centre on which an eye must be kept.

Nancy Meckler heads a group—The Freehold—not a theatre. Her first work in this country was with an English offshoot of New York's La Mama Company. But a quick look at The Freehold's repertoire shows that when Nancy Meckler came to form her own troupe it was not to pursue the American preoccupations of the parent off-Broadway organisation. She claims that the basis of The Freehold's work is a Yoga-like exercise, called The Cat, which enables those who learn it not only to discipline their bodies but also to make them sensitive instruments, capable of expressing a person's deepest feelings. The Freehold's theatre is therefore primarily physical and non-literary. But it has drawn heavily on classical not to say literary sources. Sophocles' **Antigone**, Webster's **The Duchess of Malfi** and The Bible for **Genesis** have all been given The Freehold's physical interpretation. Its **Mary Mary** programme, on the other hand, drew on a newspaper report of a little girl in the north of England who had murdered two little boys. It is interesting to note that though Freehold's workshops are run to explore expression in physical terms, the best work the group has produced is with the assistance of a writer—Peter Hulton in the case of **Antigone** and Roy Kift in the case of **Genesis** and **Mary Mary**.

Oddly enough Pip Simmons (born 1942), whose group produced admired works inspired by American events and themes, is an Englishman who has never been to the States. With **Superman** based on the comic strip cartoon treatment of the rock 'n roll scene, **Do It!**, based on Jerry Rubin's account of the 1968 attempt to break up the Democratic Convention and the **George Jackson Black and White Minstrel Show**, the group looked so wryly at the disintegration of the American way of life that they certainly avoided any cosy liberal humanitarian attitudes. **The George Jackson Show** was particularly adroit at incorporating criticism of both white and black Americans in the structure of the old nineteenth century Minstrel Show. But in **The Pardoner's Tale**, based on Chaucer, and **Alice in Wonderland**, based on Lewis Carroll, Pip Simmons showed that he could rework a diversity of English sources to produce material as explosive as his excursions into American problems.

Any conspiracy theory about Americans having taken over the British Alternative Theatre can be countered by invoking the Portable Theatre. As its name implies, this is a touring group whose productions are mounted with the minimum of sets and costumes so as to ensure swift moving productions, not to mention a practical touring unit. Founded in 1968 by two Cambridge graduates—David Hare and Tony Bicat—Portable has launched a number of new writers, most notably in the field of composite authorship. Portable's **Layby** (1971) was a seven-handed play reflecting the reaction of a group of dramatists to a newspaper clip about fellatio in a roadside layby. Some of the same writers again collaborated on **England's Ireland** (1972). This reworked facts and statistics on Britain's involvement with Northern Ireland to provide a scathing assessment of successive British governments' handling of the Ulster Problem. Personalities on both the Roman Catholic and the Protestant side were debunked in strip cartoon style. It was characteristic of the work of the Portable writers that **England's Ireland** did not attempt to offer any solutions.

The most writer-orientated of the groups working in Alternative Theatre, Portable have explored the areas of decay and moral break down in modern society. Where commercial theatre's entertainmen commitment necessitates a turning away from this area, the bes Alternative Theatre groups have, on the contrary, seized on th

Members of the Pip Simmons Theatre Group in *The George Jackson Black and White Minstrel Show*

104 Alternative Theatre

decadent and the immoral and thrown the result straight in the face of their public. It is in its assault tactics and in the nihilism of its outlook that the Alternative Theatre of today differs from that of Bernard Shaw's generation. If Ibsen with **Ghosts** and Shaw with **Mrs Warren's Profession** shocked the public of their day, it was in the context of carefully plotted full-length plays aimed at involving the spectator compassionately as well as cerebrally. And if Shaw and his followers saw the theatre as a debating hall or as a pulpit it was because they felt that with compassion and thought they might bring about a more just and humane society. Although there is an acute sense of injustice and inhumanity in the Alternative Theatre of today, the Punch and Judy-like harshness of the productions themselves is rarely conducive to compassion or reflection.

Better known in Britain's Alternative Theatre than either Pip Simmons or the Portable group is the international figure of Peter Brook. His questioning of our basic concepts of theatre and his search for a new theatrical language have been conducted in the research centre provided for him by the French authorities in Paris. He received more overseas backing when invited to unveil the results of his first year's work in France at the 1971 Shiraz/Persepolis Festival under Iranian auspices. In London this research programme has never been shown. So for British theatregoers, his richest work in this area was at the LAMDA Theatre in 1964 when the theories of Antonin Artaud (1896 – 1948) were investigated in the now-famous Theatre of Cruelty season. The most satisfactory aspect of this season was that the experience gained from it was fed back into the Royal Shakespeare Company, whose 1965 production of **The Marat/Sade**, directed at the Aldwych by Brook, would certainly never have met with the international acclaim it did without the groundwork of the LAMDA season.

Brook has been fortunate in that his experimental work has been conducted with the subsidised Royal Shakespeare Company or else abroad under French or Iranian subsidy. The humbler and less internationally well-known would-be avant-gardists in London have to get by on more modest subsidies—from the Arts Council, the local authority or the Department of Education. Although the subsidies are indeed small, it is a healthy sign that a minority theatre that is often fiercely critical of the Establishment is given official grants to go on questioning the validity of the society that helps it to get by.

It should not be forgotten, however, that the most important and reliable source of subsidy for Alternative Theatre comes from the actor. He works in this theatre for nothing or for fees that barely cover the expenses involved. The working conditions, moreover, are often frankly appalling, with no proper dressing rooms and with inadequate heat, light and sanitation. The attraction for the actor is the showcase potential of Alternative Theatre work. The actor may undertake work in a well-paid television serial and receive no press coverage of any kind even when watched by audiences that are numbered in millions. In the Alternative Theatre he may be seen in a lunch-hour production where the public at most totals two or three hundred and then be reviewed in the daily and even more influential Sunday press. When seen by a casting director or good agent in the Alternative Theatre or when receiving some valuable critical coverage, this field does have something to offer the actor. But compared to commerical theatre—and judged in terms of working conditions—it otherwise offers a pretty poor alternative.

TRAINING

Where did Shakespeare train to become a great dramatist? At what school did Peter Brook acquire the specialist instruction that has enabled him to be considered a director of genius? Which acting academy taught Michael Redgrave to perform with such skill that he has been given a knighthood? What business institution gave Peter Saunders the know-how to become celebrated as the manager responsible for staging the world's longest running play, **The Mousetrap**? What course on theatre criticism did Harold Hobson take to have survived some 26 years as **The Sunday Times'** drama reviewer and become, arguably, Britain's most powerful critic?

The answer in each case is that the knowledge, insight and technical skills required were picked up in the professional theatre itself. None arrived flourishing recherche diplomas certifying their proven ability to achieve what they were to achieve. And the first thing the would-be theatre trainee has to bear in mind is that this tradition of learning on the job survives, with all its apparent unfairness, nearly three quarters of the way through the twentieth century.

It could well happen, therefore, that a student might train at a school like London's Royal Academy of Dramatic Art for three years only to find himself then joining the two thirds of the acting profession who are always out of work. And, at the same time, a director like Joan Littlewood or Franco Zeffirelli could come across some young person with absolutely no theatre background and intuit that they had just the qualities needed for their latest productions. Clearly, as in most theatrical spheres, training for the stage has to be approacned in Britain with the expectation of an outcome as apparently illogical as the most bizarre adventure that befell Alice in Wonderland.

Even so, those desiring to join Britain's entertainment wonderland have more chances to train for it than ever before. At the academic level, for instance, 1973 saw six British universities with graduate departments of drama whereas in the late 1940s there was none. Bristol University—the first in Britain to have such a drama department—now passes out 30 students a year with degrees in drama and there are similar opportunities at the Universities of Birmingham, Exeter, Glasgow, Hull and Manchester. By no means all the students who have passed through these three-year courses then proceed directly into the professional theatre. Education claims a good many of them. And this particular background obviously provides good candidates for local authority posts like that of the County Drama Adviser, whose job encompasses liaison between schools and the professional theatre.

The greatest possible contrast with the university entree to the theatre is the old-fashioned one of becoming a dogsbody—or what is known as assistant stage manager—with a regional repertory company. Many now middle-aged actors in their stagestruck youth answered advertisements in **The Stage** weekly newspaper for jobs of this kind. By becoming a jack-of-all-trades with a shoe-string seaside repertory company they received a practical though exhausting training in their calling. As the cheerfully impoverished weekly repertory companies have been replaced by Arts Council and Local Authority subsidised repertoire theatres so this hit and miss apprenticeship of the untrained novice is rapidly becoming a thing of the past.

But the regional theatre does remain very much a training ground. The Arts Council runs a scheme whereby directors, designers and writers of promise are awarded grants to enable them to spend a year working with approved companies. In all three cases, however, applicants will need to have some solid proof of their training and of their promise. They have to be able to offer experience or sponsorship that was quite beyond the reach of the good-looking young man or woman who got a walk-on in the reps of the twenties and thirties thanks to their boundless enthusiasm and willingness to work for next to nothing. The backstage movie biographies of rags-to-riches so affectionately parodied in Sandy Wilson's musical **The Boy Friend** will soon have to be rewritten—with the man from the Arts Council possibly playing a romantic lead.

A surviving means of bypassing the drama schools remains the amateur theatre. This movement is particularly strong in Wales and in Southern Ireland. In fact many actors in Eire's national theatre company—the Abbey—have been recruited from those who put on an impressive appearance at an amateur drama festival. But to be a member of the Abbey, you have to pass an examination in Gaelic, so that is a backdoor approach firmly closed to those who are not nationals.

In England probably the richest recruiting area in amateur theatre has been provided by the National Youth Theatre. Although it does not set out to provide training for the professional theatre, the National Youth Theatre has in fact provided it with both acting and technical personnel. A good example is Helen Mirren, who appeared as Cleopatra when the NYT gave **Antony and Cleopatra** in its season at the Old Vic in the summer of 1965. Since then Helen Mirren has gone on to join the Royal Shakespeare Company where she played Cressida in **Troilus and Cressida** and Ophelia in **Hamlet**.

Yet another non-professional door that bypasses the acting academy is through the work of undergraduate productions at the universities. Probably the best-known actor of the 1970s to arrive by this route is Ian McKellen. He achieved something of a reputation as an actor whilst at Cambridge and then with an arts degree in his pocket, moved on to work through good regional companies like the Belgrade, Coventry, and the Nottingham Playhouse to the National Theatre and the West End. His is a good example of what might be lost to the theatre if entry to it were limited to those who have passed through recognized drama schools.

If the actors' Trade Union—Equity—were to bow to pressures to restrict entry to its members' overcrowded profession in this way, what sort of schools would it have to deal with? Basically there are two classes. The first, like the Italia Conti and Corona Schools in London, take on students from the ages of 5-16. Others, like the Royal Academy of Dramatic Art and the Central School of Speech and Drama, also in the capital, do not admit students under the age of 18.

The schools that take on students from the age of 5 and dovetail their general education with training for the stage have the advantage of bringing young people into the area of professional theatre from the childhood. Students of such schools often find themselves doing practical work like television commercials when still little older than Shirley Temple in her Hollywood prime.

In one case—the Aida Foster School—the establishment has gone over to becoming an agency specialising in child actors. Parents who send their children to these schools have ultimately to decide whether an early preparation for a stage career is more important than taking basic school-leaving examinations. The Prospectus of one school for the 5 to 16-year-olds warns, 'It must be clearly understood that professional work may have to be excluded in order to give the child a fair chance of passing in the subjects chosen. Parents and Headmistress get together over this point when the child is 14 and his earning capacity must be measured against the need he might eventually have for O level examination passes, should he eventually fail as an actor.

This is an important long-term decision often overlooked by stage-struck parents who see their offspring as child prodigies or at least as child breadwinners. The truth is that actors who are popular in their childhood rarely go on to exert the same spell as adults. The classic example of this in the British theatre is Master Betty (1791 — 1874) who so took London by storm in Shakespeare tragedy roles at 14 that the House of Commons actually adjourned to watch him as Hamlet. But he lingered on until his eighties in total obscurity, having failed to make a comeback at the age of 20.

For the drama schools that take on students from the age of 18 upwards, purely academic qualifications are not essential, though the Royal Academy of Dramatic Art notes in its Prospectus that 'the advantage to an actor of a good education need hardly be stressed.' Admission to RADA or similar schools in London (like the London Academy of Music and Dramatic Art) is initially by audition. And to get even thus far the would-be student must pay an average audition fee of £6.00 and offer two audition pieces (one from Shakespeare) neither of which should last more than three minutes. It does not seem long to make up your mind whether somebody is fit to devote the next three years (and some £1,750 in fees) to completing an acting course. But there are follow-up interviews for the most promising. And though the RADA Prospectus tactfully points out that candidates 'must be prepared to curtail their audition if so instructed', those who find favour with the adjudicators might be asked to go through their paces a second time in the afternoon.

The important post-war development with regard to drama schools is a change of attitude towards the best of them on the part of Local Authorities. There was a time when councillors administering public funds felt that something as fanciful as the stage was not a direction into which public money should be channelled. This meant that in the inter-war years drama academies were for the well-to-do and within their four walls you would hear the debutante-like tones of uppercrust English. No doubt this was well suited to the smart drawing-room comedies students might go on to perform in a professional theatre where the working-classes were chiefly used to provide a dramatist's comic relief.

The new readiness of Local Authorities to pay fees for promising drama students meant a new type of actor, actors with working class backgrounds and regional accents of the calibre of Albert Finney and Tom Courtenay who were in turn able to play the parts written by the

new generation of writers taking a less patronising attitude to the poor or the character with a regional background.

Other developments in the drama schools have included the need to prepare the student for camera, particularly television camera work, as well as for the stage proper. The first terms concern an exploration of theories of the nature of an actor's creativity as well as developing the voice and the body to, as the RADA Prospectus neatly puts it, gain maximum expressiveness with minimum effort.' The last two terms move into the more practical area of rehearsal for public productions which will be attended, hopefully, by lots of agents and casting directors.

Different schools, of course, place emphasis in different areas. Most, however, now accept that even the classically-gifted actor must also be given opportunities to develop the skills needed for a musical. Paul Scofield's career in switching from the verse of Shakespeare and T S Eliot to a musical like **Expresso Bongo** (1958) vividly illustrates the collapse of the restricting boundaries between what **Variety** still calls the Legit stage and the popular areas where an actor needs to be able to sing and dance.

Another important area of development is the increasing technical skills needed for stage management. Thus, the London Academy of Music and Dramatic Art, in conjunction with Theatre Projects Ltd, runs a five-term course (fees £150 per term) with instruction on stage management techniques, particularly in the use of lighting and sound equipment. This Prospectus warns that 'students will be required to work hard, and for long hours, often in the evenings and at the weekends; for these are the conditions they will meet in the profession they have chosen.'

The Rose Bruford College, half an hour out of London in Kent, specialises in training those who want to teach drama. This college's Diploma Course lasts three years and the student will need £1,650 fee money either personally or through a grant to complete it. Many Colleges of Education now run similar courses, some of them leading to degrees.

Most schools seem aware of the great interest overseas students have in training for the stage in Britain. And some have special arrangements for auditions to be held outside Britain. RADA, for example, holds three auditions a year in New York. Foreign students, whether undertaking the full three-year acting course or shorter courses in stage management, are warned that in 1973 a rock-bottom minimum of £60 a month is needed for living in London. This, of course, is quite apart from monies needed for tuition fees and specialist books and equipment.

Assuming a student is able to live on £800 a year in London, he can reckon that in the three years it takes to complete a drama school training course he will have spent a minimum of £2,000 in fees and £2,400 in keeping himself fed and accommodated. In other words, the student who is unable to obtain a grant or full scholarship must earmark a minimum of £4,400 to train for the stage in London.

It's a sobering thought that at the end of so much expenditure of

The National Youth Theatre (seen here in *The Apprentices*) has proved to be a training ground for many of Britain's new generation of young professional actors time and money, only those specialising in the technical field of stage management can expect any sort of guarantee of employment. Those who take pleasure in British theatre will be glad that each year a thousand newcomers take this risk. But only those who have absolutely no chance of finding satisfaction in any other career would be wise to join their ranks.

Part 2   Reference Section

Theatre Collections, Libraries & Galleries

London

The British Theatre Museum,
Leighton House, 12 Holland Park Road, W14. 602 3052

Opening hours: Tuesday, Thursday and Saturday 11 am to 5 pm
Underground: High Street Kensingtor
Buses: 9, 27, 28, 33, 49, 73

The Museum, still housed in temporary premises, contains the Henry Irving archives comprising 4,000 items of a personal and professional nature ranging from his stage costumes to diaries and letters. Also the Harley Granville—Barker Collection of original manuscripts and a wealth of other general theatre material.

The Victoria and Albert Museum,
Cromwell Road, South Kensington, SW7. 589 6371

Opening hours: Library 10 am to 5.45 pm Monday to Saturday. Enthoven Collection 10 am to 4.50 pm Monday to Friday
Underground: South Kensington (entrance direct from station)
Buses: 14, 30, 74, 39a, 45.

The V & A contains the famous Gabrielle Enthoven Collection of over a million playbills and programmes, 6,000 engravings, newspaper cuttings, prompt books, autographed letters, photographs and other material immaculately catalogued. The Museum also houses the London Archives of the Dance, and material on the Ballet donated by Dame Marie Rambert.

The British Theatre Association.
9 Fitzroy Square, W1. 387 2666

Opening hours: 10 am to 5 pm (to 8 pm on Wednesday and to 12.30 pm on Saturday)
Underground: Warren Street
Buses: 14, 24, 29, 73, 176 to Tottenham Court Road

The BTA runs an Information and Advice Bureau, and has a drama library of 150,000 volumes available to its members for a small annual fee. The library includes material on or collected by Miss Horniman, William Archer, Harley Granville—Barker, Nigel Playfair and Edward Gordon Craig.

The London Museum,
Kensington Palace, Kensington Gardens, W8. 937 0146

Opening hours: April to September, 10 am to 6 pm Monday to Saturday, 2 to 6 pm Sunday. During October, February and March closes 5 pm, during November to January closes 4 pm.
Underground: High Street Kensington or Queensway
Buses: 9, 12, 14, 33.

This Museum, concerned with the life and history of London, contains many items of theatrical interest consisting of costumes, stage jewellery and props used by famous artists, as well as playbills, photographs, programmes and prompt books.

The British Museum,
Great Russell Street, WC1. 636 1555

Opening hours: Printed Books Department 10 am to 5 pm Monday, Wednesday and Saturday. 10 am to 9 pm Tuesday, Thursday and Friday
Underground: Tottenham Court Road or Holborn
Buses: 7, 8, 19, 22, 25, 38

The Printed Books Department houses a large collection of play scripts submitted for licensing between 1821 and 1903 and passed to the Museum by the Lord Chamberlain's Office. Also the Burney Collection of theatre playbills and the Harris Collection of London theatre notices.

Dulwich College Library and Picture Gallery,
Dulwich, SE 21.

Opening hours: Library: during school term only by special permission by writing to the Librarian. Gallery: Tuesday to Saturday. From May 1 to August 31 10 am to 6 pm. September 1 to October 15, and March 16 to April 20 10 am to 5 pm. October 16 to March 15 10 am to 4 pm. Sundays: May 31 to August 31 2 to 6 pm. April and September only 2 to 5 pm.
Train: Southern Region from Victoria to West Dulwich

Bus: 3

The Library of the College contains over 11,000 books, the correspondence, diary, account books and papers belonging to its founder, Edward Alleyn, the Elizabethan actor and contemporary of Shakespeare. The Gallery includes portraits of Alleyn himself as well as of Burbage, Mrs Siddons, Kemble and Moliere.

The National Portrait Gallery,
St Martin's Place, Trafalgar Square, WC2. 930 8511

Opening hours: 10 am to 5 pm Monday to Friday. 10 am to 6 pm Saturdays. 2 to 6 pm Sundays
Underground: Trafalgar Square
Buses: 1, 6, 9, 11, 13, 15, 24, 29, 77, 77a, 176

Situated just round the corner from the National Gallery, the Portrait Gallery houses a large collection of canvases, drawings, busts, photographs and death masks of famous people. Among the many connected with the theatre are:

Henry Ainley
George Alexander
Mary Anderson
Squire & Lady Bancroft
James Barrie
Max Beerbohm
Brendan Behan
Thomas Betterton
Dion Boucicault
The Bronte sisters
Geoffrey Chaucer
Colley Cibber
C B Cochran
William Congreve
Clemence Dane
Ninette de Valois
John Dryden
Gerald du Maurier
T S Eliot
Lily Elsie
Nellie Farren
John Fletcher
Johnstone Forbes-Robertson
David Garrick
John Gay
W S Gilbert
Harley Granville-Barker
Lady Gregory
Joseph Grimaldi
William Hazlitt
Seymour Hicks
Mrs Horniman
Leslie Howard
Jack Hylton
Henry Irving
Henry James
Ben Jonson
James Joyce
Charles Kean
John Philip Kemble
D H Lawrence
Charles Macklin
Wm Charles Macready
John Martin-Harvey
Cyril Maude
W Somerset Maugham
Charles Morgan
Sean O'Casey
Anne Oldfield
Samuel Phelps
Stephen Phillips
Arthur Wing Pinero
Nigel Playfair
William Poel
George Robey
William Shakespeare
George Bernard Shaw
Richard Brinsley Sheridan
Sarah Siddons
Henry Wriothesley,
    Earl of Southampton
J M Synge
Ellen Terry
Dylan Thomas
J L Toole
Herbert Beerbohm Tree
Irene Vanbrugh
Oscar Wilde
Peg Woffington
William Wycherley
Charles Wyndham
W B Yeats

Vic-Wells Association Library,
housed jointly at The Old Vic, Waterloo Road, SE1, and Sadler's Wells, Rosebury Avenue, EC1. Hon Secretary: 274 6903

Opening hours: Tuesday, Thursday and Saturday 6.30 to 8.30 pm except when theatre is closed.
Underground: Waterloo for the Old Vic. Angel for Sadler's Wells
Buses: 1, 68, 176, 188, 196, for Old Vic. 19, 38, 171, 172 for Sadler's Wells

A comprehensive record of productions and artists connected with Theatre, Opera and Ballet performances at both these theatres, as well as a library of books on the theatre in general.

Mander & Mitchenson Theatre Collection,
5 Venner Road, Sydenham, SE26. 778 6730

Opening hours: by appointment only
Train: Southern Region from London Bridge to Sydenham
Bus: 12

A unique and comprehensive private collection built up over the past 30 years by two ex-actors in their own home. Engravings, paintings, souvenirs, photographs, china figures, files of programmes of London and provincial theatres, and a library of several thousand books. The Collection is extensively used by everyone engaged in theatre research.

Pollock's Toy Museum,
1 Scala Street, W1. 636 3452

Opening hours: 10 am to 5 pm Monday to Saturday
Underground: Goodge Street
Buses: 14, 24, 29, 73, 176

The "penny plain and tuppence coloured" plates of the juvenile drama published by Benjamin Pollock are a feature here, and copies can be bought. There is also a display of model theatres, cardboard cut-outs and other theatre toys.

Madame Tussaud's
Marylebone Road, NW1. 935 6861

Opening hours: Every day except Christmas Day. Weekdays: 10 am to 5.30 pm, (to 6.30 pm from April to September). Saturday & Sunday: 10 am to 6.30 pm all the year round.
Underground: Baker Street
Buses: 1, 2, 2b, 13, 18, 26, 27, 30, 59, 74, 74b, 113, 159, 176.

In the Entertainers section of this internationally famous exhibition are wax portraits of Julie Andrews, the Beatles, Richard Burton and Elizabeth Taylor, Brigitte Bardot, Sammy Davis Jnr, Tony Hancock, Alfred Hitchcock, Audrey Hepburn, Bob Hope and Morecambe and Wise. Shakespeare and Agatha Christie, Chaucer and Dickens appear in the new Grand Hall.

Bear Gardens Museum
Bear Gardens, Southwark, SE1.

Opening hours: Tuesday to Friday 10 am to 4 pm. Saturday and Sunday 2 to 5 pm. Admission free. For schools and party bookings, telephone 928 4229.
Buses: 8a, 10, 21, 35, 40, 43, 44, 47, 48, 133, Red Arrows 501, 503 all to London Bridge. 18, 95, 149, 176a to Sumner Street off Southwark Bridge. 70 to Guildford Street off Southwark Street. Then follow RAC signs.
Underground: London Bridge (which is also on Southern Region) and Mansion House.
On foot: Through the grounds of Southwark Cathedral, past St Mary Overy wharf and Clink Street to the Anchor Pub, then along Bankside under Southwark Bridge to Bear Gardens Alley.

The Globe Playhouse Trust runs this museum on a site a few yards from the present temporary playhouse structure, on Shakespeare's south bank of the Thames. The museum is housed in a converted 18th century warehouse on the actual site of the 16th century bear-baiting ring and The Hope playhouse, both operating at the time of Shakespeare's Globe, as well as the Rose and the Swan playhouses on Bankside.

The exhibitions mounted here are changed about every four months. That for the summer of 1973 covered the Elizabethan theatre and included contemporary prints, news-sheets and models of the playhouses of the period. The Folger Library in Washington also lent two exhibits.

Outside London
AYOT ST LAWRENCE
Shaw's Corner,
Ayot St Lawrence, near Welwyn, Herts.

Opening hours: Every day except Tuesday, 11 am to 1 pm, 2 to 6 pm (or dusk)
Train: From King's Cross to Welwyn Garden City. 20 miles. Then local bus for 5 miles.
Bus: Green Line coach 716a to Welwyn, then local bus for 1½ miles.

A Victorian rectory and garden which was Bernard Shaw's home for the last 40 years of his life. Now a National Trust property. The study and summer house complete with writing desks are kept as they were on his death in 1950, and the house also contains many personal effects of Shaw and his wife.

BIRMINGHAM
Birmingham Public Libraries,
Ratcliff Place, Birmingham. 021 235 9944

Opening hours: Monday to Saturday 9 am to 9 pm
Train: From Euston to New Street Station, Birmingham. 110 miles

The Shakespeare Memorial Library here contains one of the most important Shakespeare collections in the world: a set of five First Folios, nine Quartos, a complete set of Restoration Quartos and about 35,000 books, periodicals and volumes of music on Shakespeare productions. Also playbills and programmes of productions staged throughout the world.

BOURNEMOUTH
Russell-Cotes Gallery & Museum,
East Cliff, Bournemouth, Hants. 0202 21009

Opening hours: Monday to Saturday 10 am to 6 pm. Sunday 2.30 to 6 pm (closes 5 pm during November to March)
Train: From Waterloo to Central Station, Bournemouth. 108 miles

A collection of Henry Irving memorabilia is housed here including costumes and jewellery worn by Sir Henry and his sons and contemporaries.

BRISTOL
Bristol University: Richard Southern Collection,
Drama Department, The University, Bristol 8. 0272 24161 (ask for Drama Dept.)

Opening hours: Term-time Monday to Friday 9.30 am to 12.45 pm, 2 to 8 pm. (Closes 5 pm during vacation)
Train: From Paddington to Temple Meads Station, Bristol. 118 miles

Bristol University's Special Lecturer in Theatre Architecture and Scenery, Dr. Richard Southern, has made a collection of 10,000 items illustrating the history and modern techniques of theatre architecture and stage machinery.

CHATSWORTH
The Library,
Chatsworth House, Edensor, near Bakewell, Derbyshire.

Opening hours: by special permission on written application from April to October only
Train: From St Pancras to Bakewell. 153 miles

The main item in this collection is the designs of Inigo Jones for masques and plays presented at Court in the early part of the 17th century.

OXFORD
Bodleian Library,
Radcliffe Square, Oxford. 0865 44675.

Opening hours: Weekdays: 9 am to 7 pm. Camera Reading Room: 10 am to 10 pm.
Train: From Paddington to Oxford. 63 miles.

This internationally famous University Library contains a lot of Shakespeariana as well as the Edward Malone Collection of printed books and editions of plays from 1500 to 1800, the Robert Ross collection of the works and papers of Oscar Wilde, and manuscripts of John Galsworthy and T. S. Eliot.

SMALLHYTHE
The Ellen Terry Memorial Museum,
Smallhythe, near Tenterden, Kent. 058 06 2334

Opening hours: by appointment with the Curator
Train: From Charing Cross to Headcorn. 45 miles. Then local bus to Smallhythe (approximately 10 miles).

The 15th century cottage which was Ellen Terry's home for many years up to her death in 1928, preserved as she knew it and containing many of her personal relics.

STRATFORD-UPON-AVON
Train: From Paddington. 103 miles.

Royal Shakespeare Theatre Picture Gallery, Waterside.

Opening hours: April to October: weekdays 10 am to 1 pm, 2 to 6 pm, matinee days: 10 am to 6 pm. Sundays 2 pm to 6 pm. November, closes 4 pm. December to March, opens Saturday and Sunday only.

This Gallery adjoins the Royal Shakespeare Theatre, and houses portraits of famous actors and actresses from the 18th and 20th century in character in Shakespeare productions. The collection is dominated by the Benson Memorial Window, dedicated to the actor-manager Sir Frank Benson.

The Shakespeare Birthplace Trust, Henley Street.

Opening hours: 10 am to 5 pm Monday to Friday. 9.30 am to 12.30 pm on Saturday.

The Shakespeare Centre was opened in 1964, thus bringing together under one roof two separate library collections, one belonging to the Birthplace Trust and the other to the Royal Shakespeare Theatre. They form an important part of the Centre's collection.

Shakespeare's Birthplace, Henley Street.

Opening hours: From April to October: 9 am to 7 pm (10 am to 6 pm on Sundays). From November to March: 9 am to 4 pm (2 to 4.30 pm on Sundays).

This is the half-timbered house where Shakespeare was born.

**Anne Hathaway's Cottage,
Shottery, near Stratford-upon-Avon.**

Opening hours: The same as for Shakespeare's Birthplace.

One mile outside Stratford is the home of Shakespeare's wife before their marriage. It stands in an attractive English garden.

**New Place,
Chapel Street.**

Opening hours: April to October: 9 am to 6 pm (2 to 6 pm on Sundays). November to March: 2 to 4 pm (closed on Sunday).

The foundations of Shakespeare's last home, preserved in an Elizabethan knot garden, with Nash's house adjoining.

**Mary Arden's House,
Wilmcote, near Stratford-upon-Avon.**

Opening hours: April to October only, from 2 to 6 pm.

Three miles outside Stratford in the village of Wilmcote stands the Tudor farmhouse where Shakespeare's mother lived.

Statues in London

William Shakespeare.
Leicester Square, WC2.
Sculptor: Fontana, after Scheemakers.
Unveiled: July, 1874

This statue is a reproduction of the Peter Scheemakers figure from the design of William Kent in Westminster Abbey. The foundation, surmounted by a white marble statue, shows the poet with his elbow resting on three books placed on a small column and with his right hand pointing to the words: "There is no darkness but ignorance."
Underground: Leicester Square
Buses: 1, 24, 29, 176

Sarah Siddons.
Church Street, Paddington Green, W2.
Sculptor: Leon Joseph Chavilliaud.
Unveiled: 1897

Mrs Siddons, the great 18th century tragic actress, is represented by a white marble statue at the north end of the churchyard of St Mary's Church, now a recreation ground. It was unveiled by Irving, and was inspired by Joshua Reynolds' painting of her as the Tragic Muse.
Underground: Edgware Road
Buses: 6, 8, 16, 176 to Edgware Road. 18a to Paddington Green.

Sir Henry Irving.
Charing Cross Road (Trafalgar Square end), WC2.
Sculptor: Sir Thomas Brock. Unveiled: December, 1910

Sir Henry, the first actor to be knighted, lived from 1838 to 1905. This bronze statue stands on a granite pedestal and shows him standing bare-headed, wearing the gown of a Doctor of Literature. He holds a manuscript in his left hand. There is an inscription: "Erected by English actors and actresses and by others connected with the theatre in his memory."
Underground: Leicester Square or Trafalgar Square
Buses: 1, 6, 9, 11, 13, 15, 24, 29, 77, 77a, 176

Peter Pan
Kensington Gardens, W2.
Sculptor: Sir George Frampton, RA.
Unveiled: 1911

This, probably the most popular of all London statues, was commissioned by Sir James Barrie himself. It stands on the west bank of the Long Water in Kensington Gardens and is of the art nouveau period, with the central figure surrounded by mice, rabbits and squirrels.
Underground: Queensway
Buses: 9, 14, 33, 73

Blue Plaques

The idea of placing plaques on the homes of famous people originated with an anonymous writer to the Royal Society of Arts in 1864, and the first one was put up on 24 Holles Street, Westminster (now demolished) where Byron was born in 1788. The idea was taken over by the London County Council in 1901. There are now over 300 plaques on houses in Greater London; some of the earlier ones were a reddish-brown colour, and there is one in bronze to Benjamin Franklin at 36 Craven Street in Charing Cross. There are also many unofficial plaques put up by private individuals, e.g. one to Ellen Terry at 215 King's Road, Chelsea.

PLACES

Collins Music Hall, 1862 to 1958
10/11 Islington Green, Islington, N1. Erected 1968

The Theatre, 1577 to 1598
86-88 Curtain Road, Shoreditch, EC2. Erected 1920
Within a few yards of the site of the Priory of St John the Baptist, Holywell, stood the first London building specially devoted to the performance of plays.

Adelphi Terrace,
The Adelphi, Strand, WC2. Erected 1952
The present building stands on the site of Adelphi Terrace, built by the brothers Adam in the late 18th century. Among its famous residents were David Garrick, Richard D'Oyly Carte (promoter of the Savoy Operas), George Bernard Shaw and Thomas Hardy.

Bow Street,
19-20 Bow Street, Westminster, WC2. Erected 1929
Built around 1637, these premises were the homes of many notable men, among them Henry Fielding, the novelist; Charles Macklin, the actor; and William Wycherley, dramatist.

PEOPLE

Sir George Alexander, 1858 to 1918, actor-manager, 57 Pont Street, SW1. Erected 1951

Sir James Barrie, 1860 to 1937, novelist and playwright, 100 Bayswater Road, Paddington, W2. Erected 1961

Sir Max Beerbohm, 1872 to 1956, artist and writer, 57 Palace Gardens Terrace, Kensington, W8. Erected 1969

Albert Chevalier, 1861 to 1923, music hall comedian, 17 St. Ann's Villas, St. Ann's Road, Kensington, W11. Erected 1965

John Dryden, 1631 to 1700, poet and playwright, 43 Gerrard Street, W1. Erected 1875

John Galsworthy, 1867 to 1933, novelist and playwright, Grove Lodge, Hampstead Grove, NW3. Erected 1950. Lived here from 1918 to 1933

David Garrick, 1717 to 1779, actor, Garrick's Villa, Hampton, Middlesex. Erected 1970

W S Gilbert, 1836 to 1911, dramatist and co-author of the Savoy Operas, 39 Harrington Gardens, Kensington, SW7. Erected 1929

Kenneth Grahame, 1859 to 1932, author of **Wind in the Willows**, 16 Phillimore Place, Kensington, W8. Erected 1959. Lived here from 1901 to 1908

Sir Philip Ben Greet, 1857 to 1936, actor-manager, 160 Lambeth Road, Lambeth, SE1. Erected 1961

George Grossmith (senior), 1847 to 1912, actor and author, 28 Dorset Square, NW1. Erected 1963

George Grossmith (junior), 1874 to 1935, actor-manager, 3 Spanish Place, W1. Erected 1963

William Hazlitt, 1778 to 1830, essayist and theatre commentator, 6 Frith Street, W1. Erected 1905. Died here

Sir Henry Irving, 1838 to 1905, actor-manager 15a Grafton Street, W1 Erected 1950. Lived here from 1872 to 1899

Henry James, 1843 to 1916, writer and playwright, 34 De Vere Gardens, Kensington, W8. Erected 1949. Lived here from 1886 to 1902

Sir Harry Lauder, 1870 to 1950, music hall artist, 46 Longley Road, SW17. Erected 1969

D H Lawrence, 1885 to 1930, novelist and poet and playwright, 1 Byron Villas, Vale of Health, Hampstead, NW3. Erected 1969

Dan Leno, 1860 to 1904, music-hall comedian, 96 Akerman Road, Lambeth, SW9. Erected 1962

Sir Gerald du Maurier, 1873 to 1934, actor-manager, Cannon Hall, 14 Cannon Place, Hampstead, NW3. Erected 1967

Samuel Phelps, 1804 to 1878, tragedian, 8 Canonbury Square, Islington, N1. Erected 1911

Sir Arthur Wing Pinero, 1855 to 1934, playwright, 115a Harley Street, W1. Erected 1970

Sir Nigel Playfair, 1874 to 1934, actor-manager, 26 Pelham Crescent, Kensington, SW7. Erected 1965

Richard Brinsley Sheridan, 1751 to 1816, dramatist, 14 Savile Row, W1. Erected 1881 **and** 10 Hertford Street, W1. Erected 1955

Dame Ellen Terry, 1847 to 1928, actress, 22 Barkston Gardens, Kensington, SW5. Erected 1951

Sir Herbert Beerbohm Tree, 1853 to 1917, actor-manager, 31 Rosary Gardens, Kensington, SW7. Erected 1950

Sir Charles Wyndham, 1837 to 1919, actor-manager, 43 York Terrace, St. Marylebone, NW1. Erected 1962

Edgar Wallace, 1875 to 1932, writer, 6 Tressillian Crescent, Deptford, SE4. Erected 1960

Oscar Wilde, 1854 to 1900, dramatist and wit, 34 Tite Street, Chelsea, SW3. Erected 1954

Churches

Westminster Abbey,
Parliament Square, SW1.

Underground: Westminster
Buses: 3, 11, 12, 24. 29, 39, 53, 59, 76, 77, 77a, 159, 170, 172, 184.

Poet's Corner, in the South Transept of the Abbey, has over the years been appropriated by poets and others connected with the arts. A monument to William Shakespeare, who is buried in Stratford, was erected by subscription in 1740 (the central part of it has been copied for the statue in Leicester Square). Next to it are the graves of David Garrick and Henry Irving, both marked by statues, and nearby lies Richard Brinsley Sheridan. There are busts of John Dryden, Poet Laureate and playwright; and of Francis Beaumont (of Beaumont and Fletcher). Geoffrey Chaucer's elaborate monument is one of the main features of Poet's Corner, and Alfred Tennyson and Robert Browning lie buried in front of it. A recently-unveiled stone commemorates T S Eliot, who died in 1965. Ben Jonson, whose body lies in the Nave of the Abbey, has a monument here, and both places bear the same inscription: ''O rare Ben Jonson.'' Barton Booth, the 17th century actor, and Mrs Pritchard, 18th century actress; Jane Austen and the three Bronte sisters (Charlotte, Emily and Anne); John Gay (author of **The Beggar's Opera**); Oliver Goldsmith and Sir William D'Avenant (Poet Laureate, theatre manager and staunch Cavalier) all have monuments in Poet's Corner.

Elsewhere in the Abbey, William Congreve has a wall monument and Anne Oldfield, the 17th century actress, a commemorative stone in the floor, both in the South Aisle of the Nave; Thomas Betterton, the 17th century actor and his contemporary, Mrs Bracegirdle, are buried in the East Walk of the Cloisters; Samuel Foote, 18th century actor and dramatist, and Spranger Barry, rival and contemporary of Garrick, lie in the North Walk of the Cloisters; while in St Andrew's Chapel are statues of Mrs Siddons (who is buried in Paddington Green) and her brother, the actor John Kemble.

St. Paul's Church
Covent Garden, WC2.

Underground: Covent Garden
Buses: 1, 6, 9, 11, 13, 15, 77, 77a, 77b, 77c, 170, 176.

Inigo Jones (Surveyor of the King's Works under Charles I, and a theatre designer) built the church in 1633, and it has an unbroken connection with the theatre. Known as ''the actors' church,'' it houses the offices of the Actors' Church Union. David Garrick worshipped at St. Paul's; W S Gilbert was baptised and Sir Peter Lely, William Wycherley, Grinling Gibbons, Thomas Arne and Charles Macklin were all buried there. Ellen Terry's ashes are contained in a delicate silver casket on the south wall. Among the plaques decorating the west wall are those dedicated to Vivien Leigh, Ivor Novello, C B Cochran, Marie Lloyd, Jose Collins, Ada Reeve, Baliol Holloway, Bransby Williams, Leon Quartermaine, Clemence Dane, Leslie Henson, Edouard Espinosa, Sophie Fedorovitch (the designer), and W Macqueen-Pope (the theatre historian). Close to Ellen Terry's memorial on the south wall is a plaque to Dame May Whitty and her husband Ben Webster, and opposite is a recently-erected one to Sir Lewis Casson.

Theatre Shops

General

The Prop Shop & Gallery,
51 Old Church Street, Chelsea, SW3.
352 6370

Run by actor/producer Louis Negin and designer Charley Dunlop, The Prop Shop sells to the public clothes, jewellery, furnishings and props from theatre and film productions as well as making for the profession, and they will make to order. It also mounts exhibitions to coincide with important London play and cinema productions.
Underground: Sloane Square, then by bus along King's Road
Buses: 11, 19. 22

The Stanley Hall Shop & Art Gallery
69 George Street, W1 (off Baker Street). 486 0771

Stanley Hall of Wig Creations has opened a shop and art gallery selling original theatre designs, playbills, posters, prints, original postcards of Edwardian beauties and famous actors of the day, books on the theatre and also jewellery, icons, ties, scarves, artificial flowers and a wealth of similar material. The premises have themselves been designed by Carl Toms.
Underground: Marble Arch or Baker Street
Buses: 1, 2, 2b, 13, 26, 30. 59, 74, 74b, 113, 159

Professional

The following selection of firms specialise in services to the professional theatre under the heading indicated:

Costumes

Morris Angel & Sons Ltd,
119 Shaftesbury Avenue,
Cambridge Circus, WC2. 836 5678.

Berman & Nathan Ltd,
18 Irving Street. WC2. 839 1651

Theatreland Ltd,
14 Soho Street, W1. 437 2245

Make-Up

Leichner (London) Ltd,
436 Essex Road, N1. 226 6601

Max Factor Hollywood & London Ltd,
16 Old Bond Street, W1. 493 6720

Light & Sound Equipment

Strand Electric Ltd,
29 King Street, WC2. 836 4444

Theatre Projects Ltd,
10 Long Acre, WC2. 836 0386

Stagesound (London) Ltd,
11 King Street, WC2. 240 0955

Wigs

Wig Creations Ltd,
25 Portman Close, W1. 486 0771

Theatre Bookshops

The bookselling heart of London is the Charing Cross Road, which neatly divides the West End as it runs south from Oxford Street to Trafalgar Square. Of the general bookshops, new and second-hand, that line it, there are two of particular interest to the theatre enthusiast, Foyle's and Better Books. At Solosy's (no 50) airmail editions of **Variety** and **Billboard** can be obtained by visitors homesick for Broadway. Just off Charing Cross Road is St Martin's Lane; one of the pedestrian streets that link the two is Cecil Court, which houses a number of specialist and other bookshops. A little to the east of St Martin's Lane, behind Covent Garden market, is London's largest bookshop specialising in drama, French's.

W & G Foyle
119 Charing Cross Road, WC2. 437 5660

The Drama Department of 'The World's Largest Bookshop,' on the third floor, has a predictably large stock of books on technique and criticism as well as plays.

Better Books Up the Street
136 Charing Cross Road, WC2. 836 1885

Poetry, drama and cinema branch of the main Better Books shop a little further down at no 94, this holds a good selection of new British and imported drama books, particularly on modern movements.

Sterling's Bookstore,
57 St Martin's Lane, WC2. 836 2597

Always one of the first shops to have copies of the latest book on the theatre and ballet, as well as stocking a number of "remaindered" books at reduced prices. Has no Theatre Section as such.

Robert Chris,
8 Cecil Court, WC2. 836 6700

A general bookseller whose stock includes new and second-hand theatre books.

Ballet Bookshop,
9 Cecil Court, WC2. 836 2314

Holds a large selection of play scripts and a more limited one of second-hand books on theatre and cinema. Comprehensive coverage of books on the ballet in this country and the United States.

Pleasures of Past Times
11 Cecil Court, WC2. 836 1142

As well as second-hand books on the theatre, holds a stock of 'Theatre Bygones'—playbills, programmes, postcards and other collector's items.

Suckling & Co,
13 Cecil Court, WC2. 836 2177

A general second-hand and antiquarian bookseller who stocks the occasional theatre book. Also sells prints.

Travis & Emery Ltd.,
16 Cecil Court, WC2. 240 2129

Essentially a music shop specialising in all material connected with music and music scores. But also holds a stock of second-hand books on the theatre as well as playbills and programmes and prints, plus some books on ballet and stage design.

All the above shops are within a short distance of one another.
Underground: Leicester Square; for Foyle's, Tottenham Court Road.
Buses: 1, 14, 19, 22, 24, 29, 176.

French's Theatre Bookshop,
26 Southampton Street, Strand, WC2E 7JE. 836 7513.

A 24-hour telephone enquiry service is offered by this bookshop, famous for its "acting editions" of plays. A wide range of books on the theatre and of play scripts in stock.
Underground: Covent Garden
Buses: 1, 6, 9, 11, 13, 15, 60, 77, 77a, 170, 176.

Leading Ticket Agencies

The ticket agencies sell seats for all the main London theatres and for festivals such as Stratford-upon-Avon. For the convenience of this service they charge a commission of approximately 45p on a top-price seat and slightly less for a cheaper one. The list below gives the principal London agents. Some have provincial branches and these will be found in the appropriate section of the Yellow Pages directory.

Abbey Box Office Ltd, 27 Victoria Street, SW1. 222 2992.

H J Adams Ltd, 5 Grosvenor Street, W1X 0AE. 629 4775 and 493 8311

Also at: Ambassador Travel Service, 441 Oxford Street, W1. 499 1313
Blackheath Travel Ltd, 13 Blackheath Village, SE3. 852 0025
The Charles Dickens Hotel, 66 Lancaster Gate, W2. 262 5090
Curzon Hotel, Stanhope Row, Park Lane, W1. 493 7222
Gateway Travel, 12a Radnor House, Regent Street, W1. 437 9514
Hotel Russell, Russell Square, WC1. 837 6470
Lamertons World Travel, High Street, W5. 567 6677
Lunn-Poly Holidays & Travel, 36 Edgware Road, W2. 262 3156
Milbanke Travel Ltd, 104 New Bond Street, W1. 493 8494
Harvey Nichols & Co Ltd, Knightsbridge, SW1. 235 7274
Park Plaza Hotel, Bayswater Road, Lancaster Gate, W2. 262 2953
Royal Lancaster Hotel, Lancaster Terrace, W2. 262 6737
Sherlock Holmes Hotel, Baker Street, W1. 486 6161

Albemarle Booking Agency Ltd. 13 Liverpool Street, EC2. 283 5314

Also at: Albany Travel Services Ltd, 7 Princes Street, W1. 499 7050
Bank of New South Wales, 29 Threadneedle Street, EC2. 588 4020
Elliotts Travel Ltd, 10 Goswell Road, EC1. 253 6156
W Kearsley & Co Ltd, 170 Piccadilly, W1. 499 4181
Travelworld Olympic Ltd, 24 Queensway, W2. 727 8050

Wakefield Fortune Ltd, 3a Aldwych, WC2. 836 1566

Army & Navy Stores, Victoria Street, SW1. 834 1234 (ask for Theatre Bookings)

Edwards & Edwards, 7 Southampton Row, Holborn, WC1. 242 4001
Also at: 115 Cannon Street, EC4. 623 4441
33 Coventry Street, W1. 930 2592
Palace Theatre, Shaftesbury Avenue, W1. 437 4695
The Arches, Ludgate Hill, EC4. 236 8256

Harrods Ltd, Knightsbridge, SW1, 730 1234 (ask for Theatre Bookings)

Lacon and Ollier, 60 South Audley Street, W1. 499 3631
Also at: 1 Angel Court, EC2. 606 8216

G S Lashmar Ltd. 18 South Molton Street, W1. 493 4731

Leader's Box Office, 14 Royal Arcade, Old Bond Street, W1. 629 3711

Keith Prowse & Co. Ltd, 90 New Bond Street, W1. 493 6000
Also at: Mayfair Hotel, Stratton Street, W1. 493 4236
Chappell's, 50 New Bond Street, W1. 493 2444
Churchill Hotel, Portman Square, W1. 486 5746
Claridge's Hotel, Brook Street, W1. 629 8860
5 Coventry Street, W1. 437 2103
Dorchester Hotel, Park Lane, W1. 629 8888
Earl's Court Exhibition Building, Warwick Road, SW5. 385 4444
Grosvenor House, Park Lane, W1. 499 6363
Mount Royal Hotel, Marble Arch, W1. 629 8040
Park Lane Hotel, Piccadilly, W1. 499 6321
Portman Hotel, Portman Square, W1. 935 8390
Ritz Hotel, Piccadilly, W1. 493 8181
Westbury Hotel, 22 New Bond Street, W1. 629 7755

23 St Martin's Court, WC2. 836 1029
Victoria Station, SW1. 834 5495

Rake's Ticket Agency Ltd, 12 Great
Newport Street, WC2. 240 0681

Cecil Roy Ltd, 74 Old Brompton
Road, SW7. 589 0121
    Also at: 44 Shaftesbury Avenue,
W1. 437 8976
5 The Pavement, Worple Road,
Wimbledon, SW19. 946 0510

Simpson's of Piccadilly Ltd, 203 Piccadilly, W1. 734 2080 (ask for Theatre
Bookings)

Webster & Girling Ltd, 211 Baker
Street, NW1. 935 6666

Webster & Waddington Ltd, 74
Mortimer Street, W1. 580 3030

Some Theatre Pubs

NOTE: for pubs offering theatre performances, see the Theatre Guide section on **Fringe and Lunchtime.**

The Anchor,
Bankside, Southwark, SE1. 407 1577

Buses: 8a, 10, 21, 35, 40, 43, 44, 47, 48, 133, and Red Arrows 501, 503, all to London Bridge. Also 18, 95, 149, 176a to Southwark Bridge.
Underground: London Bridge (which is also on Southern Region)
Parking: The Anchor has its own car park

Close to the site of Shakespeare's Globe, and to Sam Wanamaker's 1970s version of it, the Anchor is the only remaining Bankside tavern of the original seven "stews" (an Elizabethan term for inns of ill-repute). The first building on this site was destroyed by fire in 1676 and the present one was built on the same spot some years later, with many of the original parts and timbers retained in the reconstruction.

There is a Globe Bar, containing a model of the original playhouse, a Shakespeare Room, and the Elizabethan Long Gallery restaurant, specialising in traditional English dishes. Mrs Thrale's Room on the ground floor also has a snack bar. The restaurant is not open early enough in the evening for pre-theatre meals, but the snack bar serves salads and sandwiches from 5.30 pm.

The Black Swan (The Dirty Duck),
Waterside, Stratford-upon-Avon, Warwickshire. 0789 2104

By road: Stratford-upon-Avon is 92 miles from London
By rail: Trains take 2¼ hours from Paddington

"The Duck," as it is affectionately known, is a little over 300 years old, and stands on the town's Waterside, along the river from the Royal Shakespeare Theatre. On summer days the balcony overlooking the Avon is crowded with company and staff from the theatre.

Sir Frank Benson, Director of the (then) Shakespeare Memorial Theatre for thirty years from 1886 to 1916, used a large wooden building just behind the pub as a rehearsal room, and on the backstage call-board he would never announce the following day's rehearsal schedule at The Black Swan but always at The Dirty Duck. As such it has now become known to generations of artists and audiences all over the world.

The walls of the saloon bar are to-day covered with autographed photographs of members of the Royal Shakespeare Company from past and present seasons.

The George Inn,
Borough High Street, Southwark, SE1. 407 2056

Buses: 8a, 10, 21, 35, 40, 43, 44, 47, 48, 133, Red Arrows 501 and 503 all to London Bridge.
Underground: London Bridge (which is also on Southern Region)

This 16th century coaching inn, destroyed by the Fire of London in 1666 and rebuilt ten years later, is London's oldest inn, and its only remaining galleried one, only the south wing of which is still left standing. The George is now a National Trust property. It stands back from the Borough High Street and is entered through an archway into its own cobbled courtyard. Shakespeare **could** have drunk here; Dickens certainly did, and he used it as a background to his novel **Little Dorrit.**

On the ground floor is the tap room with its five-shilling levy clock and a bar hung with pewter mugs, and two dining rooms with their high-backed settles where traditional English dishes (steak and kidney pie) are served. Upstairs are two balustrade balconies leading to the old four-poster bedrooms, unhappily no longer used for overnight guests. Each summer a Shakespeare play is performed by an amateur group in the Inn's courtyard.

The restaurant is open from midday until 2 pm for lunch, and from 6.30 until last-orders at 9.15 pm for dinner. It is advisable to book a table in advance. Cold snacks are also served from the bar during opening hours.

Gilbert & Sullivan,
28 John Adam Street, London, WC2. 839 2580

Buses: 1, 1a, 6, 9, 9a, 11, 13, 15, 77, 77a, 77b, 77c, 170, 176 to the Strand, then turn down Villiers Street.
Underground: Charing Cross

Formerly the St Martin's Tavern, this pub was redecorated and renamed the Gilbert & Sullivan in 1962, for two good reasons: it stands close to the site of the old Adelphi Terrace where Richard D'Oyly Carte lived and where, in the 1880s, many plans for the future of the Gilbert and Sullivan operas were hatched and discussed between the three men. It is also only a few minutes' walk away from the Savoy Theatre, original home of the operettas which were to become internationally known as the Savoy Operas.

The Gilbert & Sullivan's bars and walls are liberally decorated with mementoes of the Savoy Operas, and among the many original designs are those by Charles Ricketts for the **Mikado** production of 1926, still in use to-day, and by Peter Goffin, present Artistic Director of the company, who also made the sketches from which the model sets in the bar were constructed. W S Gilbert's own sketches for the first production of **Ruddigore** in 1887 are exhibited, alongside various portraits, lithographs and cartoons of Gilbert, Sullivan, Richard D'Oyly Carte, and his grand-daughter Bridget, who since 1958 has been head of the company. Also on display are letters, programmes of first nights, sets of cigarette cards of the operas, and photographs of the principals in some of the early productions.

The restaurant, decorated with Peter Goffin's engraved glass panels showing scenes from the operas, serves pre-theatre dinner from 6 pm but closes at 9.30 pm. Sandwiches, sausages and other snacks are available from the bar from 5.30 onwards from Monday to Friday only.

The Nag's Head
10 James Street, Covent Garden, WC2. 836 4678

Buses: 1, 1a, 6, 9, 9a, 11, 13, 15, 77, 77a, 77b, 77c, 170, 172, 188, 196 to the Aldwych
Underground: Covent Garden

This 19th century inn, rebuilt by the first Samuel Whitbread, the brewer, on the site of an earlier hostelry (said to be a favourite haunt of Edmund Kean and his contemporaries) lies in the centre of Covent Garden, and is patronised by artists and audiences from the neighbouring Aldwych, Covent Garden, Drury Lane, Duchess, Strand and Fortune theatres. Its walls and corridors are so closely packed with theatre memorabilia that it can almost be regarded as a museum in its own right.

In the Saloon Bar are original Cruikshank engravings of Whitbread (who was largely responsible for the rebuilding of Drury Lane in 1812) seen with Sheridan (whose disastrous financial mishandling of the earlier theatre made the establishment of the new one almost impossible), also of Edmund Kean, together with playbills of Kean as Richard III, Hamlet Romeo, all at Drury Lane; engravings and playbills of Garrick who gave his last performance at Drury Lane in 1776; of Mrs Siddons alongside two of her letters; of Grimaldi, "the Garrick of the clowns"; of John Philip, Charles and Fanny Kemble, Peg Woffington Master Betty the child actor, Betterton, Foote, Macklin, Macready, and many others down to Irving and Dan Leno and other artists and playwrights whose fame is associated with Drury Lane and Covent Garden theatres. The Public Bar has an engraving of "The overflowing of the Pitt" at Drury Lane in 1771, and other prints of both theatres, and in the upstairs restaurant are original costume designs for theatre, opera and ballet productions by Cecil Beaton, Oliver Messel, Loudon Sainthill, Tanya Moiseiwitsch and others.

The restaurant is open for pre-theatre dinner from 6 pm but last orders are taken at 9 pm. Cold snacks (salads and sandwiches) are served in the Saloon Bar from 5.30 pm.

The Old Bull & Bush
North End Way, Hampstead, NW3. 455 3685

Buses: 210, 268
Underground: Golders Green or Hampstead on the Northern Line

This famous Hampstead hostelry began life as a farm house in 1645 and it still retains part of its Queen Anne architecture, with bay windows facing the road down from Hampstead Heath. William Hogarth, the 18th century painter and caricaturist, lived here for some years after the building had become an inn.

The Old Bull & Bush achieved the height of its fame in "the gay 90s" a the time of the Edwardian music-hall when one of its best-loved artists, Florrie Forde, immortalised the place in her song "Down at the Old Bull & Bush." At that time, Londoners came out to Hampstead by wagonette, horse-drawn buses and on horseback to spend the evening in the gardens of the Old Bull & Bush dancing "to the strains of Harrington's Blue Hungarian Band."

Some years ago the present owners redesigned the bars to bring back the atmosphere of those days. One of the bars has been named after Florrie Forde, and is decorated with her photographs, song titles and other mementoes; another is named after Hogarth.

Throughout the summer, although the Hungarian Band has long since departed, drinks are served on the terrace here. There is also a snack bar where the chef will cook grills to order.

The Salisbury
90 St Martin's Lane, London, WC2. 836 5863

Buses: 1, 24, 29, 176 to Charing Cross Road
Underground: Leicester Square or Trafalgar Square

Probably the best-known theatre pub in London, the Salisbury has been a favourite drinking and meeting place for members of the profession for decades. This is natural enough for it stands in the centre of the St Martin's Lane theatre area, with the Duke of York's and Albery's almost next door, the Coliseum opposite, the Ambassadors, the St Martin's and the Cambridge just up the road, Wyndham's and the Garrick just behind, and Shaftesbury Avenue only five minutes' walk away.

The Salisbury's ornate Victorian interior, with its red plush furnishings, gas-light fittings and decorative glass panels, has been beautifully preserved. As well as the spacious bar, there is a large well-stocked snack bar serving salads and hot snacks from 5.30 until 10.30 pm.

The Victoria Tavern
10a Strathearn Place, London, W2. 262 7474

Buses: 12, 88
Underground: Lancaster Gate

As its name suggests, the Victoria Tavern (where Charles Dickens is said to have been a regular customer) seeks to retain the atmosphere of that period. On the first floor is the Gaiety Bar, where all the furnishings have comes from the old Gaiety Theatre, the walls are ornamented with silk hats, opera gloves, and other Victoriana, and customers sit in miniature theatre boxes.

A new restaurant has recently opened in the formerly derelict cellars here, to commemorate the 100th anniversary of the publication of Dickens' last complete novel, **Our Mutual Friend**, and it is named after that work. The decor recreates the street scenes and the sounds of mid-Victorian London with the use of real paving stones and rough brick walls, with diners sitting on the "pavement" outside the bow-fronted windows of The Old Curiosity Shop and Mr Micawber's front door.

The restaurant is open from 6.30 pm to last-orders at 10.45 pm, and a ground-floor snack bar is open from 5.30 until 10 pm.

The White Horse
Rupert Street, London, W1. 437 1756

Buses: 9, 9a, 14, 19, 22, 38 to Shaftesbury Avenue
Underground: Piccadilly

This Soho pub, situated between Shaftesbury Avenue and Coventry Street, has recently opened an upstairs cocktail bar called The Theatre Bar.

Its walls are decorated with posters, playbills and photographs of actors and actresses appearing in the many theatres in the neighbourhood, many of whom are regular customers here. The Theatre Bar caters for anyone who wants a drink and a cold buffet meal either before or after the performance. At the beginning of 1973 it opened from 5.30 to 11 pm, with the intention of extending the licence to midnight.

Recommended Reading

NEW WRITING

Martin Esslin. **The Theatre of the Absurd.** Penguin
John Russell Taylor. **Anger and After.** Methuen
John Russell Taylor. **The Second Wave.** Methuen

ACTORS

Michael Billington. **The Modern Actor.** Hamish Hamilton

DIRECTION

Peter Brook. **The Empty Space.** Penguin

LIGHTING DESIGN

Richard Pilbrow. **Stage Lighting.** Studio Vista

OPERA AND BALLET

Peter Brinson and Clement Crisp. **Ballet For All.** David & Charles and Pan (paperback).
Eric Walter White. **Benjamin Britten. His Life and Operas.** Faber & Faber.

REGIONAL THEATRE

John Elsom. **Theatres Outside London.** Macmillan

YOUNG PEOPLE'S THEATRE

Peter Slade. **Child Drama.** University of London Press
Brian Way. **Development Through Drama.** Longmans

REFERENCE

Oxford Companion to the Theatre. Edited by Phyllis Hartnoll.
Penguin Dictionary of the Theatre. John Russell Taylor.
Who's Who in the Theatre. Pitman

MAGAZINES AND JOURNALS

Lists of current West End productions appear in the entertainment columns of the national daily and Sunday newspapers, and in the two London evening newspapers. **Time Out** magazine (weekly) gives this information and a very full listing of London fringe and lunchtime productions. **The Stage** newspaper (weekly) has a listing of current productions in the regional and outer London theatres.

Magazines for the theatregoer include the monthly **Plays and Players** and **Theatre Quarterly.** Dance is covered by **Dance and Dancers** and **Dancing Times,** opera by **Opera** and **Music and Musicians,** all monthly.

Part 3

Theatre Guide

The following pages are not intended as an exhaustive list of every professional theatre in Great Britain, but as a guide to playhouses and companies considered to be providing the best work in this country now.

Readers wishing to telephone London theatres from outside London should use the prefix 01.

130 Map of Central London Theatres

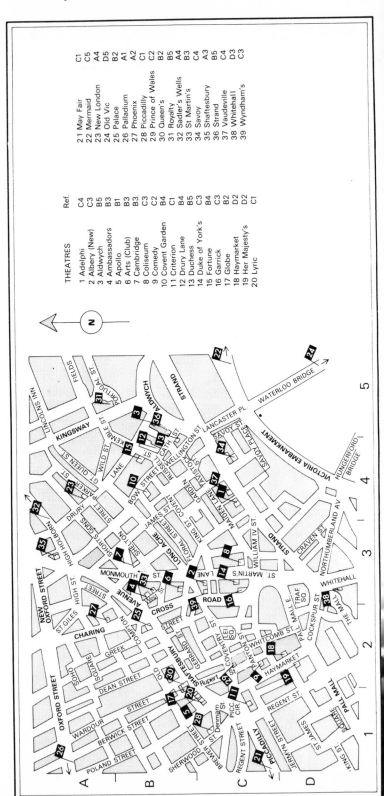

THEATRES	Ref.
1 Adelphi	C4
2 Albery (New)	C3
3 Aldwych	B5
4 Ambassadors	B3
5 Apollo	B1
6 Arts (Club)	B3
7 Cambridge	B3
8 Coliseum	C3
9 Comedy	C2
10 Covent Garden	B4
11 Criterion	C1
12 Drury Lane	B4
13 Duchess	B5
14 Duke of York's	C3
15 Fortune	B4
16 Garrick	C3
17 Globe	B2
18 Haymarket	D2
19 Her Majesty's	D2
20 Lyric	C1

21 May Fair	C1
22 Mermaid	C5
23 New London	A4
24 Old Vic	D5
25 Palace	B2
26 Palladium	A1
27 Phoenix	A2
28 Piccadilly	C1
29 Prince of Wales	C2
30 Queen's	B2
31 Royalty	B5
32 Sadler's Wells	A4
33 St Martin's	B3
34 Savoy	C4
35 Shaftesbury	A3
36 Strand	B5
37 Vaudeville	C4
38 Whitehall	D3
39 Wyndham's	C3

Central London

ADELPHI
Adelphi Theatre, Strand, WC2.
Box office: 836 7611.

The present theatre, the fourth on this site in just over a hundred years, opened in 1930. In its first few years it was the home of many Charles Cochran successes, as well as the long runs of **Bless The Bride**, and Novello's **The Dancing Years** transferred from Drury Lane. A macabre historical note: one of the previous theatres on the site was the scene of the murder of William Terriss, idol of London theatregoers in the 1890s, who was fatally attacked by a lunatic as he entered the stage door one evening. In recent years, the Adelphi has continued its policy of staging spectacular musicals, and the record run of **Charlie Girl** in the 1960s has been followed by the current one of the revival of **Show Boat**. The proscenium stage faces on to a 3-tier auditorium seating 1,470. There are 6 bars. The usual price reductions are offered for parties. Two wheelchairs can be accommodated in each of the 4 boxes. Nearest car parks: in Savoy Place behind the Savoy Hotel, or in St. Martin's Lane behind the Odeon Cinema.

Nearest underground: Trafalgar Square Buses: 1, 1a, 6, 9, 11, 13, 15, 77, 77a, 77b, 77c, 170, 176. Also Red Arrow 605.

ALBERY'S
Albery's Theatre, St Martin's Lane, WC2.
Box office: 836 3878.

Built in 1903 and, until 1973, known as the New Theatre. The name change is in honour of Sir Bronson Albery (stepson of Sir Charles Wyndham, founder of Wyndham's Theatres) who died in 1972 and whose son and grandson now control the company. The theatre is probably best known as the wartime home of the Old Vic Company during the 1940s when the famous Olivier/Richardson seasons were presented here. In its early days, the New was the scene of many successful runs of **The Scarlet Pimpernel** with Fred Terry and Julia Neilson, of

Matheson Lang's personal triumph in **The Wandering Jew,** and of Sybil Thorndike's first appearance as **Saint Joan** in 1924. John Gielgud's first big personal success, in **Richard of Bordeaux,** was at this theatre in 1933 and it was followed by the long run of his **Hamlet,** and the famous **Romeo and Juliet** production in which he and Laurence Olivier alternated in the roles of Romeo and Mercutio. After the last war, there was **The Cocktail Party** and **I Am A Camera,** and Lionel Bart's **Oliver!** which had its 5-year run here from 1960. The Royal Shakespeare Company production of **London Assurance** played here for almost a year in 1972. The theatre has a proscenium stage facing on to a 959-seat auditorium on 3 levels. There are 4 licensed bars. Disabled patrons can most easily be seated in the boxes and at the back of the dress circle, which is at street level. There are 2 car parks in St Martin's Lane—one behind the Odeon Cinema and one at the entrance to Upper St Martin's Lane.

Nearest underground: Leicester Square. Buses: 1, 24, 29, 176.

ALDWYCH
Aldwych Theatre, The Aldwych, WC2.
Box office: 836 6404.

This Edwardian theatre opened in 1905 with a revival of **Bluebell in Fairyland** starring Seymour Hicks and Ellaline Terriss, followed by the first London production of **The Cherry Orchard** in 1911. Between the wars, the theatre became famous as the home of the "Aldwych farces"—those series, mostly by Ben Travers, which hilariously brought together a team headed by Tom Walls, Ralph Lynn and Robertson Hare. **Watch on the Rhine** with Anton Walbrook was a success of the last war; Gertrude Lawrence made her last appearance here in **September Tide** in 1948, and Vivien Leigh starred in **A Streetcar Named Desire** in 1949. The Royal Shakespeare Company have made the Aldwych their London home for the past 12 years, but are soon to vacate it when their new theatre in the Barbican Arts Centre is completed. The

RSC's London programme comprises a repertoire of world and British premieres of new plays (Pinter's **The Homecoming, Landscape** and **Silence** and **Old Times**; also David Mercer's **After Haggerty** had their first performance here, and Jules Feiffer's **Little Murders** and Albee's **A Delicate Balance, Tiny Alice** and **All Over** their British premieres) as well as classics from an international repertoire and the most successful of their Shakespeare productions from Stratford-upon-Avon. During the spring of each year the Company has vacated the Aldwych to make way for visiting companies from abroad in the form of the World Theatre Season. The building underwent a major redecoration and modernisation at a cost of over £70,000 in 1971 when air-conditioning was one of the many new amenities installed. There is a seating capacity of 1,024, and bars on each of the 3 levels, as well as a stalls coffee bar. Price concessions operate at matinees. Parking space is available in side streets or in the Aldwych after meter-time. There is a car park in Upper St Martin's Lane, about 5 minutes' walk away.

Nearest underground: Covent Garden or Holborn. Buses: 1, 4a, 6, 9, 11, 13, 15, 68, 77, 77a, 170, 172, 188, 196.

AMBASSADORS

Ambassadors Theatre, West Street, WC2H 9ND.
Box office: 836 4105.

Built in 1913, the Ambassadors was the theatre where both Vivien Leigh (in **The Mask of Virtue** in 1935) and Ivor Novello (in **Deburau** in 1921) made their London debuts. During the last war, the famous **Sweet and Low** revue series was presented here. Since 1952 it has had the distinction of continuously housing London's longest-running play of all time—Agatha Christie's **The Mousetrap**, now in its 21st year. There is a proscenium stage and a seating capacity of 453 divided between stalls and dress circle. Two licensed bars. A large car park is in Upper St Martin's Lane, 20 yards away.

Nearest underground: Leicester Square. Buses: 1, 14, 19, 22, 24, 29, 176.

APOLLO

Apollo Theatre, Shaftesbury Avenue, W1.
Box office: 437 2663.

This Victorian theatre, built at the turn of the century, had its most recent renovation in 1972. In 1907 Cicely Courtneidge made her London debut here in the original production of **Tom Jones**, and during the First World War **Hobson's Choice** had a long run. In the 1930s its successes included O'Casey's **The Silver Tassie**, Ian Hay's comedy **The Housemaster**, Sherwood's **Idiot's Delight** and Patrick Hamilton's thriller **Gaslight**. **Seagulls Over Sorrento** ran for over 1,500 performances just after the last war, and the theatre's present policy is still one of mainly comedy. The auditorium seats 796 facing on to a proscenium stage. There is an air-ventilation system, and 4 licensed bars. Nearest car parks are in Denman Street or Brewer Street, 3 minutes away.

Nearest underground: Piccadilly. Buses: 14, 19, 22, 38.

ARTS THEATRE CLUB

Arts Theatre Club, 6-7 Great Newport Street, WC2.
Box office: 836 3334.

Opened in 1927, the Arts became London's most important club theatre —described as a miniature National Theatre—under the direction of Alec Clunes from 1942 until the early 50s. Ten years later the Royal Shakespeare Company presented some of their experimental work here, and in 1955 Peter Hall directed the British premiere of **Waiting For Godot**. The Arts has since 1967 been the headquarters of Caryl Jenner's Unicorn Theatre for Young People. The Company's policy is to present as much new work as possible, mainly for children but with the occasional adult play given for short evening runs. A members-only club (for details, telephone 240 2076) with bar and restaurant facilities. Seating capacity: 346. There is a large car park in Upper St Martin's Lane, just round the corner.

Nearest underground: Leicester Square. Buses: 1, 14, 19, 22, 24, 29, 176.

THE CAMBRIDGE

Cambridge Theatre, Earlham Street, WC2.
Box office: 836 6056.

London's fifth largest theatre, the Cambridge opened in 1930 with an Andre Charlot revue starring Beatrice Lillie, and called **Masquerade**. The theatre has been used for visiting opera companies and for musicals as well as drama. In the 1950s Albert Finney had a big success here in **Billy Liar**, and in

1963 Tommy Steele starred in the musical **Half a Sixpence**. The National Theatre Company took a short lease in 1970, and their productions of **The Beaux' Stratagem** and **Hedda Gabler** with Maggie Smith both played to full houses. A highly-praised revival of **Journey's End** played here in 1972. At the end of that year, Larry Parnes took over the theatre on a 12-year lease with a plan for turning it into a centre for musicals and revue and other activities including a theatre club, housed in the spacious downstairs bar. This new 12-hours-a-day policy will also cover the presentation of regular children's matinees, lunch-time theatre and Sunday evening "Cambridge Footlights" revue. The Cambridge has a seating capacity of 1,285 divided between stalls, dress circle, upper circle and boxes, and it has a proscenium stage. Two wheel-chairs are allowed into the stalls at each performance. There are 5 bars, including a champagne bar. Nearest car park is in Upper St Martin's Lane, 2 minutes' walk away.

Nearest underground: Leicester Square or Tottenham Court Road. **Buses:** 1, 14, 19, 22, 24, 29, 176.

COCHRANE

Jeannetta Cochrane Theatre, Southampton Row, WC1.
Box office: 242 7040.

Built in 1963, this small 344-seat theatre with a proscenium stage is named after the founder of the Department of Theatre Design at the Central School of Art & Design.

Jim Haynes' London extension of the Traverse Theatre had a season here in 1966 and Charles Marowitz' productions of **The Bellow Plays** and **Loot** transferred to the West End. It is normally open only during school holiday time, and its policy is the presentation of professional education attractions for short seasons. This includes visits by the National Youth Theatre and Ballet Rambert, among others. There are catering facilities, but no restaurant or licensed bar. Wheelchairs can be accommodated. Car parks in Museum Street, by the British Museum, and in Bloomsbury Square, both 5 minutes' walk away.

Nearest underground: Holborn. **Buses:** 5, 19, 38, 55, 172 to Theobalds Road, or 68, 77, 77a, 77b, 77c, 170, 188, 196, 239 to Kingsway.

COLISEUM

The Coliseum, St Martin's Lane, WC2N 4ES.
Box office: 836 3161.

London's largest theatre, built by Sir Oswald Stoll in 1904 as a rival to Drury Lane, was originally a variety house where spectacular entertainments of all kinds were staged, from rodeos to symphony concerts. The first musical to be seen here was **White Horse Inn** in 1931, to be followed by **The Vagabond King** and then by a series of American hits like **Annie Get Your Gun, Kiss Me, Kate, Call Me Madam, Guys and Dolls** and **The Pajama Game**. The Coliseum has been the home of Sadler's Wells Opera since their move from Sadler's Wells itself in 1968. Under the direction first of Stephen Arlen and now of Lord Harewood, the company presents opera in English in repertoire, with occasional ballet seasons during the early summer when the opera company is on tour. During the past 5 years they have given the British premiere of Prokofiev's opera **War and Peace** and the world premiere of Malcolm Williamson's new work **Lucky Peter's Journey**. The theatre is closed for a short period each July. There is a large proscenium stage, and a seating capacity of 2,354. Bars and buffets are on each level throughout the building, which is open 45 minutes before each performance. Reduced prices are offered to parties of 20 and over. Wheelchairs can be accommodated in stalls boxes only. A National Car Park is at the rear of the theatre.

Nearest underground: Leicester Square or Trafalgar Square. **Buses:** 1, 14, 19 22, 24, 29, 176.

COMEDY

Comedy Theatre, Panton Street, SW1.
Box office: 930 2578.

Built in 1881, the Comedy became the first theatre-management venture for Herbert Beerbohm Tree in the 1890s. John Barrymore made his London debut here in 1905, and Gerald du Maurier one of his biggest hits in **Raffles** just before the First World War. The New Watergate Theatre Club presented a notable series of productions here from 1956, including **A View from the Bridge, Cat on a Hot Tin Roof** and **Five Finger Exercise**. More recently, Spike Milligan had a success here in **Son of Oblomov**, and **There's a Girl in my Soup** played the second half of its 6-year London run here. The Comedy has a proscenium stage and a seating capacity of 820 on 4 levels. Air-conditioning has been installed. There are 4 bars, and wheelchair accommodation for 4 in the auditorium. Parking: nearest garage is in Whitcomb Street, just round the corner.

Nearest underground: Piccadilly. Buses: 9, 9a, 14, 19, 22, 38 to Piccadilly Circus.

COVENT GARDEN OPERA HOUSE
Royal Opera House, Covent Garden, WC2E 7QA.
Box office: 240 1066.
Information service: 240 1911.

The present Royal Opera House, the third on this site and built in 1858, is the home of both the Royal Opera and Royal Ballet companies. The artistic policy of both is the presentation of opera and ballet of the classical, well-established school and of modern works, and to continue to build a repertoire of productions using international and national artists. In the past 5 years, the Royal Opera has given the world or British premieres of new works ·by Tippett, Searle, Rodney Bennett and Maxwell Davies. New ballets have included Debussy's **Afternoon of a Faun** and Stravinsky's **Requiem Canticles** both choreographed by Jerome Robbins, and Berio's **Field Figures** choreographed by Glen Tetley. The Royal Ballet undertakes regional and overseas tours, and their off-shoot Ballet For All company tours smaller theatres and halls throughout the country. The Opera House is normally closed for 6 weeks around August and mid-September.

The auditorium seats 2,117 divided between orchestra stalls, stalls circle, grand tier, balcony stalls, amphitheatre and boxes. A new ventilation system has recently been installed. There are many bars and buffet bars, and cold suppers are served in the Crush Bar and in some boxes by arrangement before 1 pm on the day of performance with the Catering Manager (ring 240 1200). Box 66 is suitable for a disabled person unable to leave a wheelchair; safety regulations preclude wheelchairs elsewhere in the auditorium, although by arrangement suitable seats are reserved for those able to be transferred to theatre seats. Photographs, posters, publications and records relating to Covent Garden productions are available from foyer bookstalls and the box office. Late-comers are provided with a television monitor in the Crush Bar and the Upper Amphitheatre Foyer. Parking in the side streets available in after-meter hours.

Underground: Covent Garden. Buses: 1, 1a, 6, 9, 9a, 11, 13, 15, 77, 77a, 77b, 77c, 170, 172, 188, 196.

CRITERION
Criterion Theatre, Piccadilly Circus, W1.
Box office: 930 3216.

A Wyndham's theatre, founded by Sir Charles Wyndham, it opened in 1903 as one of London's first theatres to be lit by electricity. It came into the news in 1972 when its demolition was threatened by a new plan for Piccadilly Circus, later abandoned. Terence Rattigan's first play, **French Without Tears** ran for over 1,000 performances here from 1936; more recently Iris Murdoch's **A Severed Head** just exceeded that record, and Simon Gray's **Butley** ran for 13 months from 1971. A proscenium stage faces on to a 607-seat auditorium on 3 levels. There are 2 licensed bars, and air-conditioning is installed. Two special seats are provided for the disabled in the grand circle, which is at street level. The nearest car park is in Whitcomb Street, or in Denman Street over the road.
Nearest underground: Piccadilly. Buses: 9, 9a, 14, 19, 22, 25, 38.

DRURY LANE
Theatre Royal, Drury Lane, WC2.
Box office: 836 8108.

One of London's oldest, most famous and most beautiful theatres, the present building, the 3rd on the site, was opened in 1812. It was in the first Drury Lane that Nell Gwynne is reported to have sold her oranges before making her debut there in 1665, and in the second Drury Lane that Garrick, as actor-manager, rescued Shakespeare and restored his original texts to the stage. Sheridan's **School for Scandal** opened here in 1777, and Siddons, Kean and Macready all played here. Henry Irving and Ellen Terry gave successful seasons, as did Forbes-Robertson. In the 1920s large-scale musicals like **Rose Marie, The Desert Song, Show Boat, Cavalcade** and Ivor Novello musicals filled the theatre. Novello played **Henry V** in a spectacular production here in 1938. Re-opening after the last war, the list of successes began again with **Oklahoma!, Carousel, South Pacific, The King and I, Hello Dolly!** and, most successful of all, **My Fair Lady** which ran for over 2,000 performances. The theatre has a seating capacity of 2,283 divided between stalls, circle, upper circle, balcony and boxes. There is a proscenium stage, and a system of water-cooled air-conditioning. There are 2 bars on each level. Parking space is available in surrounding streets in after-meter hours, but car parks in Drury Lane and Upper St Martin's Lane are only about 5 minutes' walk away.

Nearest underground: Covent Garden or Holborn. Buses: 1, 1a, 6, 9, 9a, 11, 13, 15, 77, 77a, 77b, 77c, 170, 172, 188, 196.

DUCHESS
Duchess Theatre, Catherine Street, Aldwych, WC2.
Box office: 836 8243.

Built in 1931, the Duchess is one of the West End's smallest theatres with a seating capacity of 474 divided between stalls, dress circle and upper circle. Emlyn Williams had two of his biggest successes—Night Must Fall and The Corn is Green—here before the last war, and Coward's Blithe Spirit had some of its nearly 2,000 performances here during the war itself. Terence Rattigan's The Deep Blue Sea and Pinter's The Caretaker have been among its more recent successes. Until the recent long run of The Dirtiest Show in Town, however, its attractions have in the past few years been mainly modern thrillers and comedies. There is a proscenium stage, and bars in the foyer and at the back of the stalls. Parking space is available in surrounding streets in after-meter hours; the nearest car parks are in Savoy Place, just behind the Savoy Hotel in the Strand, or in Upper St Martin's Lane.

Nearest underground: Covent Garden. Buses: 1, 1a, 6, 9, 9a, 11, 13, 15, 77, 77a, 77b, 77c, 170, 188, 196.

DUKE OF YORK'S
Duke of York's Theatre, St Martin's Lane, WC2.
Box office: 836 5122.

This Victorian theatre first opened in 1892 under the management of an eccentric actress, Violet Melnott, and was later taken over for 20 successful years by the American manager, Charles Frohman, who presented the premieres of a number of plays by James Barrie, including The Admirable Crichton in 1902 and Peter Pan in 1904. During the last war, there were long runs of Pink String and Sealing Wax and Is Your Honeymoon Really Necessary? and in the 1960s The

Killing of Sister George, Goodnight Mrs Puffin and Relatively Speaking. The Duke of York's has a seating capacity of 756 on 4 levels. There are 3 bars as well as a coffee bar. Reduced prices are offered for Friday matinees, for parties of 10 and over, and for pensioners. There are National Car Parks behind the Odeon Cinema, almost opposite, and in Upper St Martin's Lane just up the road.

Nearest underground: Leicester Square. Buses: 1, 14, 19, 22, 24, 29, 176.

FORTUNE
Fortune Theatre, Russell Street, WC2.
Box office: 836 2238.

One of the smaller of London's theatres, the Fortune, built in 1924, seats 426 divided between stalls, dress circle and upper circle. There is a proscenium stage. Probably the theatre's biggest successes in recent years have been the long runs of the Flanders and Swann entertainment At the Drop of a Hat followed by Beyond the Fringe in the early 1960s. The thriller Suddenly at Home began a long run in 1971. There are bars at both stalls and upper circle levels. Parking space is available in surrounding streets during after-meter hours, but the nearest car park is either in Savoy Place just behind the Savoy Hotel in the Strand, in Drury Lane, or in Upper St Martin's Lane.

Nearest underground: Covent Garden. Buses: 1, 1a, 6, 9, 9a, 11, 13, 15, 77, 77a, 77b, 77c, 170, 176, 188, 196.

GARRICK
Garrick Theatre, 2 Charing Cross Road, WC2
Box office: 836 4601.

Built in 1886, this proscenium-stage theatre has had many major renovations and improvements since then. Mrs Patrick Campbell and Jack Buchanan made successful appearances here in the 20s and 30s, and the theatre had its biggest hit with Love On The Dole in 1935. During the last war it was the home of the Robertson Hare—Alfred Drake series of Vernon Sylvaine farces. Since 1967 the Garrick has been the London headquarters of Brian Rix's company, following his long and famous tenure of the White-hall. The seating capacity is 800, and air-conditioning is in the form of fresh air trunking. There are full licensed bar facilities. Wheelchairs can be admitted to the dress circle, which is at street level, but occupants then have to transfer to theatre seats. There is a National Car Park behind the Odeon Cinema in St Martin's Lane, a few minutes away.

Nearest underground: Leicester Square or Trafalgar Square. **Buses:** 1, 14, 19, 22, 24, 29, 176.

GLOBE

Globe Theatre, Shaftesbury Avenue, W1.
Box office: 437 1592.

Opened in 1906 as the Hicks, named after the actor-manager Sir Seymour Hicks, this theatre was renamed the Globe 3 years later. Among the most famous productions associated with it are the long run of **Robert's Wife** with Edith Evans in the 1930s, and Terence Rattigan's **While the Sun Shines** which ran for over 1,000 performances during the last war; Robert Sherwood's **Petrified Forest** in which Owen Nares made his last appearance in 1942; Fry's **The Lady's Not For Burning;** Graham Greene's **The Potting Shed,** and Bolt's **A Man for all Seasons.** The auditorium seats 885 on 3 levels facing on to a proscenium stage. There is an approved air-ventilation system. Also 3 licensed bars. Nearest car parks are in Denman Street and Brewer Street; both 2 minutes' walk away.

Nearest underground: Piccadilly. **Buses:** 14, 19, 22, 38.

HAYMARKET

Theatre Royal, Haymarket, SW1.
Box office: 930 9832.

The second oldest working playhouse in London, this beautiful Nash theatre, the second on the site, opened in 1821 with Sheridan's **The Rivals.** The previous building, opened just a hundred years before, was the scene of many colourful non-theatrical events, including a riot begun by the Duke of Cumberland (the "butcher of Culloden") who leapt on to the stage during a performance and attacked the scenery with his sword. A Royal Patent was granted in 1767, even though further riots took place during a Royal Command Performance 17 years later, when many people were trampled to death. Beerbohm Tree took control of the present theatre in the 1890s before moving across the road to his new theatre, Her Majesty's, which he built with profits made from his successful Haymarket production of **Trilby.** Wilde's **An Ideal Husband** had its first performance at the Haymarket in 1895, **Ghosts** in 1914, Barrie's **Mary Rose** in 1920, **Ten Minute Alibi** in 1933, and Coward's **Design for Living** in 1939. Since the last war, productions of **Waters of the Moon, The Chalk Garden, Flowering Cherry, Ross** and a visit by Helen Hayes in **The Glass Menagerie** have been the highlights, as well as John Gielgud's last appearance as **Hamlet** in 1944. John Mortimer's **A Voyage Round My Father** ended a run of over a year here in the autumn of 1972. The Haymarket's proscenium stage faces on to an auditorium seating 905 divided between stalls, dress circle, upper circle, gallery and 4 boxes. There are licensed bars at stalls, dress circle and upper circle levels. Nearest car park is in Whitcomb Street, at the top of Haymarket.

Nearest underground: Piccadilly or Trafalgar Square. **Buses:** 9, 9a, 14, 19, 22, 38.

HER MAJESTY'S

Her Majesty's Theatre, Haymarket, SW1.
Box office: 930 6606.

The fourth theatre on the site, the present building opened in 1897 as the permanent home of Herbert Beerbohm Tree's company; Tree staged here some of the most elaborate productions of Shakespeare London has seen. **Chu Chin Chow** began its 2,000 performances here in 1916, followed by Coward's **Bitter Sweet,** Priestley's **The Good Companions,** and Ivor Novello and Vivien Leigh in **The Happy Hypocrite.** More recently, **Edward My Son** in 1947, **West Side Story** in 1958 and **Fiddler on the Roof** have been outstanding productions. The proscenium stage faces on to a 4-tier auditorium seating 1,260. There is an approved air-ventilation system, and 3 licensed bars. Nearest car park is in Whitcomb Street at the top of Haymarket.

Nearest underground: Piccadilly. **Buses:** 9, 9a, 14, 19, 22, 38.

LYRIC

Lyric Theatre, Shaftesbury Avenue, W1.
Box office: 437 3686.

Built in 1888, the Lyric was the scene of the London debuts of both Eleanore Duse, the Italian tragedienne, and her French counterpart, Sarah Bernhardt. **Floradora, The Chocolate Soldier, Lilac Time,** Tallulah Bankhead in **The Gold Diggers, Autumn Crocus, Reunion in Vienna** and **Victoria Regina** were all pre-war successes here, and in

1946 **The Winslow Boy** had a long run, succeeded by Eliot's **The Confidential Clerk** and **Irma La Douce** and **Robert and Elizabeth**. Recently, Alan Ayckbourn's comedy **How the Other Half Loves** ran for nearly 900 performances. The Lyric has a seating capacity of 920 on 3 levels facing on to a proscenium stage. There are 3 licensed bars. One wheelchair can be accommodated in a stalls box. Multi-storey car parks are in Denman Street and Brewer Street, both only 2 minutes' walk away.

Nearest underground: Piccadilly. **Buses:** 14, 19, 22, 38.

MAY FAIR
May Fair Theatre, Stratton Street, W1.
Box office: 629 3036.

This 310-seat theatre, built into the Mayfair Hotel, opened in 1963 with a production of Pirandello's **Six Characters in Search of an Author** starring Ralph Richardson and Barbara Jefford. Its biggest success since then has been the long run of Christopher Hampton's **The Philanthropist** which transferred here from the Royal Court in September, 1970. There are two restaurants (tables reserved by ringing the box office), a coffee shop and 3 licensed bars. There is room for 2 wheelchairs in the auditorium. Parking space available in Berkeley Square and adjoining streets at night.

Nearest underground: Green Park. **Buses:** 9, 9a, 14, 19, 22, 25, 38.

MERMAID
The Mermaid, Puddle Dock, Blackfriars, EC4.
Box office: 248 7656.

One of London's first new theatres to open after the last war, the Mermaid is built into the shell of Blackfriars Wharf and is the brainchild of its founder and director, Bernard Miles and his wife, Josephine Wilson. Its first production in 1959 was Lionel Bart's musical, **Lock Up Your Daughters** which had a long and successful run. In recent years, probably its most famous transfer to the West End has been Peter Luke's **Hadrian VII**. The Mermaid policy is to present limited runs of at least 6 new, classical or musical plays each year. The open stage faces a steeply-raked one-tier auditorium seating 498. Air-conditioning is installed. A foyer bookstall sells programmes, books and Mermaid souvenirs. There are 2 licensed restaurants overlooking the Thames (248 2835 for reservations) as well as a coffee and snack bar and 2 other bars. Reductions in ticket prices are made for parties and members of the Mermaid Association. Wheelchairs can be accommodated by prior arrangement. Parking available in adjoining streets, specifically in Upper Thames Street.

Nearest station: Blackfriars (on the Southern Region as well as the underground Circle and District lines). **Buses:** 6, 6a, 9, 11, 13, 15 to Ludgate Hill, and 17, 45, 63, 76, 109, 155, 168, 177 and 184 to Blackfriars.

NEW LONDON
New London Theatre, Drury Lane, WC2B 5PW.
Box office: 405 0072.

Part of the New London Centre which also contains a restaurant, nightclub, flats, showrooms, shops and a multi-storey underground car park. The administrators are EMI under the personal supervision of Bernard Delfont. Built on the site of the Winter Garden at the junction of Parker Street and Drury Lane, which opened in 1919 and was demolished in 1963, this £3 million construction is London's newest theatre. It opened in January, 1973 with Peter Ustinov starring in and directing his own play **The Unknown Soldier and His Wife**. The 911-seat auditorium is the first of its kind, having stage, seating, lighting and even walls which can change position "at the throw of a switch." Thus a conventional stage and auditorium can be transformed into theatre-in-the-round within a few minutes. It can also be changed into a conference or lecture hall for daytime use. Air-conditioning, of course, is installed. The theatre is reached by lift from the underground car park (which takes 450 cars, and space in which can be reserved at the same time as booking a ticket) to the main entrance foyer on the ground floor. An escalator reaches up to the main reception area immediately beneath and behind the auditorium. There are circular bars and a spacious lounge area. The restaurant, seating 400, is open before and after the performance for early dinner and late-night supper with cabaret. Wheelchairs can be accommodated by prior arrangement with the Manager; there is a special WC for disabled patrons.

Nearest underground: Holborn and Covent Garden. **Buses:** 19, 55, 68, 77, 77a, 77b, 77c, 170, 172, 188, 196, 239 to Kingsway.

OLD VIC

The Old Vic, Waterloo Road, SE1.
Box office: 928 7616 (situated 3 minutes' walk away, at 76 The Cut).

The temporary home of the National Theatre Company since its formation in 1963 and until its own theatre is completed in 1974 on the South Bank of the Thames. Built in 1818 and then called the Coburg, the theatre later became internationally famous as the Old Vic under the devoted management of Lilian Baylis who rescued it from its gin palace existence to stage Shakespeare, and for a while opera and ballet, productions from 1914. The Old Vic between the wars became a nursery for the talent of the great names in the British theatre, among them Gielgud, Olivier, Redgrave, Richardson, Ashcroft, Evans, Thorndike. Here, too, the complete Shakespeare First Folio was first presented, by Robert Atkins in the 1920s, and again by Michael Benthall in the 1950s. The Old Vic Company disbanded in 1963 on the formation of the National Theatre. Under the direction of Laurence Olivier, the NT has since presented many world and British premiérés including work by Arrabal, Peter Nichols, Tom Stoppard and John Osborne. It has also given new life to some neglected classics as well as producing better-known works from an international repertoire. Outstanding among Olivier's own performances are his Othello in 1964 and his James Tyrone in O'Neill's Long Day's Journey Into Night in 1972. Productions are presented in repertoire. A new proscenium was designed in 1963 with an apron extension, and the seating capacity of the Old Vic is now 878. There is a restaurant serving cold pre-performance dinners (928 2033 for reservations) as well as 3 bars and 2 buffets (including one serving hot savouries in the upper circle). A foyer bookstall sells the texts of plays in the company's repertoire as well as souvenir programmes, posters, books and theatre magazines. Price concessions are offered to parties of 20 or more. There is accommodation for 1 wheelchair in the stalls. A large car park is adjacent to the theatre.

Nearest underground: Waterloo. Buses: 1, 1a, 4, 68, 70, 176, 188, 196, 239. Red Arrows to Waterloo Station: 501, 502, 503, 505, 507, 513.

OPEN AIR, REGENT'S PARK

Open Air Theatre, Queen Mary's Gardens, Regent's Park, NW1.
Box office: 486 2431.

The Open Air Theatre has become one of London's regular summer institutions, and has been performing on this particular piece of greensward since 1932. Many structural improvements for both performers and audience have been added since then. David Conville's New Shakespeare Company has been occupying the theatre for the past few years, and during a 12-week season from June to late August there are 2 productions of Shakespeare plays, each presented for a 6-week run. The auditorium seats approximately 1,600, the front few rows in deck chairs, the rest in rather less comfortable seats, but cushions and rugs are available on hire. If it rains, ticket-holders are given seats for another performance (in the case of school parties unable to attend another performance, money is refunded.) There are price concessions for parties of 10 or more and for schools. A feature of the Open Air Theatre is the Wine Tent. It is licensed until after midnight, and the restaurant (935 4139 for reservations) serves dinner before and after evening performances. You can also get snacks, glasses of wine, beer, iced champagne and hock, and mulled claret on chillier evenings. Wheelchairs can be accommodated in the auditorium. There is plenty of parking space outside Queen Mary's Gardens.

Nearest underground: Baker Street. Buses: 1, 2, 2b, 13, 18, 26, 30, 59, 74, 74b, 113, 159 to Baker Street.

PALACE

Palace Theatre, Cambridge Circus, W1.
Box office: 437 6834.

This large Victorian theatre, built in 1891, was originally an opera house, and its opening production under the D'Oyly Carte management was Arthur Sullivan's grand opera Ivanhoe. During its Palace of Varieties period soon after, Pavlova made her London debut here, as also did Mistinguette. In 1911 the first Royal Command Variety Performance was held here. No, No, Nanette had a long run from 1925, and in the period just before the last war Jack Hulbert and Cicely Courtneidge staged 3 successful shows opening with Under Your Hat in 1938. Since then, the biggest and longest success has been The Sound of Music which ran from 1961 to 1967. Before that, in 1949 Ivor Novello's last musical, King's Rhapsody opened, and during its long run here, Novello died. The auditorium has a seating capacity of 1,500 on 5 levels facing on to a proscenium stage. There are 6 bars, and coffee is also available. Two wheelchairs can be accommodated in the stalls, which are at street level. Nearest car park is in Upper St Martin's Lane, or in an open-air park off Gerrard Street.

Nearest underground: Leicester Square or Tottenham Court Road. Buses: 9, 22, 38.

PALLADIUM
Palladium, Argyll Street, W1A.
Box office: 437 7373.

A Moss Empires theatre, the Palladium opened in 1909 as a variety house, with Nellie Wallace and Martin Harvey incongruously sharing the top billing. From 1929 to the end of the last war it was the home of George Black's spectacular revues and pantomimes. It is still London's leading variety house, with its large-scale Christmas panto-mimes an important feature of the year's programme. The annual Royal Variety Performance is held here. The Palladium has a seating capacity of 2,271 on 3 levels before a proscenium stage. There are 4 licensed bars and a snack bar. GLC regulations restrict wheelchairs in the auditorium to 1 each performance. There is a car park in Poland Street, a few minutes' walk away.

Nearest underground: Oxford Circus. Buses: with the continuous changes in one-way and no-traffic schemes in this area, it is only safe to recommend any bus going to Oxford Circus or to the top of Regent Street.

PHOENIX
Phoenix Theatre, Charing Cross Road, WC2.
Box office: 836 8611.

Built in 1929, this 1,028-seat theatre opened with the original production of Coward's Private Lives. The musical Canterbury Tales ran here for five years from March 1968. The pros-cenium stage faces on to an auditorium on 3 levels. There are 4 bars including a sandwich bar. Also a Paralok self-service cloakroom system, and wheel-chair facilities. The Phoenix car park is next door.

Nearest underground: Tottenham Court Road. Buses: 1, 14, 19, 22, 24, 29, 176 to Charing Cross Road, or 1, 7, 8, 25, 73 to Oxford Street/Tottenham Court Road junction.

PICCADILLY
Piccadilly Theatre, Denman Street, W1V 8DY.
Box office: 437 4506.

Built in 1928, the Piccadilly was almost immediately taken over by Warner Brothers for the showing of Vitaphone films, and the first talkies ever seen in this country were screened here, among them Al Jolson in The Singing Fool. The theatre reverted to live entertainment with The Student Prince which was revived the following year. A revue by Dion Titheradge and Vivian Ellis, Folly to be Wise, was the theatre's first big success in 1931; then came Bridie's A Sleeping Clergyman with Robert Donat and Ernest Thesiger in 1933. After a bad period in the late 1930s, Coward's Blithe Spirit played the first part of its long run here in 1941, followed by Gielgud's Macbeth the next year and the musical Panama Hattie in 1943. The building was badly damaged by flying-bomb blast in 1944 and closed for some months. In 1960 Donald Albery took over and carried out extensive renovations both front and backstage; and the Piccadilly became London's first fully air-conditioned theatre. Since then, the theatre's best remembered productions have been Who's Afraid of Virginia Woolf? the musical Man of La Mancha and The Ruling Class. The Piccadilly has a proscenium stage facing on to a 1,138-seat auditorium on 3 levels. There is a licensed bar at each level. A self-service Paralok cloakroom system is installed. Wheelchairs can be accommodated in some boxes in the royal circle which is at street level. The nearest car park is in Denman Street, almost next door.

Nearest underground: Piccadilly. Buses: 9, 9a, 14, 19, 22, 38.

PLAYERS' THEATRE CLUB
Players' Theatre, Villiers Street, Strand, WC2.
Box office: 839 1134.

This theatre club, housed since 1946 in the former home of Gatti's Under the Arches Music-Hall, is continuing the Victorian tradition of music hall, complete with white-tie-and-tails Chair-man. Here the Late Joys Victorian Music-Hall recreates the atmosphere of a hundred years ago, and presents all the songs made famous by the stars of the past. There is a complete change of programme every fortnight, and after the show you can come up and use the stage for dancing. This is a club theatre, but for overseas visitors there is a temporary membership of £1 for a week, or £2.50 for 3 months. The Supper Room (box office number for reservations) is open from 7 to 11.30 pm, and there is a coffee bar serving sandwiches, as well as 2 licensed bars. Wheelchairs can be accommodated in the auditorium by prior arrangement. Nearest car park is in Savoy Place, just behind the Savoy Hotel.

Nearest underground: Charing Cross, just round the corner. Buses: 1, 1a, 6, 9, 9a, 11, 13, 15, 77, 77a, 77b, 77c, 170, 172, 176, to the Charing Cross end of the Strand.

PRINCE OF WALES
Prince of Wales Theatre, Coventry Street, W1.
Box office: 930 8681.

The first theatre on this site opened in 1884 as the Prince's, changing to its present title 2 years later, significantly after Lily Langtry's appearance there. Mrs Patrick Campbell, Forbes-Robertson and Marie Tempest all had successes in that theatre. The present building opened in 1937—its foundation stone was laid by Gracie Fields—and for many years George Black successfully presented revue and variety. Sid Field had a personal triumph when he played in **Harvey** here in 1943, and in recent years the Prince of Wales has staged a number of large-scale musicals, outstanding among them **Funny Girl** with Barbra Streisand. The air-conditioned auditorium seats 1,139 on 2 levels before a proscenium stage. There is a champagne bar, a dress circle bar and a double stalls bar. Nearest car park is in Whitcomb Street.

Nearest underground: Piccadilly. Buses: 9, 9a, 14, 19, 22, 38.

QUEEN'S
Queen's Theatre, Shaftesbury Avenue, W1.
Box office: 734 1166

The original building opened in 1907, and among its early successes was **The Barretts of Wimpole Street** in 1930, and a John Gielgud season in 1937 in which, with Peggy Ashcroft, he presented and appeared in productions of **Richard II, School for Scandal, Three Sisters** and **The Merchant of Venice. Dear Octopus** opened here in 1939, followed by **Rebecca**, during the run of which the theatre was badly damaged in the blitz. Entirely re-designed inside, the Queen's re-opened in 1959 with Gielgud's solo programme, **The Ages of Man**. The theatre's most recent success has been the Maggie Smith-Robert Stephens revival of Coward's **Private Lives,** directed by Gielgud. The proscenium stage faces on to a 950-seat auditorium divided between stalls, circle and upper circle. Air-conditioning is installed. There are 3 bars and a coffee bar. For the disabled, the front of the dress circle has some convenient seating, but wheelchairs cannot be accommodated in the auditorium. Nearest car park is in Denman Street, or Brewer Street, both only a few minutes' walk away.

Underground: Piccadilly. Buses: 14, 19, 22, 38.

ROYAL COURT
Royal Court Theatre, Sloane Square, SW1.
Box office: 730 1745.

Home of the English Stage Company under its current director, Oscar Lewenstein. The present theatre first opened in 1888, temporarily dropped the Royal from its title 14 years later, and from 1904 to 1906 staged the famous J E Vedrenne/Granville—Barker seasons of plays by Shaw and Galsworthy, as well as the classics and Greek tragedy. J B Fagan succeeded them in the 1920s and continued their high standard. Bad times eventually turned the theatre into a cinema in 1932, and it was closed after bomb damage in 1940. George Devine formed the English Stage Company in 1955 and under his direction the Royal Court became internationally known for its productions of work by new writers, beginning an entirely new chapter in our theatre history with Osborne's **Look Back In Anger** in 1956. In the past 5 years, world premieres have been presented of plays by Osborne, Edward Bond, Angus Wilson, John Arden, Christopher Hampton, David Cregan, John Hopkins, David Storey, E A Whitehead, Charles Wood, Arnold Wesker and many others. Its present policy is straight runs of 5 or 6 weeks, with the longer-running productions transferring to the West End. There is a proscenium stage, seating capacity of 401 on 2 levels, and an air-conditioning system. No restaurant, but 2 bars and a coffee bar. Price concessions are made to students. No wheelchair facilities as such, but the staff are willing to help carry disabled theatregoers. A small auditorium above the main one, The Theatre Upstairs, stages experimental work (see under separate entry). Parking space fairly easy to find in side streets off Sloane Square.

Nearest underground: Sloane Square. Buses: 11, 19, 22, 46, 137.

ROYALTY
Royalty Theatre, Portugal Street, Kingsway, WC2.
Box office: 405 8004.

One of London's newer theatres, the Royalty (built on the site of the former Stoll Opera House) opened in 1960 with Durrenmatt's **The Visit** starring Alfred Lunt and Lynn Fontanne. The theatre shortly ran into trouble financially, and after being used as a cinema for some years it eventually closed. Paul Raymond took over in 1970 and, shortly after, **Oh! Calcutta!** began a long run here. The Royalty seats 912 on 2 levels before a proscenium stage. Air-conditioning is installed. There are 2 spacious bars and a snack bar serving coffee. Up to 5 wheel-chairs can be accommodated in the auditorium, and the most convenient place for disabled patrons is a box at the back of the circle, with easy access from street level. Plenty of parking space in Lincoln's Inn Fields in after-meter hours.

Nearest underground: Holborn. Buses: 55, 68, 77, 77a, 77b, 77c, 170, 172, 188, 196, 239.

SADLER'S WELLS
Sadler's Wells Theatre, Rosebery Avenue, EC1.
Box office: 837 1672.

Sadler's Wells gets its name from a medicinal spring discovered on the site, then the grounds of one Thomas Sadler's house in Islington. The area was turned into a spa with pleasure grounds, and a theatre was erected in 1765 where both Kean and Grimaldi appeared. Samuel Phelps took over in the 1840s to present productions of Shakespeare. After an unhappy period as an ice-rink, a boxing ring and a cinema it was brought back to life by Lilian Baylis who rebuilt and re-opened it in 1931 as the North London equivalent of the Old Vic. From then until its closure in 1940 it was to become the home of the famous opera and ballet companies. In 1945 it opened again, the ballet company transferring to Covent Garden to become the Royal Ballet and the opera company occupying the theatre full-time. In 1968 Sadler's Wells Opera moved to the centre of London to the Coliseum, and since that time Sadler's Wells itself has been providing a platform for visiting opera, dance and drama companies from home and overseas. The proscenium stage faces on to an auditorium on 3 levels, seating 1,500. Mr. Sadler's original well can still be seen under a trap-door in the stalls. There are 3 bars and a buffet service (sandwiches and salads) in the Wells Room (278 6563 for reservations). Special rates for party bookings on application to Peter Hampson, Promotions Manager, at the same number. Sadler's Wells is usually closed during the whole of August. There is plenty of space for parking in streets around the theatre; no meters.

Nearest underground: Angel. Buses: 19 and 38 from Piccadilly. 172 from Holborn. 171 from Waterloo, or 77, 188, 196 change at Holborn.

ST MARTIN'S
St Martin's Theatre, West Street, WC2.
Box office: 836 1443.

Built in 1916, this 550-seat theatre was renovated and modernised in 1961. In the 1920s Galsworthy's **The Skin Game** and **Loyalties** were staged here. **The Shop at Sly Corner** had a long run after the last war, and the theatre's two most recent successes have been **The Killing of Sister George** in 1966 and the long run (till 1973) of **Sleuth**. The air-conditioned auditorium is on 3 levels, facing on to a proscenium stage. There are bars at both stalls and circle levels. There is a multi-storey car park in Upper St Martin's Lane, just a few yards away.

Nearest underground: Leicester Square. Buses: 1, 14, 19, 22, 24, 29, 176.

SAVOY
Savoy Theatre, Strand, WC2.
Box office: 836 8888.

The early history of this theatre is dominated by the Savoy Operas—the Gilbert and Sullivan light operas presented by D'Oyly Carte from the opening of the theatre in 1881 until the turn of the century. Vedrenne and Granville—Barker took over the theatre in 1907 after their success at the Royal Court, and classical seasons followed. In the late 1920s **Young Woodley** and **Journey's End** had their London runs here. **The Man Who Came to Dinner** ran for 700 performances during the last war, and Alan Melville's **A La Carte** revue was staged in 1948. There have been many seasons of Gilbert and Sullivan since the original ones, but the Savoy's present policy is one of straight plays, with a line of long-running comedies to its credit, the latest being William Douglas Home's **The Secretary Bird** and **Lloyd George Knew My Father.** The proscenium stage faces on to a 1,122-seat auditorium on 3 levels. There are 4 bars, and coffee is also served in the intervals. Wheelchairs have easy access from the Embankment entrance into the dress circle. Nearest car park: Savoy Place on the Embankment immediately behind the Savoy Hotel.

Nearest underground: Trafalgar Square. **Buses:** 1, 1a, 6, 9, 9a, 11, 13, 15, 77, 77a, 77b, 77c, 170, 176.

SHAFTESBURY
Shaftesbury Theatre, Shaftesbury Avenue, WC2.
Box office: 836 6596.

Opened in 1911, this theatre was originally called the New Princes, changing its name to the Princes soon after, and to the Shaftesbury in 1962. Sacha Guitry appeared here in the early 1920s, and Sybil Thorndike and Henry Ainley starred in a production of **Macbeth** in 1926. Jessie Matthews made a wartime appearance in **Wild Rose** in 1942. Since then, the theatre has presented mainly musicals, although Eric Portman played for over 500 performances in **His Excellency** in 1950. American musicals such as **Pal Joey** and **How to Succeed in Business Without Really Trying** both had successful runs here in the 1950s. More recently the "tribal love-rock musical," **Hair,** occupied the stage here for five years from September, 1968. Seating 1,253 on 4 levels before a large proscenium stage, the Shaftesbury has the usual licensed bars on each level. Limited facilities for wheelchairs. Reduced prices for parties of 20 and over. The Shaftesbury was sold to a property development company in 1973. Nearest car park is in Upper St Martin's Lane.

Nearest underground: Tottenham Court Road. **Buses:** 7, 8, 19, 22, 25, 38.

STRAND
Strand Theatre, Aldwych, WC2.
Box office: 836 2660.

The theatre was built in 1905 and in its early years, under the direction of the American Shubert brothers, such artists as Irving, Tree and Eleonora Duse appeared here, along with seasons of Italian opera. Subsequent lessees have included Arthur Bourchier (who presented Mrs Patrick Campbell in the first performance of **Mrs Warren's Profession** and also Adele and Fred Astaire), George Grossmith, and Leslie Henson who with Firth Shepherd produced a series of hilarious farces in the early 1930s. Ivor Novello lived for many years up until his death in 1950 in a spacious flat built into the roof of the theatre and did much of his writing and composing here. Donald Wolfit gave his wartime performances of lunchtime Shakespeare at the Strand, and **Arsenic and Old Lace** had its record run here from 1942. Peggy Mount had a big personal success after the last war in **Sailor, Beware!** (1955) which was followed by Frankie Howerd in **A Funny Thing Happened on the Way to the Forum.** More recently, C P Snow's **The Affair** ran for a year, and there have been revivals of **An Ideal Husband** with Margaret Lockwood, **Dear Octopus** with Cicely Courtneidge and Jack Hulbert, and **When We Are Married** with Peggy Mount and Fred Emney. **Not Now, Darling** co-starred Donald Sinden and Bernard Cribbins, and was followed by the latest long-running comedy, **No Sex, Please, We're British** in 1972. The Strand's proscenium stage faces on to a 1,092-seat auditorium. There are 5 bars, and wheelchairs can be accommodated in the front row of the dress circle. Parking space is available in side streets in after-meter hours.

Nearest underground: Covent Garden or Holborn. **Buses:** 1, 1a, 6, 9, 11, 13, 15, 77, 77a, 77b, 77c, 170, 172, 176, 188, 196.

VAUDEVILLE
Vaudeville Theatre, Strand, WC2. ONH.
Box office: 836 9988.

Built in 1870, this intimate 559-seat theatre underwent a major redecoration by its present owner, Peter Saunders, just 100 years later. In the 1890s the first productions in this country of **Hedda Gabler** and **Rosmersholm** were presented here for matinee performances. **Quality Street** had a big success in 1902. Gertrude Lawrence made her first London appearance here as principal dancer and understudy in 1916. And during the last war **Acacia Avenue** and **No Medals** both played to full houses. The theatre's longest run was given by the Julian Slade-Dorothy Reynolds musical, **Salad Days** which transferred from the Bristol Old Vic in the 1950s and went on to beat **Chu Chin Chow** as a record-breaker. The Vaudeville's most recent successes have been the first London run of **The Man Most Likely To**, **The Jockey Club Stakes** and **Move Over, Mrs Markham**. The auditorium has a proscenium stage, and is divided between stalls, dress circle and upper circle. There is a licensed bar on each level, and air-conditioning is installed. Parking space can be found in the side streets off the Strand or in the Savoy Adelphi car park immediately behind the Savoy Hotel.

Nearest underground: I Charing Cross or Trafalgar Square. **Buses:** 1, 1a, 6, 9, 9a, 11, 13, 15, 77, 77a, 77b, 77c, 170, 176.

VICTORIA PALACE
Victoria Palace, Victoria Street, SW1.
Box office: 834 1317.

This Moss Empires theatre was built in 1911 as a variety house. Gracie Fields played here in the early 1930s, and **Me and My Girl** began its epic run in 1937. The Crazy Gang took over in 1949, and for the past 10 years the theatre has been the home of successive Black and White Minstrel shows. The proscenium stage faces on to a 1,541-seat auditorium, and air-conditioning is installed. There are 4 licensed bars. Wheelchairs are not allowed in the auditorium because of licensing regulations. There is a large car park in Buckingham Palace Road.

Nearest underground: Victoria. **Buses:** 10, 16, 25, 29, 38, 52, 149, and Red Arrows 500, 503, 506, 507 all to Victoria Station.

WESTMINSTER
Westminster Theatre, Palace Street, Buckingham Palace Road, SW1E 5JB.
Box office: 834 0283.

Built in 1931, the Westminster underwent a major renovation in 1972. Westminster Productions Ltd in association with Moral Re-Armament have occupied the theatre for the past 10 years. Straight runs of plays following the Moral Re-Armament line are presented between seasons of their perennial pantomime, **Give a Dog a Bone** by Peter Howard. The theatre has a seating capacity of 599 on 2 levels before a proscenium stage. A new ventilation system has been installed. There is a good restaurant (834 7781 for reservations) as well as a snack bar. Space is available for on-street parking in the evening and for Saturday matinees in the surrounding area.

Nearest underground: Victoria. **Buses:** 10, 16, 25, 29, 38, 52, 149, and Red Arrows 500, 503, 506, 507 all to Victoria Station.

WHITEHALL
Whitehall Theatre, Whitehall, SW1.
Box office: 930 6692.

Built in 1930, this theatre stands at the top of Whitehall close to Trafalgar Square. It has always been associated with lighter forms of theatre, and during the last war Phyllis Dixey's famous non-stop revue occupied the theatre for a number of years. In 1945 **Worm's Eye View** ran for over 2,000 performances. Brian Rix took over in 1950, and from then until 1967, when he moved to the Garrick, he established the Whitehall as the home of British farce. Under his management were launched such successes as **Reluctant Heroes**, **Dry Rot** and **One for the Pot**. The theatre is now under lease to Paul Raymond, whose show **Pyjama Tops** has been running since 1969. The 620-seat auditorium is divided between stalls and circle, and faces on to a proscenium stage. There are 3 bars as well as a snack bar. One wheelchair can be accommodated in the stalls. Parking space is available in Horse Guards Parade and in the side streets off Whitehall.

Nearest underground: Trafalgar Square or Charing Cross. **Buses:** 1, 1a, 6, 9, 9a, 11, 13, 15, 77, 77a, 77b, 77c, 170, 176.

WYNDHAM'S
Wyndham's Theatre, Charing Cross Road, WC2.
Box office: 836 3028.

A Wyndham's Theatre, built in 1899. One of its early successes was James Barrie's **Dear Brutus** in 1917. Edgar Wallace ran the theatre for a period in the 1920s during which his own thrillers enjoyed a popular appeal lasting from **The Ringer** in 1926 to **The Case of the Frightened Lady** in 1931, and revived with the long run of **Saloon Bar** in 1939. **George and Margaret** had a big success here from 1937, and during the last war **Quiet Wedding** and **Quiet Weekend** broke box office records. Edith Evans in **Daphne Laureola**, Ustinov's **The Love of Four Colonels** and Dorothy Tutin in **The Living Room** are the best remembered plays of the 1950s. Sandy Wilson's musical **The Boy Friend** ran here for 5 years from 1954, and among the theatre's more recent successes have been **The Prime of Miss Jean Brodie** and **Godspell**. A proscenium stage faces on to a 770-seat auditorium on 3 levels. There are 7 licensed bars including a Wine Bar in the foyer. A wheelchair can be accommodated in a stalls box. Nearest car park is in St Martin's Lane, behind the Odeon Cinema.

Nearest underground: Leicester Square. Buses: 1, 24, 29, 176.

YOUNG VIC
Young Vic, The Cut, Waterloo, SE1. 8LP.
Box office: 928 6363.

Formed in 1970 as a branch of the National Theatre Company at the Old Vic up the road, this theatre presents a repertoire of plays for young audiences as well as acting as host to visiting groups from this country and abroad. The artistic director is Frank Dunlop.

One of the Young Vic's most recent "firsts" has been the world premiere of the stage version of **Joseph and the Amazing Technicolor Dreamcoat** with music by Andrew Webber and lyrics by Tim Rice. The building, which has been constructed inside the shell of a former butcher's shop, seats 456 in an adaptable acting area. It is air-conditioned and there is a coffee bar. Price reductions for parties of 10 or more are offered. Also facilities for wheelchairs in the auditorium. Parking space is available in surrounding streets and in the large car park adjacent to the Old Vic in the Waterloo Road.

Nearest underground: Waterloo.
Buses: 1, 1a, 4, 68, 70, 176, 188, 196, 239, and Red Arrows 501, 502, 503, 505, 507, 513 all to Waterloo, and 17, 45, 63, 109, 141, 184 to Blackfriars Road at the junction with The Cut.

London: Fringe & Lunchtime

ACT INN

Act Inn Theatre Club, 37 Brewer Street, W1.
Box office: 734 2997.

This lunchtime club has its premises over a pub called The Duke of Argyle. Their 2 to 3 week runs of new experimental work provide a showcase for actors, writers and directors. Recent British premieres have included Mrozek's Out At Sea, Pirandello's A Dream but Perhaps It Isn't, and Anouilh's Humulus the Muted Lover. There is seating for up to 100 around an adaptable acting area. Food and drink are available in the pub below. Membership is 25p, and price concessions are made for group bookings. The Act Inn is 150 yards from Piccadilly, and there are multi-storey car parks in Brewer Street itself and in adjoining Denman Street.

Nearest underground: Piccadilly. Buses: 9, 14, 19, 22, 38.

ALMOST-FREE

Almost-Free Theatre, 9-19 Rupert Street, W1.
Box office: 485 6224.

The Almost-Free, home of the Ambiance Lunch-Hour Theatre Club and of Interaction, was founded by Ambiance director Ed Berman in 1971 with the object of presenting lunchtime productions of British and world premieres by known and unknown authors. So far they have presented one-act plays by such writers as Tom Stoppard, Peter Nichols, David Rudkin and Berman himself. The Interaction company takes over the theatre in the evening to present folk and poetry festivals and other activities as well as plays, replacing the work of The Other Company which disbanded in 1972 on the sudden death of its young director, Naftali Yavin. Interaction also operates a street theatre called Dogg's Troupe which visits schools, youth clubs, mental hospitals, community centres and remand homes. There is also a Fun Art Bus touring the London streets during the summer. Seating capacity is approximately 100 before a flexible open-type stage. Air-conditioning is installed, and there is a licensed bar and a coffee bar. As its name suggests, the Almost-Free Theatre has an unusual price system. To quote their official brochure: "In order that Inter-Action productions are available to everyone, all members may determine both their own membership fee and ticket prices from 1p upwards. Please pay as much, not as little, as you can." Wheelchairs can be accommodated in the auditorium, which is at ground level, and for the disabled the services of a backstage WC (more accessible than the public one) are offered. Nearest car parks are in Denman Street and Brewer Street, both a few minutes away.

Nearest underground: Piccadilly. Rupert Street runs between Shaftesbury Avenue and Coventry Street, and among the many buses are: 9, 9a, 14, 19, 22, 38.

BUSH

Bush Theatre, The Bush Hotel, Shepherd's Bush, W12.
Box office: 743 5050.

This fringe theatre opened early in 1972 with its premises an adapted hall above a pub. Their programme aims at catering for their own area as well as for a wider public, and the emphasis is on new work. There is a basic permanent company augmented from outside for each production, and the Bush plays host to many visiting companies, usually alternating in fortnightly intervals. Their performances are in the evening with only the occasional lunchtime production. Since their formation, they have presented the first performance of John McGrath's Plugged In performed by a guest company and themselves produced John Arden's The Ballygombeen Bequest. The Bush seats 115 around a moveable open-plan stage. The pub downstairs provides refreshment as well as sandwiches and snacks which can be taken into the theatre. Membership fee: 25p a year. Wheelchairs cannot be accommodated in the theatre, but the staff are willing to carry disabled patrons if necessary.

There is a new car park at the junction of Shepherd's Bush Green and Uxbridge Road, and space is also available in surrounding streets.

Nearest underground: Shepherd's Bush. **Buses:** 12, 49, 88, 207, 220.

COCKPIT
Cockpit Theatre and Arts Workshop, Gateforth Street, off Church Street Market, Marylebone, NW8.
Box office: 402 5081.

Run by the Inner London Education Authority, the Cockpit opened in January, 1970. Under its Artistic Director, Alec Davison, it acts as host to the best of youth companies, both amateur and professional, experimenting in new drama, music, mixed media and environmental work. It is open 7 days a week throughout the year except for 2 weeks in August, and among its many other activities is the organising of courses and conferences for teachers and youth leaders conducted by 3 professional teams. The Cockpit was London's first officially-licensed in-the-round theatre. It has an open flexible stage with seating for 250 in the round, 170 for a thrust stage, and 120 for an end-stage arrangement. Air-conditioning is installed. There is a good coffee bar with a "dish of the day" and snacks. A pub is directly opposite. Price concessions offered to parties, pensioners and students. Ample facilities for wheelchairs if prior notice is given. Nearest car park is in Marylebone Road, but there is plenty of space in surrounding streets after 6.30 pm.

Nearest underground: Marylebone or Edgware Road.
Buses: 6, 7, 8, 15, 16, 36, 36a, 36b, 59, 159, 176 to Edgware Road or Lisson Grove.

DARK & LIGHT
The Dark and Light Theatre, Longfield Hall, Knatchbull Road, SE5.
Box office: 274 4070.

The Dark and Light Theatre Company, under its founder and director, Frank Cousins, has occupied these premises since August, 1971. The first multi-racial theatre with multi-racial casts to be established in this country, it is essentially a London-based touring group, subsidised by the Arts Council and local education authorities to take its productions around the country, mainly to community halls and schools in urban areas with large immigrant populations who do not normally visit a theatre. Among the new work presented by the Company since its beginning are Athol Fugard's **Blood Knot** and Leroi Jones' **The Slave**. The theatre seats 200, all at stalls level, with a basically proscenium stage which can be adapted. Light refreshments are available but at present there is no bar. Parking is available in surrounding streets.

Nearest underground: Brixton (on the Victoria line, as well as Southern Region) which is 10 minutes' walk away down Burton Road with Knatchbull Road at the end. **Buses:** 3, 59, 95, 109, 133, 159, 172 to Brixton Road.

THE HALF MOON
The Half Moon, 27 Alie Street, E1.
Box office: 480 6465.

A former synagogue in the East End built in 1894 and used as a warehouse for some years was taken over in January, 1972 by a young director and two actors who had met at drama school—Guy Sprung, Maurice Colbourne and Michael Irving, and they were later joined by another actor, William Gregory. They formed The Half Moon Theatre Club, with a policy of putting on principally new work whenever it was financially possible, and with the aim not only of attracting audiences from other parts of London but also of involving the neighbourhood in their activities by presenting plays with a familiar background to the area, and by giving children's shows and working with local schools and youth groups. Their opening production was the British premiere of Brecht's **Jungle of the Cities**, and since then probably their most outstanding shows have been **Sawdust Caesar** written and directed by Andy Smith; **Dan Dare**, their Christmas 1972 children's play; and Terence Greer's musical about Jack the Ripper, called **Ripper!** Productions are presented in the round, and the seating capacity is usually 100 on one level, although the auditorium is variable. The theatre has no licence but soft drinks are obtainable, and the pub next door (The White Swan) acts as the theatre bar. Annual subscription is 10p, and ticket prices are around 50p for adults and 30p for children; reductions are offered for parties of 10 and over. The auditorium is at street level, so there is easy access for wheelchairs, and 2 or 3 can be accommodated. There is no nearby car park, but street parking is unrestricted in the evening.

Nearest underground: Aldgate East, just round the corner. **Buses:** 5, 10, 15, 23, 25, 40, 67, 253.

KING'S HEAD

King's Head Theatre Club, 115 Upper Street, Islington, N1.
Box office: 226 1916.

This Victorian pub has been taken over by King's Head Theatre Productions under the direction of Dan Crawford, and new plays are presented every 4 to 6 weeks at evening performances. Lunchtime shows are also put on, occasionally in partnership with Basement Theatre Productions. One of the King's Head's most signal successes has been their production of David Mercer's Let's Murder Vivaldi. The auditorium here consists of accommodation for about 60 seated at dining tables arranged round an open stage. An inclusive ticket can be bought for both dinner and performance if required. Club membership is 25p annually. Full pub facilities are available, of course. Local street parking is unrestricted.

Nearest underground: Angel on the Northern line, or Highbury and Islington on the Victoria line. Buses: 4, 19, 30, 43, 104.

LITTLE

Quipu, Little Theatre Club, Garrick Yard, St Martin's Lane, WC2.
Box office: 240 0660.

Founded by dramatist David Halliwell, Quipu is one of the oldest established lunchtime theatre clubs. They eventually took over this theatre (originally a sewing-machine factory) in 1971. With a policy of encouraging new drama, their productions are staged for fortnightly straight runs at lunchtime, with the occasional evening show. There is no permanent company; a director and artists are recruited for each play. The theatre has a seating capacity of 50 on one steeply-raked tier, with an acting area at the far end. There is a licensed bar which also serves coffee and sandwiches. Membership fee: 25p annually, or 5p for one performance. Nearest car park in Upper St Martin's Lane, or behind the Odeon Cinema just down the road.

Nearest underground: Leicester Square. Buses: 1, 14, 19, 22, 24, 29, 176.

LAMB & FLAG

The Lamb & Flag, Rose Street, off Garrick Street, Covent Garden, WC2.
Box office: 836 4108.

This 16th century public house (to be preserved under the new Covent Garden scheme) is the home of one of the first pub theatres to operate in London. The Recreation Ground Theatre Company presents lunchtime performances of new short plays by known and unknown authors, among them the London premiere of Henry Livings' Pongo Plays, the professional premiere of Arrabal's Picnic on the Battlefield, Triangle by James Saunders, and Better Days Better Knights by Stanley Eveling. There is room for an audience of 40 around an open acting area. Refreshments from the pub bar, which is famous for its game pie and other delicacies, can be consumed during the performance. There is a multi-storey car park in Upper St Martin's Lane, a few minutes away, or on-street parking in the side streets.

Nearest underground: Leicester Square, Trafalgar Square or Covent Garden. Buses: 1, 14, 19, 22, 24, 29, 176.

OPEN SPACE

Open Space, 32 Tottenham Court Road, W1.
Box office: 580 4970.

This is a members-only theatre, subsidised by the Arts Council and Camden Borough Council. Under the direction of Charles Marowitz it has gained a reputation for experimental theatre since its formation in 1968, and has over 50 world premieres to its credit, including Marowitz' own treatments of Macbeth, Othello and Hamlet. Occasional lunchtime productions are also presented. Seating for 130 round an open stage. Vent-Axia air-conditioning is installed. Tickets are £1 plus 25p membership (50p plus 25p for students) or £3 full membership for a year. There are no wheelchair facilities but staff will help to carry disabled patrons. Nearest car parks in Ridgemount Place off Store Street just behind Tottenham Court Road, or in Museum Street by the British Museum.

Nearest underground: Tottenham Court Road or Goodge Street. Buses: 14, 24, 29, 73, 176.

ORANGE TREE

The Orange Tree, 45 Kew Road, Richmond, Surrey.
Box office: 940 0944.

The Richmond Fringe Theatre Group have been presenting lunchtime performances at this pub since the beginning of 1972, and their success is acknowledged by the granting of a small subsidy jointly by the local Borough Council and the Arts Council. Each production here runs for 10 days, and their programme includes neglected classics as well as a main policy of presenting new and experimental work. A major renovation of the premises was carried out in 1973 when an improved snack-bar and a fully-equipped studio theatre with air-conditioning were installed. Activities were then to be extended to the evenings as well as lunchtime, and it was hoped to engage a resident company. Price concessions are offered to groups of 8 or more. Parking space available in nearby Borough car parks

Train: Richmond Station, on the District line or Southern Region main line, is 50 yards from the theatre.

Buses: 27 or 65.

OVAL HOUSE
Oval House Theatre Club, 52 Kennington Oval, SE11.
Box office: 735 2786.

Housing two separate studio theatres, one seating 150 and the other 60, the Oval House has adaptable seating and acting areas. Short seasons and weekend festivals of experimental theatre are given here, and in the past 5 years world and British premieres of plays of John Arden, Howard Brenton, Megan Terry, Alan Sillitoe and John Grillo have been presented as well as the first appearance in this country of groups like the Bread and Puppet Theatre and the New York Theatre Company. The Freehold, Portable Theatre, Contemporary Theatre, Inter-Action and the Pip Simmons Group have all produced new work here in the past few years. The Oval House is closed during August. There is a coffee bar with reasonably-priced home-cooked food. Membership is 50p annually. There is accommodation for wheelchairs in the two auditoria, and parking is fairly easy in adjoining streets.

Nearest underground: The Oval. **Buses:** 36, 36a, 59, 185.

PINDAR OF WAKEFIELD
The Pindar of Wakefield, 328 Gray's Inn Road, WC1.
Box office: 837 7269.

The Aba Daba Music Hall, housed for the past 2 years in a pub in the Gray's Inn Road, presents evening performances only. Music Hall on Friday and Saturday, jazz for 2 nights a week, and folk music another night. The director

is Shaun Curry. Performances are given in the Music Hall Room of the pub, which can seat 120 round an open acting area. The usual pub facilities are instantly available, plus chicken-in-the-basket and scampi-in-the-basket. Accommodation can be found for wheelchairs, as the pub is at street level. Nearest car park is in Museum Street by the British Museum.

Nearest underground: King's Cross. **Buses:** not recommended, although the 17, 18, 45, 46 are the nearest.

THE PLACE
The Place, 17 Duke's Road, Euston, WC1.
Box office: 387 0031.

Home of the London Contemporary Dance Theatre, this little one-tier theatre, seating 255, was opened in 1969 and is used mostly for contemporary dance, with outside companies presenting drama, music and mixed-media shows. (In 1971 the Royal Shakespeare Company gave a season here during which they presented the British premieres of Trevor Griffiths' **Occupations** and **Subject To Fits** by Robert Montgomery as well as Michael Meyer's translation of Strindberg's **Miss Julie**). The Place is open 3 or 4 times each year for seasons of from 5 to 8 weeks. The stage is adaptable to both proscenium or open-stage productions. A foyer bar is open during performances, and there is a members-only licensed restaurant for suppers. Club membership is 50p annually; non-members pay 10p extra for tickets. Price concessions for parties of 10 or more. Parking space available in surrounding streets in the evening.

Nearest underground: Euston or King's Cross or Euston Square. **Buses:** 14, 18, 30, 73, 77a, 77b, 77c, 239 to Euston Road, (St Pancras Church).

SOHO POLY
The Soho Poly, 16 Riding House Street, W1.
Box office: 636 9050.

The Soho Theatre's founder-director, Frederick Proud, took over a students' basement workshop in March, 1972 and turned it into one of the most successful of the fringe theatres. Before then the Soho Theatre Company had for 2 years been presenting seasons at the King's Head in Islington and other places before establishing their own home. Their policy is to present lunchtime, evening and late-night performances to new audiences drawn mainly from local office workers and anyone else in the district. Their programme ranges from neglected classics (they recently presented a season of little-known work by Chekhov, Cervantes, Shaw and Sheridan) to basically new plays: since the Company's inception they have given over 40 productions of world or British premieres. The auditorium seats between 50 and 60 depending on the stage arrangement, which is variable. Access is difficult for wheelchair patrons because of steep stone steps to the auditorium. The theatre is not licensed, but coffee and soft drinks are available as well as bread and cheese, and soup. The Soho Poly is a club theatre, and annual membership is 25p. Parking is easy in surrounding streets in after-meter hours, but bad at lunchtime and there are no convenient car parks. Riding House Street is close to the BBC in Great Portland Street.

Nearest underground: Oxford Circus.
Buses: 3, 53, 137 to Great Portland Street, or any number going to Oxford Circus.

THEATRE UPSTAIRS
Theatre Upstairs at the Royal Court, Sloane Square, SW1.
Box office: 730 2554.

The Theatre Upstairs opened in February, 1969 and is literally upstairs from the Royal Court's main auditorium. In its first few years it has established itself as an expansion of the Court itself as a writer's theatre, able to take risks and explore new and experimental forms of theatre. There is a new show each month, with a different writer, director, designer and cast. Frequent late-night shows and other events are included in their programme. Among the many world or national premieres presented here have been Athol Fugard's **Boesman and Lena**, Heathcote Williams' **AC/DC,** E A Whitehead's **The Foursome** (which transferred to the West End); N F Simpson's **Was He Anyone?** and work by Howard Brenton, Peter Gill, Wilson John Haire and many others. The totally flexible acting/audience area seats between 60 and 90 arranged in a number of different ways. The theatre is open from Tuesday to Sunday but closed on Monday. There is air-conditioning. Also a bar, where you can buy sandwiches. The Theatre Upstairs is a club theatre, and full membership costs around £2 a year, but only 25p for students.

Nearest underground: Sloane Square.
Buses: 11, 19, 22, 137.

Outer London

ASHCROFT, CROYDON (touring date)

Ashcroft Theatre, Fairfield Halls, Park Lane, Croydon, CR9 1DG.
Box office: 688 9291.

Built in 1962 as part of the Fairfield Halls arts complex, the Ashcroft is principally a touring-date theatre, with the occasional presentation of its own productions for short seasons. The theatre is closed for 2 or 3 weeks during August. Seating capacity is 744 on 2 levels before a proscenium stage. The auditorium is air-conditioned. There is a restaurant (box office number for reservations) as well as a buffet and licensed bars. Up to 4 wheelchairs can be accommodated in one of the boxes, and for the disabled there are also specially-designed WCs. Ample space for parking in adjacent underground car park.

Trains: main line from Victoria to East Croydon, takes 15 minutes.

BANKSIDE GLOBE

The Bankside Globe Playhouse, 40 Bankside, Liberty of the Clink, Southwark, SE1
Box office: 928 1812..

This new project, built on the original site of Shakespeare's Globe, is under the direction of Sam Wanamaker and has the financial backing of John Player & Sons. Their first season was presented in the summer of 1972. The 1973 season, extending from June to September, aimed to continue a policy of presenting plays from the English classic repertoire, as well as Sunday evening concerts, a second annual Shakespeare Film Festival in the Bankside Globe Playhouse Classic cinema, and exhibitions at the Bear Gardens Museum of Elizabethan theatre—all under the title of **The Southwark Fair.** The Playhouse consists of a tent-like structure which is open at the sides, seating approximately 800. It operates only during the summer months. Cloakroom and WC facilities exist but are rather primitive. Good pub and snack bar arrangements, though, from an adjacent specially-constructed tavern. There is an open car park nearby.

Nearest underground: London Bridge.
Buses: 8a, 10, 21, 35, 40, 43, 44, 47, 48, 133 to London Bridge, or 501, 503 Red Arrows. Also 18, 95, 149, 176a to Southwark Bridge. Use stops nearest to Sumner Street, then follow the RAC signs to the Playhouse.

GREENWICH

Greenwich Theatre, Crooms Hill, Greenwich, SE10.
Box office: 858 7755.

The Greenwich Theatre was opened in October, 1969, and under the control of its artistic director, Ewan Hooper, has quickly gained a reputation for presenting some of our best new drama, with no fewer than 22 premieres and 3 transfers to the West End to its credit. Peter Nichols' **Forget-Me-Not Lane** and John Mortimer's **A Voyage Round My Father** had their first performances here, and there have also been productions of the classics. In January, 1973, Company Theatre, founded by Robin Phillips, Jeremy Brett and Joe Mandel, joined Greenwich with the object of forming a permanent company here, augmented from time to time with appearances by guest artists. Other regular features at Greenwich include Sunday night concerts, Sunday lunchtime jazz sessions and a thriving youth theatre and schools touring company called Bowsprit which is sited in Woolwich. A permanent exhibition of paintings, photographs and sculpture is mounted in the theatre's Art Gallery. The seating capacity is 426 around an open stage, and partial air-conditioning is installed. There is a restaurant (858 1318 for reservations) as well as 2 bars and a coffee bar. Price concessions of up to 50% are granted in certain cases. A large free car park is opposite the theatre.

Trains: Southern Region from Charing Cross to Greenwich, takes 19 minutes.
Buses: 177, 180, 180a, 185, to Greenwich Church.

HAMPSTEAD THEATRE CLUB

Hampstead Theatre Club, Swiss

Cottage Centre, NW3.
Box office: 722 9301.

Founded by James Roose-Evans in 1961, it receives a grant from the London Borough of Camden and also from the Arts Council. The building was virtually torn apart in 1970 and moved to a new site a few yards away. Since its formation, the Hampstead Theatre Club has presented 4-weekly straight runs almost entirely consisting of new plays by such writers as Frank Marcus, David Hare, Peter Ransley and many others, and it has a high rate of transfers to central London. It also mounts late-night shows. There is no permanent company. Michael Rudman, from the Edinburgh Traverse, took over the theatre's artistic direction in June 1973. The 157-seat auditorium has an end-stage and there is a licensed bar. Space for 2 wheelchairs is available in the front of the auditorium, which is on ground-level. A large car park is a few yards away, and off-street parking available at the back of the theatre. Club membership is £1 a year, but only 15p for late-night shows.

Nearest underground: Swiss Cottage.
Buses: 31, 187, 268.

QUEEN'S, HORNCHURCH
The Queen's Theatre, Station Lane, Hornchurch, Essex.
Box office: 49 43333.

Hornchurch Urban District Council was the first local authority after the last war to establish a theatre, and the Queen's (then a disused cinema) was acquired and converted in 1953 to its present purpose. A modern new building on an adjacent site is now under construction for possible opening late in 1973. Hornchurch Theatre Trust Ltd. under the direction of Antony Carrick, presents 3-weekly straight runs of contemporary and some classical plays, as well as special celebrity concerts and children's shows. The Queen's is closed for 6 weeks each summer from mid-June to early August. Seating capacity is 379 before a proscenium stage. Price concessions are made to parties of 12 and over, and to pensioners at certain matinees. There are no wheelchair facilities. One licensed bar. Free public car park adjacent to the theatre.

Underground: District Line trains take about 45 minutes from central London to Hornchurch underground station, 5 minutes' walk away.

RICHMOND
Richmond Theatre, The Green, Richmond, Surrey.
Box office: 940 0088.

A Victorian theatre with 675 seats on 2 levels before a proscenium stage, plus a 200-seat gallery which is only used when the house is sold out. The building is now on the GLC list as being of architectural merit, notably for the relief-work of Shakespeare characters in the auditorium and the gold leaf decoration on plasterwork and decorative mouldings. The theatre has a varied policy of some fortnightly repertory, some straight runs of new plays and some touring companies, with the emphasis on light entertainment. There is a small cafe and 2 bars, and wheelchairs can be accommodated in the front stalls. Concessions operate for parties, pensioners and schoolchildren. There is no private parking but plenty of space on Richmond Green after meter hours, and 2 car parks close by.

Nearest station: Richmond, on the District underground line and on Southern Region. Buses: 27, 33, 37, 65, 290, Green Line Coaches: 714, 716, 716a.

ROUND HOUSE
Round House, Chalk Farm Road, NW1 8BG.
Box office: 267 2564.

The Round House, built in 1846 as a locomotive turntable shed, has been used as an Arts Centre since 1968 and is run by The Round House Trust Limited, a registered charity. Presents 4 to 6 week runs of experimental theatre, plus films, children's events, concerts and exhibitions. **Godspell, Oh! Calcutta!,** and Arnold Wesker's **The Friends** had their first London performances here, and **Rabelais** its English-language premiere. Seating in the main auditorium for between 500 and 650, with an additional 100 seats in the gallery. There is an open-plan stage with adaptable arena. Restaurant (267 2541 for reservations) and full bar and snack bar facilities. The theatre is open from 10 am to midnight. Price concessions offered to party bookings and to students at most performances. The Round House has its own car park adjacent to the building, and there is also easy street parking.

Nearest underground: Chalk Farm.
Buses: 24, 31, 68.

SHAW
Shaw Theatre, 100 Euston Road, NW1

Box office: 388 1394.

Opened in July 1971, the Shaw is leased by Camden Borough Council at a peppercorn rent to Michael Croft for his National Youth Theatre and the professional Dolphin Theatre Company, and their productions alternate. The NYT's repertoire is composed of Shakespeare productions and new plays specially commissioned for them, notably by Peter Terson who has given them probably their biggest success, **Zigger Zagger**. The Dolphin Company provides new plays and the classics presented for short runs. The theatre has a seating capacity of 510 on 2 levels. The stage is proscenium-arched with a semi-thrust, and air-conditioning is installed. There is a licensed bar and a coffee bar. Price concessions vary, but are emphasised during NYT seasons, with very cheap rates for students and young people. Wheelchairs can be accommodated in the auditorium. A car park is opposite the theatre entrance.

Nearest underground: Euston, King's Cross or St Pancras. **Buses** passing the theatre are: 14, 30, 73, 77a, 77c.

THEATRE ROYAL, STRATFORD E
Theatre Royal, Salway Road, Stratford, E15.
Box office: 534 0310.

This lovely little Victorian theatre (now officially listed as a historic monument) set in the East End of London is the home of Joan Littlewood's Theatre Workshop. It was here that **Oh! What a Lovely War**, and many other Theatre Workshop successes had their first performance under her direction in the 1950s and early 1960s. The theatre is usually closed during the whole of August. There is a proscenium stage facing on to a 508-seat auditorium on 3 levels. No restaurant, but a good bar service. A limited number of wheelchairs can be accommodated in the stalls. Good parking space in surrounding streets.

Nearest underground: Stratford, on the Central line. **Buses:** not recommended as there is no direct route from central London.

WATFORD PALACE
Palace Theatre, Clarendon Road, Watford WD1 1JZ, Herts.
Box office: 92 25671

Built in 1908 as a music hall, the Palace has a new foyer/box office area added in 1964. It is now the home of the Watford Theatre Company run by Watford Civic Theatre Trust. The present Director, Stephen Hollis, runs a policy of 2½ week repertory, and in the past few years the theatre has presented the British premieres of Tennessee Williams' **Sweet Bird of Youth**, Maureen Duffy's **The Silk Room** and Kevin Laffan's **The Superannuated Man**. There is a Theatre in Education group attached to the company, as well as frequent lunchtime shows, Sunday concerts, after-the-play discussions, lectures and other events. The theatre is usually closed during August. A proscenium stage faces on to a 690-seat auditorium on 3 levels. A licensed bar opens for both evening and lunchtime performances and for the latter you can also eat your sandwiches to musical accompaniment. Numerous price concessions available. There is a large municipal car park at the back of the theatre.

Nearest underground: Watford Junction, on the Bakerloo line; also London Midland Region, which takes 20 minutes from Euston. **Buses:** not recommended as there is no direct route from central London.

WIMBLEDON (touring date)
Wimbledon Theatre, Wimbledon Broadway, London, SW19.
Box office: 946 5211.

Built in 1910, this Edwardian theatre is protected by a Preservation Order; its last major renovation was in 1969 and it has a yearly refurbishing. Wimbledon is a touring-date theatre, and there is also an annual pantomime season here and a summer repertory season presented by Newpalm Productions from early July to mid-August. The theatre is closed during Wimbledon Tennis Fortnight each June. It has a seating capacity of 2,000 divided between stalls, circle and gallery, facing on to a proscenium stage. There are 4 licensed bars, and sandwiches and coffee are also available in the circle bar. Substantial price concessions are offered at mid-week matinees to school parties, students and pensioners. For disabled people, there is space in the stalls for 4 wheelchairs, and access to lavatories without negotiating steps. A car park for 600 cars is within 200 yards of the theatre, and there is parking space in side streets in the evening.

Underground: Wimbledon, on the District line, also Southern Region. **Buses:** 14, 22, 30 and 74 to Putney Bridge, then change to 93.

Festivals

ALDEBURGH

Snape Maltings Concert Hall, Snape, Saxmundham, Suffolk.
Box office: 072885 2935.

The Aldeburgh Festival of Music and the Arts (festival office: High Street, Aldeburgh, Suffolk) was founded as an annual one-week Festival in June each year in 1948 by Benjamin Britten, Eric Crozier and Peter Pears—Aldeburgh being Britten's home town. Britten premieres have included **Let's Make An Opera** (1949), **Noyes Fludde** (1958), **A Midsummer Night's Dream** (1960) and **Death in Venice** (1973).

The Maltings Concert Hall at Snape, which now houses spring and summer arts festival programmes as well as the major June festival, was built in 1969 and opened in 1970 after a fire had destroyed the original Concert Hall. It has an open stage and seats 820 for opera and 760 for ballet. Air conditioning is installed. In 1973 ticket prices ranged from £2 to £3 but concessions are made for parties of 20 or more for the spring and summer weekend festival programmes. There is a self-service restaurant which does not take reservations. Refreshments may also be found at the nearby Plough and Sail Pub. Arrangements can be made to accommodate wheelchair visitors providing notice is given 24 hours beforehand.

Aldeburgh is 100 miles from London by road. The journey by rail takes approximately three hours from London's Liverpool Street Station. There is only one through train per day to the Festival's closest station, Saxmundham. All other trains for Saxmundham involve a change at Ipswich. Saxmundham is four miles from the Maltings and special theatre buses meet trains 45 minutes before the start of the performance. A local bus service meets most trains but visitors wanting further details should ring the Festival Office: 072885 2935 where advance booking arrangements for tickets are also made. Convenient hotels: The Wentworth (072885 2312), The Brudenell (072885 2071) The White Lion (072885 2720) and The Uplands (072885 2420).

CHICHESTER

Chichester Festival Theatre, Oaklands Park, Chichester, Sussex.
Box office: 0243 86333.

The theatre opened in July, 1962 under the direction of Laurence Olivier, and on his appointment as Director of the National Theatre he managed both. One of the highlights of this period was the now famous production of **Uncle Vanya** directed by Olivier and in which he co-starred with Michael Redgrave and Joan Plowright. John Clements succeeded him as Director from 1966-73 and is himself to be succeeded by Keith Michell in 1974. A summer season is presented here each year, extending from May to September, when four new productions are given, ranging from Shakespeare and the classics to modern plays. World and British premieres have included Robert Bolt's **Vivat! Vivat Regina!**, Anouilh's **The Fighting Cock** and **Dear Antoine** and Ustinov's **The Unknown Soldier and his Wife**. It is usual for one of the season's productions to transfer to London at the end of the Festival. At Christmas, 1972, for the first time a Christmas production was mounted. A foyer bookstall sells souvenir programmes, books and theatre magazines. The theatre seats 1,394 round an open thrust stage—a design inspired by Sir Tyrone Guthrie's Shakespeare Festival Theatre at Stratford, Ontario, Canada. Air-conditioning is installed. Price reductions are made for block bookings of 20 and over. There is a restaurant (0243 82219 for reservations) and 2 bars. A large car park is at the back of the theatre. Wheelchair facilities are available on request.

Chichester is 70 miles by road from London. Trains take 1 hour 40 minutes from Victoria to Chichester station, 15 minutes' walk away. Convenient hotels: The Dolphin & Anchor, West Street (0243 85121); The Ship, North Street (0243 82028); and the Chichester Motel (0243 86351).

154 Theatre Guide

EDINBURGH

The Edinburgh International Festival takes place each year for three weeks in the late summer. (The 1973 Festival ran from August 19 to September 8.) During this time, drama, opera and ballet companies, conductors, solo musicians and orchestras from all over the world as well as from the UK and Scotland, are invited to perform in the City's many theatres and concert halls. There is also a 2-week Film Festival. A highlight of each year is the floodlit Military Tattoo staged by the Army against the background of the Castle esplanade. The Festival's present Director is Peter Diamand. Inaugurated in 1947, the Edinburgh Festival had as its first Director Rudolf Bing, at that time Director and General Manager of Glyndebourne Opera, whose long-cherished ambition it had been to make Edinburgh an international centre for the arts.

In recent years the official Festival programme has been enlarged with an increasing number of "fringe" productions presented by university and other drama and folk groups in church halls, cellars and any other available space. It was, in fact, as part of this "fringe" activity during the 1960 Festival that **Beyond The Fringe** made its first appearance, and helped launch the satire boom in Britain in the 1960s, with its offshoots such as the famous television weekly series, **That Was The Week, That Was** and the still-flourishing satirical magazine, **Private Eye**. Tom Stoppard also first came to notice on the fringe with the Edinburgh premiere in 1966 of his **Rosencrantz and Guildenstern are Dead**.

The Festival can also claim to have promoted a very important new trend in theatre architecture, for it was in 1948 that Tyrone Guthrie, invited to direct Sir David Lyndsay's 16th century satire **The Three Estates**, was offered the Assembly Hall of the Church of Scotland as a possible auditorium. The large projecting platform in the Hall, previously only used for church assemblies, gave Guthrie his first opportunity to experiment with virtually theatre-in-the-round conditions which he later developed in his work at Stratford, Ontario and the Guthrie Theatre, Minneapolis, and which was to lead to the radical re-thinking on stage design in new British theatres like Chichester and the Sheffield Crucible.

All information regarding details of the programme for the Edinburgh Festival, booking arrangements, membership of the Festival Club and Festival Guild, can be obtained from the Festival Offices, 21 Market Street, Edinburgh EH1 1BW, Scotland (031-226 4001) or from the Festival's London office at 29 St James's Street, SW1 (01-839 2611).

Edinburgh is 373 miles by road from London. Trains from King's Cross to Edinburgh Waverley station take 6 hours during the day, or slightly longer overnight. Flights from Heathrow to Edinburgh airport take approximately 1½ hours. Recommended hotels: Caledonian in Princes Street (031-225 2433); George in George Street (031-225 1251); North British in Princes Street (031-556 2414). The Festival Offices (see above) will also provide lists of cheaper accommodation.

GLYNDEBOURNE

**Glyndebourne Festival Opera House, Glyndebourne, Lewes, Sussex BN8 5UU.
Box office: 0273 812411 (London branch box office: 01-935 1010).**

Founded by John Christie and his wife Audrey Mildmay in 1934, Glyndebourne Opera is housed in a building dating from that year set beside Christie's beautiful Tudor country house and garden. The international festival, which started with the presentation of Mozart operas, now has a repertoire expanded to cover the whole operatic field from the earliest baroque works of the mid-17th century to modern; in 1970 Glyndebourne commissioned **The Rising of the Moon** from Nicholas Maw, and a fairly typical 1970s programme was that for the 1973 Festival, which consisted of Mozart's **Die Zauberflote** and Le Nozze di Figaro, Monteverdi's Il Ritorno d'Ulisse in Patria, Richard Strauss's Capriccio and the first production in this country of von Einem's **The Visit of the Old Lady,** with Peter Hall directing the Monteverdi and the second Mozart. The present chairman is George Christie, son of the founder who died in 1962. In 1972 the Glyndebourne Touring Opera company was formed and for the first time operas from the previous season toured larger regional centres in this country, using the original sets and costumes but sometimes with younger and lesser-known artists in the company. Glyndebourne is closed between opera festivals, which usually run from late May to mid-August. The grounds are not open to the public but to ticket-holders only. Evening dress, formal or informal, is "recommended", and performances start early (the longer ones at 4 pm) to allow for the "long interval". The intimate, very uncluttered auditorium seats just under 800 on 3 levels with boxes, before a proscenium stage. Prices are high: from £8 for a front stall to £3.50 in the upper balcony, and there are no price concessions. Even so, unless you can take advantage of the Members' priority booking scheme you have to be early on the scene to be successful in getting tickets. There is a main foyer bar, and 3 restaurants (0273 812510 for reservations) all of which serve dinner in the "long interval". Details of how to order your dinner and wine in advance are sent with your tickets, but for many people a large part of the attraction of Glyndebourne is to bring their own picnic and eat it in the grounds. There is space in the auditorium for 2 wheelchairs. A large car park is at the back of the building.

Glyndebourne, just south of Lewes, is 54 miles by road from London (allow a full 2 hours if driving through Central London). Trains take 1 hour 10 minutes from Victoria (also stopping at Clapham Junction and East Croydon) to Glynde station, where coaches meet passengers and take them direct to the Opera House. After the performance, passengers are taken by coach to Lewes for the London train. Special rail-road return tickets are available when buying rail tickets in London, on presentation of Glyndebourne Opera tickets. Recommended hotels: The Ringmer (0273 348) about 2 miles away and late meals served by arrangement; also The Grand in Brighton (0273 26301) and The Burlington in Eastbourne (0323 22724) both within a 10-mile radius.

PITLOCHRY

Pitlochry Festival Theatre, Pitlochry, Perthshire, Scotland, PH16 5DR.
Box office: Pitlochry 233 (dial 100 and ask operator for number).

The first Pitlochry Festival was held in 1951 in a tented structure replaced by the present building 2 years later. Its director is Kenneth Ireland. Festivals extend from April to September each year, during which time 8 productions are presented in repertoire, together with Sunday concerts, recitals and art exhibitions. Works by Scottish writers, especially Bridie, usually make up a good share of festival material, as well as the classics and some new plays which are given their premieres here.

The theatre is closed from October to March, when the company undertakes Scottish Arts Council-sponsored tours to Aberdeen and other arts centres. Attached to the main company is the younger Theatre in Education group, which travels over 9 counties in Northern Scotland. Each April there is a Festival preview with a Mini-Festival Weekend of concerts and poetry readings. The Festival Theatre has a wide proscenium stage with an apron, facing on to a one-tier raked amphitheatre seating 502. The usual price concessions are made for parties, pensioners and children. The Brown Trout Restaurant (box office number for reservations) serves lunch and dinner. There is also a cocktail bar serving sandwiches, tea and coffee to ticketholders only, plus a Sun Lounge Café open to the public during the day for lunch and high tea. Also a tea garden. There is easy access to the auditorium for wheelchairs from street level. Two car parks adjoin the theatre.

Pitlochry is 444 miles by road from London. Trains (overnight only) take 10 hours from Euston to Pitlochry station, which is 5 minutes away. Flights from Heathrow to Edinburgh (68 miles away) take approximately 1½ hours. Recommended hotels: Atholl Palace (Pitlochry 66); Pitlochry Hydro (Pitlochry 480); Fisher's (Pitlochry 284); Scotland's (Pitlochry 185). Pitlochry is a busy tourist centre, and accommodation enquiries will be dealt with by the Pitlochry Tourist Association (Pitlochry 215). Cheap hostel accommodation for 1 or more nights recommended at Strathtummel Youth Hostel, 3½ miles outside Pitlochry (Killiecrankie 217).

STRATFORD-UPON-AVON

Royal Shakespeare Theatre, Waterside, Stratford-upon-Avon, Warwickshire.
Box office: 0789 2271.

The present theatre (formerly known as the Shakespeare Memorial Theatre) was built in 1932 to replace the original (built 1879) on the same site, burned down 4 years earlier. The very first Shakespeare Jubilee in Stratford was presented in 1769 by David Garrick in a specially-erected pavilion by the Avon, but it was not until over a century later, with the advent of Frank Benson, that festivals of any significance were held here. The present Director of the Royal Shakespeare Company is Trevor Nunn who succeeded Peter Hall, inaugurator of the company in its present form with a

London home for the presentation of non-Shakespeare productions as well as a Stratford base. The Company's long-standing policy in Stratford is the presentation of an annual Shakespeare Season from April to December, in which up to 8 productions are given in repertoire, with possibly one non-Shakespeare Elizabethan work among them. Some of the more successful productions are later presented in London, at the Aldwych. Theatre-goround, an off-shoot company composed of members of the RSC, presents small-scale productions for touring and for the occasional performance in Stratford itself. The Royal Shakespeare Theatre's summer school is held in the Shakespeare Institute each August, providing courses of lectures and discussions in which distinguished speakers take part (details from the theatre on receipt of a stamped addressed envelope). Other amenities include the sale of posters, postcards and records concerned with RSC productions. For details of the Picture Gallery, see the **Theatre Collections** section of this book. The theatre is closed for a few weeks during the winter, but for the rest of the between-Season period it is used as a touring-date theatre. There is a seating capacity of 1,518 on 3 levels, with boxes. The proscenium stage had a number of technical additions in 1972 including the installation of hydraulic lifts. Air-conditioning is installed. There is a large licensed restaurant (0789 3226 for reservations) serving lunch, dinner and after-theatre supper as well as a self-service restaurant and bars on each level. Wheelchair facilities available by prior arrangement. Parking for 84 cars in the theatre forecourt, or in a large municipal car park by Clopton Bridge, 200 yards away.

Stratford-upon-Avon is 91 miles by road from London. Trains take 2¼ hours from Paddington to Stratford station, 15 minutes' walk away. Recommended hotels: The Arden on Waterside (0789 3874); Hilton (0789 67511); Swan's Nest (0789 66761); The Shakespeare, High Street (0789 3631). Cheap hostel accommodation for 1 or more nights available at YHA, Hemingford near Alveston (Alveston 2823—dial 100 and ask operator for number).

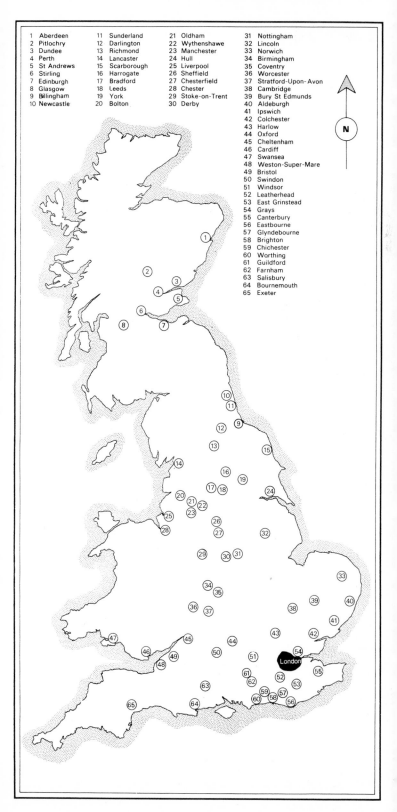

1 Aberdeen	11 Sunderland	21 Oldham	31 Nottingham
2 Pitlochry	12 Darlington	22 Wythenshawe	32 Lincoln
3 Dundee	13 Richmond	23 Manchester	33 Norwich
4 Perth	14 Lancaster	24 Hull	34 Birmingham
5 St Andrews	15 Scarborough	25 Liverpool	35 Coventry
6 Stirling	16 Harrogate	26 Sheffield	36 Worcester
7 Edinburgh	17 Bradford	27 Chesterfield	37 Stratford-Upon-Avon
8 Glasgow	18 Leeds	28 Chester	38 Cambridge
9 Billingham	19 York	29 Stoke-on-Trent	39 Bury St Edmunds
10 Newcastle	20 Bolton	30 Derby	40 Aldeburgh

41 Ipswich
42 Colchester
43 Harlow
44 Oxford
45 Cheltenham
46 Cardiff
47 Swansea
48 Weston-Super-Mare
49 Bristol
50 Swindon
51 Windsor
52 Leatherhead
53 East Grinstead
54 Grays
55 Canterbury
56 Eastbourne
57 Glyndebourne
58 Brighton
59 Chichester
60 Worthing
61 Guildford
62 Farnham
63 Salisbury
64 Bournemouth
65 Exeter

N

Regions

Aberdeen

HIS MAJESTY'S (touring date)
His Majesty's Theatre, Rosemount Viaduct, Aberdeen, Scotland.
Box office: 0224 28080.

Built in 1906, this touring-date theatre presents a programme of visiting companies ranging from opera and ballet to pantomime and straight plays. It has a seating capacity of 1,800 with a proscenium stage. Price concessions are made to students, schoolchildren and pensioners. There are 2 lounge bars but no restaurant. A multi-storey car park is 200 yards away.

Aberdeen is 492 miles by road from London. Trains take 10 hours from King's Cross to Aberdeen station, 5 minutes away. Flights from Heathrow to Aberdeen (6 miles away) take 1 hour 50 minutes. Recommended hotels: The Station (0224 27214); The Caledonian (0224 29233).

Billingham

FORUM
Forum Theatre, Town Centre, Billingham, Teesside TS23 2LJ.
Box office: 0642 552663.

Opened in 1968, the Forum is part of a large complex also housing an ice rink, swimming pool and other facilities. There is a mixed-programme policy of presenting "home productions" interspersed with visiting opera, ballet and drama companies, and some new work has been given its first performances here. The seating capacity is 630 on 3 levels before a proscenium stage. The usual price concessions are made to pensioners, students and children. A restaurant (0642 551381 ext. 67 for reservations) is open for dinner, and there is also a snack bar and 2 licensed bars. Ample free parking available.

Billingham is 247 miles by road from London. Trains take 4 hours from King's Cross to Billingham station, 10 minutes away. Flights from Heathrow to Teesside airport, 10 miles away, take 1¼ hours. Recommended hotels in Stockton-on-Tees: Billingham Arms (0642 552104); Holmesdale (0642 554935).

Birmingham

ALEXANDRA
Alexandra Theatre, Station Street, Birmingham B5 4DS.
Box office: 021 643 1231.

Built in 1901, this theatre had a new foyer added in 1969. Its policy is the presentation of fortnightly repertory for 26 weeks of the year, touring companies for 12 weeks, and pantomime for 10 weeks. The repertory company occasionally undertakes tours outside Birmingham. The Alexandra has a seating capacity of 1,664 on 3 levels, and a proscenium stage. There is a snack bar and 3 licensed bars. A multi-storey car park is close by, and street parking is available in the evening. Wheelchairs can enter direct into the stalls, which are at street level.

MIDLANDS ARTS CENTRE
Midlands Arts Centre, Cannon Hill Park, Birmingham 12 9QH.
Box office: 021-440 3838.

Built in 1967, the Centre houses both the Midlands Arts Theatre Company and the Cannon Hill Puppet Theatre. Its policy is to present plays of all kinds for all groups, beginning with the youngest of children. In recent years it has produced world premieres of Henry Livings' This Jockey Drives Late Nights and David Cregan's How We Held the Square as well as 8 puppet productions originated by the company. In addition there is a small Theatre in Schools unit, and the performance of late-night productions and experimental work. The 3 auditoria comprise a 220-seat Studio Theatre, a 100-seat Hexagon Theatre and a 1,000-seat Open Air Arena. The Studio and the Hexagon have air-conditioning and open-stage areas. Price reductions are available for certain performances for students, apprentices, children and Cannon Hill members. There is an unlicensed restaurant (021-440 4221 for reservations) as well as a coffee bar, both open from 10 am to 10.30 pm. Wheelchairs can be accommodated in the Studio Theatre only. There is ample parking facilities on the Arts Centre site.

REPERTORY THEATRE
Birmingham Repertory Theatre, Broad Street, Birmingham B1 2EP.
Box office: 021-236 4455.

This new building opened in October, 1971, to succeed the original theatre in Station Street which Sir Barry Jackson, a pioneer of the repertory movement in this country, founded in 1913, and of which he remained Governing Director until his death in 1961. The present director of the new Birmingham Rep is Michael Simpson, and under him a 3-weekly repertoire system is operated, presenting the best of world drama, both classical and modern. In recent years probably their biggest success has been the world premiere of Peter Luke's **Hadrian VII**, presented in Birmingham under Peter Dews' directorship before its eventual transfer to London. Monthly Sunday concerts are also organised. The new theatre has a seating capacity of 901 in one steep rake, with a proscenium stage convertible to partial thrust. Air-conditioning is installed. The **Brum Studio**, attached, was opened a year after the main theatre; it seats between 100 and 120 and its own independent productions tour for 1 week out of 4. The Studio is also used for late-night folk sessions. Both auditoria are closed during August. Price concessions of up to 25% are offered to parties of 10 or more, and the West Midlands Arts Association subsidises a travel voucher system. Also included in the many reduction schemes are students, pensioners and members of the Playgoers' Society. There is a restaurant (021 236 5115 for reservations) serving lunch and dinner, and a coffee bar open for snacks all day. The Mezzanine Bar serves cold lunches. Space for 6 wheelchairs in the main auditorium, with reduced-price tickets for each escort. A large public car park within 300 yards.

Birmingham is 110 miles by road from London. Trains take 1 hour 40 minutes from Euston to Birmingham New Street station, which is 5 minutes away from the Alexandra, 20 minutes (by bus) from the Midlands Arts Centre and 15 minutes away from the Repertory Theatre. The Express Coach Service running from Victoria Coach Station in London up the M1 takes about 1½ hours to Digbeth Coach Station, Birmingham. Recommended hotels: Albany (021 643 8171); Midland (021 643 2601); Royal Angus (021 236 4211); Market (021 643 1134).

Bolton

OCTAGON
Octagon Theatre, Howell Croft South, Bolton, Lancashire BL1 1SB.
Box office: 0204 20661.

Built in 1967, this new theatre has a flexible stage with a seating capacity which therefore ranges between 324 for a thrust stage, 350 for an open-end production and 420 in the round. Under its present Artistic Director, Wilfred Harrison, the Octagon presents 3-weekly straight runs of the classics, established modern work and a number of specially-commissioned local interest plays. In the past few years they have had 8 premieres. There is a small studio with no actual stage area but which can be adapted to seat 150. The Octagon acts as host to local amateur companies during the summer, and is closed for 2 weeks in July. Air-conditioning is installed. There is a licensed bar and a coffee bar open during the day as well as at performance times. Price concessions are offered to pensioners and students at some performances. There is accommodation for wheelchairs on the first level of the auditorium.

Bolton is 200 miles by road from London. Trains take 3½ to 4 hours from Euston (changing at Manchester from the local Piccadilly to Victoria stations) to Bolton station, 5 minutes away. Flights from Heathrow to Manchester airport (16 miles away) take 45 minutes. Recommended hotels: The Pack Horse (0204 26661); The Last Drop (0204 51933).

Bournemouth

PAVILION (touring date)
Pavilion Theatre, Westover Road, Bournemouth, Hants.
Box office: 0202 25861.

Built in 1929, this touring-date theatre was refurbished in 1971. Its attractions range from straight plays to music-hall, pantomime, ballet and musicals. There is a seating capacity of 1,518 on 2 levels before a proscenium stage. Refreshments are provided by The Lucullus Restaurant (0202 28404 for reservations) and a licensed bar. There are no special facilities for wheelchairs, but a limited number can be accommodated by arrangement. Parking space available in front of the theatre.

Bournemouth is 112 miles by road from London. Trains take 1 hour 40 minutes from Waterloo to Bournemouth station, 5 minutes away.

Recommended hotels: Highbury (0202 21059); The Michelmoor (0202 26145); Semel et Semper (0202 63911).

Bradford

ALHAMBRA (touring date)
The Alhambra, Morley Street, Bradford 7, Yorkshire.
Box office: 0274 27007.

A touring-date theatre which first opened in 1914, the Alhambra has a seating capacity of 1,625 facing on to a proscenium stage. It is generally closed for a few weeks in the summer. There is a bar on each floor. Parking space available by the Central Library close by.

Bradford is 195 miles by road from London. Trains take between 3 and 4 hours from King's Cross to Bradford Exchange station, 6 minutes away. Flights from Heathrow to Leeds/Bradford airport, 4 miles away, take 1 hour. Recommended hotels: Victoria (0274 28706); Midland (0274 25663).

Brighton

GARDNER CENTRE
Gardner Centre for the Arts, University of Sussex, Falmer, Brighton, Sussex BN1 9RA.
Box office: 0273 685861.

The Gardner Centre, endowed as an Arts Centre for the Brighton/Sussex region, opened in 1969. It is set in parkland on the campus of Sussex University, on the main Brighton/Lewes Road 4 miles from the centre of Brighton. There is no permanent company, and at the beginning of 1973 the Centre's artistic policy was under review, the project having had a rather uncertain beginning. However, under its first director, Walter Eysselinck, some interesting world premieres were given, including new plays by John McGrath and Michael Hastings. There is no studio theatre but in the Art Gallery exhibitions change about every 6 weeks. The single-tier auditorium has 3 separate stages with a maximum seating capacity of 391 which varies with the changes to open-stage or end-stage presentations. Air-conditioning is installed. Price concessions are made to pensioners, students and parties. There is a bar serving light meals on request (box office number for reservations) as well as a licensed bar. A large car park is nearby.

THEATRE ROYAL (touring date)
Theatre Royal, New Road, Brighton, Sussex.
Box office: 0273 28488.

Dating from around 1804, this proscenium-stage theatre seats 961, divided between stalls, royal circle, second circle, gallery and 7 boxes. A number of redecorating and modernising schemes have been undertaken this century. A large percentage of West End productions appear here on their way to London. There is no restaurant but there are 6 licensed bars. No special parking facilities, so street-parking is recommended.

Brighton is 50 miles by road from London. Trains take 1 hour from Victoria to Brighton station, 10 minutes away from the Theatre Royal, and to Falmer station (changing at Brighton), 5 minutes away from the Gardner Centre. Recommended hotels: Royal Albion (0273 29202); Shelley's (079 16 2361); The White Hart (079 16 4676). The second and third hotels are closer to Falmer.

Bristol

BRISTOL OLD VIC
The Bristol Old Vic Company controls 3 buildings: The Theatre Royal and New Vic, King Street, Bristol BS1 4ED (box office: 0272 24388) and the Little Theatre, Colston Street, Bristol BS1 (box office: 0272 21182).

The Theatre Royal, built in 1766, is the oldest theatre in the country with a continuous working history, and is one of the few surviving examples of 18th century theatre architecture in Europe. It was saved from the indignity of being the home of variety and pantomime in 1943 when, as Britain's first state-aided theatre, it re-opened as the Bristol Old Vic, with its own drama school founded 3 years later. In 1971 the building underwent major structural renovation and re-opened in 1972 with a studio theatre, The New Vic, added. The Bristol Old Vic also provides a company and stage-management team to staff the Bristol Corporation's 360-seat Little Theatre where special seasons are presented like that in the autumn of 1972 dedicated to modern American drama. The Bristol Old Vic, which is one of the leading regional companies (its Artistic Director, Val May, has held the post since 1961) presents new productions in the Theatre Royal for straight runs of 1 month, and has an impressive record for premiering new plays and musicals which have subsequently transferred to London. The Theatre Royal has a proscenium stage before an auditorium seating about 658 divided between stalls, dress circle, upper circle, boxes and gallery. The studio theatre, The New Vic, which is air-conditioned, seats about 100 and has a flexible stage. Here is presented an international repertory of avant-garde new writing as well as a whole range of projects including daytime work with children. Wheelchairs can be accommodated in the Theatre Royal in boxes only. There are 3 bars, which also serve coffee. Open sandwiches are available an hour before performance time. Price concessions at the Theatre Royal include 1 free ticket for every group of 10 or more, and a Travel Subsidy Voucher Scheme operates. A multi-storey car park is in Prince Street, 2 minutes away. The Bristol Old Vic is closed in July and August.

Bristol is 120 miles by road from London. Trains take 2 hours from Paddington to Bristol Temple Meads station, 15 minutes away. Recommended hotels: The Clifton (0272 34420); Hawthorn's (0272 38432); Grand Spa (0272 38955).

Bury St Edmunds

THEATRE ROYAL (touring date)
Theatre Royal, Westgate Street, Bury St Edmunds, Suffolk.
Box office: 0284 5469.

This lovely 17th century theatre was restored to its proper use in 1965. One of its claims to fame is that Brandon Thomas' farce **Charley's Aunt** had its first performance here in 1892. The Theatre Royal has a seating capacity of 333 divided between stalls, grand circle, dress circle and gallery. An air-cooling system is installed. The theatre is closed from June to early September. Its present policy is to operate as a touring-date theatre, although in the past efforts have been made to establish it as the home of repertory. Price concessions granted to Theatre Club members, block bookings, pensioners and students. There is a bar and a coffee bar, and wheelchairs can be accommodated in the side boxes. Parking space available in surrounding streets.

Bury St Edmunds is 65 miles by road from London. Trains take 2½ hours from Liverpool Street to Bury St Edmunds station, 10 minutes away.

Recommended hotels: The Suffolk (0284 3995); The Angel (0284 3926); Everard's (0284 5384).

Cambridge

ARTS
Arts Theatre, Peas Hill, Cambridge.
Box office: 0223 52000.

Built in 1936, the Arts seats 600 before a proscenium stage. It acts as a home base for the Cambridge Theatre Company (see under **Companies**) as well as being a touring date for companies presenting plays, ballet and opera. It also presents concerts and University shows. A Young Theatre Group meets on Saturday mornings. The Arts Cinema, 2 minutes away, is a specialist cinema showing the best films from the world's studios, un-dubbed. Price concessions are offered for parties of 20 or more. There is an Arts Restaurant (0223 59302 for reservations) in St Edward's Passage where theatre patrons get a discount, as well as a Roof Garden buffet serving lunch and supper. Parking in Lion Yard adjacent to the theatre.

Cambridge is 55 miles by road from London. Trains take 1¼ hours from King's Cross or Liverpool Street to Cambridge station, 10 minutes away. You can get back to London after an evening performance as there are trains at 10.25 pm and 12.45 am. Recommended hotels: The University Arms (0223 51241); Royal Cambridge (0223 51631).

Canterbury

MARLOWE
Marlowe Theatre, St Margaret's Street, Canterbury, Kent.
Box office: 0227 64747.

Converted into a theatre in 1951, the Marlowe has a resident company presenting repertory, but it also houses touring opera, ballet and puppet companies as well as orchestral concerts, and the occasional film show and lecture. Their repertory programme changes from Brecht and Ibsen to established London successes and some new work. The Marlowe is closed for 3 weeks in July. Seating capacity is 652 on 2 levels before a proscenium stage. There is a licensed bar and also a coffee and sandwich bar. Wheelchairs can be accommodated in the auditorium. A car park adjoins the theatre. Reduced prices are offered to pensioners, students and parties of 12 and over, and an Arts Council-subsidised transport scheme exists here for parties within a 50-mile radius of the town.

Canterbury is 60 miles by road from London. Trains take 1¼ hours from Victoria to Canterbury East station, 7 minutes away. Recommended hotels: Slatters (0227 63271); County (0227 66266); Chaucer (0227 64427).

Cardiff

CASSON STUDIO

The Casson Studio Theatre, 56 Ruby Street, Cardiff.
Box office: 0222 27500.

Home of the Welsh Theatre Company, the Casson Studio, under its present Director, Michael Geliot, operates a repertory system with occasional visits from other companies. The theatre is closed during the summer. In the past year, the Casson has given the first performances of 3 new plays, by Elaine Morgan, G O M Jones and Ewart Alexander. The theatre seats 80 before an open-plan stage. Half-price concessions are made to students at certain performances. Refreshment is provided by a bar, a soup kitchen and a coffee bar. There are no special wheelchair facilities but a few can be accommodated in the auditorium. There is easy parking in the cul-de-sac by the theatre.

NEW (touring date)

New Theatre, Park Place, Cardiff CF1 3LN.
Box office: 0222 32446.

This Victorian theatre was built in 1904, and has had a major refurbishing operation between 1970 and 1972. There is a proscenium stage facing on to a 1,180-seat auditorium divided between stalls, front circle, rear circle, upper circle and boxes. A touring-date theatre, it is also the home of the Welsh National Opera Company. It is closed during July and August. There is an active theatre society of some 3,000 members. Catering facilities comprise 3 theatre bars and a coffee bar. There is a restaurant (0222 23471 for reservations) at the adjacent Park Hotel. Up to 4 wheelchairs can be accommodated in the auditorium. A multi-storey car park is opposite.

Cardiff is 150 miles by road from London. Trains take 2½ hours from Paddington to Cardiff General station, 20 minutes away from the Casson Studio, and 5 minutes from the New. Recommended hotels: The Park (0222 23471); The Queen's (0222 30601); The Angel (0222 32633).

Cheltenham

EVERYMAN

Everyman Theatre, Regent Street, Cheltenham, Gloucestershire.
Box office: 0242 25544.

This well-preserved late Victorian theatre had as its architect Frank Matcham, who also designed the Palladium, the Coliseum and other London theatres. It is a Grade 2 listed building. The Everyman Company has a policy of 3-weekly repertory, with some visiting ballet companies and 2 weeks of local amateur productions each year. It has a number of premieres to its credit, the most recent being Andrew Rosenthal's Gathering of the Clan, and plays here range from the best of new established writing to the classics. Action Theatre, a breakaway group, takes over the theatre on some Monday evenings to present works by such writers as Arrabal, and for folk concerts, poetry recitals and other events. The theatre is closed for 5 weeks during May and June each year. Seating capacity is 679 before a proscenium stage. Price concessions operate for pensioners, and there is a half-price Travel Subsidy Scheme financed by the South Western Arts Association. A restaurant (box office number for reservations) provides pre-theatre suppers, and morning coffee is available to the public in the Long Bar. Matinee teas and interval refreshments are also available. Space is permitted for only 1 wheelchair in the auditorium. A public car park is behind the theatre, and space is also available in the surrounding streets.

Cheltenham is 98 miles by road from London. Trains take 2½ hours from Paddington to Cheltenham station, 5 minutes' drive away. Recommended hotels: The Plough, next door to the theatre (0242 22087); The Queen's (0242 54724); The George (0242 24732).

Chester

GATEWAY

Gateway Theatre, Hamilton Place, Chester.
Box office: 0244 40393.

Built in 1968, the Gateway is in the centre of a new shopping precinct. Under its Director, Julian Oldfield, there is a 3-weekly repertory system of "plays aimed at middle-of-the-road theatregoers with occasional forays into more adventurous work." They have two world premieres and an

English premiere to their credit. There is a studio theatre, where more avant-garde productions are staged. The Gateway seats between 440 and 500, depending on whether the large proscenium stage is used or whether the apron with moveable thrusts is extended from it. Seating is on one steeply-raked single tier. Air-conditioning is installed. The studio theatre, which has no set stage area, seats up to 50, and the company here runs a theatre-in-education team, a youth group and Saturday morning sessions for younger children. There are also exhibitions mounted in the Hart Room during the summer and the pre-Christmas period. A licensed bar is open at lunchtime as well as in the evening, and a coffee bar is open all day. There is no theatre restaurant, but the Gateway has a "curtain-up" arrangement with the local Berni Inn. The usual price reductions operate for pensioners, students and parties of 10 and over. There is a moveable ramp for wheelchairs, and a limited number can be accommodated in the auditorium. Plenty of parking space under and in front of the theatre.

Chester is 182 miles by road from London. Trains take 2½ hours from Euston to Chester General station, 15 minutes' walk away. Recommended hotels: Grosvenor (0244 24024); Blossoms (0244 23186); Riverside (0244 26580).

Chesterfield
CIVIC
Chesterfield Civic Theatre, Corporation Street, Chesterfield, Derbyshire.
Box office: 0246 2901.

This Victorian building, built in 1875, became a theatre in 1949. Under its present director, Derek Coleman, it runs a fortnightly repertory system, and has two premieres to its credit in the past few years. Plays range from the best of established modern work to the occasional classic and the local documentary. The proscenium stage faces on to a 549-seat auditorium. Price concessions are made to children and students at certain performances, and to parties of 15 and over. There is a licensed bar and a coffee bar. There are 3 free car parks within 200 yards.

Chesterfield is 150 miles by road from London. Trains take 2½ hours from St Pancras to Chesterfield station, 200 yards from the theatre. Recommended hotels: The Station (0246 71141); Hotel Portland (0246 4502).

Colchester
MERCURY
The Mercury Theatre, Balkerne Gate, Colchester CO1 1PT, Essex.
Box office: 0206 73948.

A hexagonal shaped 2-storey building opened in May, 1972, this new theatre, subsidised by Colchester Borough Council, has a unique adaptable stage designed by the Royal Shakespeare Company's head of design, Christopher Morley. The auditorium is flanked by mobile towers which when moved over the seating alter the shape of the auditorium and its relationship to the stage, giving an open, a hexagonal or a traditional type stage. Seating capacity ranges from 505 to 409. The Mercury's policy is the presentation of 3-weekly straight runs of both modern and classical work. The Jenny Bone Studio Theatre, seating 80, also has a flexible auditorium and is used mainly for poetry and jazz evenings, for local amateur groups and the company use it as rehearsal rooms. The theatre closes down from June to mid-July. A variety of concessions is offered to pensioners and students. There is a licensed restaurant (0206 46881 for reservations) serving lunch and dinner, a licensed bar and a coffee bar. For the handicapped, there is space for 2 wheelchairs in the auditorium (reached by lift) and a special WC on the ground floor. A multi-storey car park is adjacent to the theatre.

Colchester is 54 miles by road from London. Trains take about 1 hour from Liverpool Street to Colchester station, 10 minutes away. The last train back to London at night leaves Colchester at 10.13 pm. Recommended hotels: The George (0206 78494); Marks Tey Motor Hotel, 4 miles away (0206 210001). Colchester is on the edge of the famous Constable country, just over the Essex border into Suffolk, and is itself one of the oldest towns in Britain.

Coventry
BELGRADE
Belgrade Theatre, Corporation Street, Coventry, Warwickshire CV1 1GS.
Box office: 0203 20205.

One of the first new theatres to be built after the last war, the Belgrade—so named because the timber for the interior of the building was a gift to Coventry from the Yugoslav capital—opened in March, 1958. Arnold Wesker's Chicken Soup with Barley was given its world premiere here in 1958. The Director, Warren Jenkins, operates a 2 or 3-weekly repertory programme, with a director and cast engaged for each production. In recent years, outstanding shows have been Frankie Howerd in **The Wind in the Sassafras Trees** and Dorothy Tutin in **Ann Veronica**. The Belgrade has a studio theatre which seats 60 and has a flexible acting area and is used by the Young Stagers. The main auditorium, which has a proscenium stage, seats 899 on 2 levels with boxes. Air-conditioning is installed. There is a restaurant (0203 56431 for reservations) which serves lunch and dinner as well as morning coffee and afternoon tea. Also two licensed bars. Price concessions operate in the form of season tickets, as well as the usual price reductions for parties of 20 and over, for pensioners, students and school-children. Two wheelchairs can be accommodated in the back boxes. A Corporation car park is adjacent to the theatre.

COVENTRY THEATRE (touring date)
The Coventry Theatre, Hales Street, Coventry, Warwickshire.
Box office: 0203 23141.

This touring-date theatre, which has a total seating capacity of 2,002, opened in 1937. Autumn and spring seasonal revues are mounted here, and large-scale pantomime productions, ballet and musicals presented by visiting companies throughout the rest of the year. There are also Sunday concerts and film shows. The auditorium, facing on to a proscenium stage, is fully air-conditioned. The usual price concessions are available to parties, pensioners, etc. There is a restaurant (0203 23143 for reservations) as well as 4 licensed bars and 2 snack bars. Opposite the theatre is a multi-storey car park.

Coventry is 92 miles by road from London. Trains take 1¼ hours from Euston to Coventry station, 10 minutes away from the Belgrade and 15 from the Coventry. Recommended hotels: Leofric (0203 21371); Smithfield (0203 20456); Berkeley (0203 25952).

Darlington

CIVIC
Civic Theatre, Parkgate, Darlington,

County Durham.
Box office: 0325 65774.

This early Edwardian theatre underwent its most recent major renovation in 1968. It has a policy of presenting resident repertory seasons supplemented by other attractions for one performance only. Plays range from Ibsen, Shaw and Wilde to Agatha Christie and modern comedy. There is a seating capacity of 600 on 2 levels before a proscenium stage. The theatre is usually closed from late July to late August. Price concessions operate for pensioners, children and parties. A licensed lounge bar also sells coffee. After-the-show buffet meals can be arranged for parties on a week's notice. Two wheelchairs can be accommodated in the stalls, which are at street level. Parking space available adjacent to the theatre.

Darlington is 242 miles by road from London. Trains take 3 hours from King's Cross to Darlington station, 5 minutes away. Flights from Heathrow to Teesside (4 miles away) take about 1 hour. Recommended hotels: The King's Head (0325 67612); North Eastern (0325 4373). The Europa Lodge (0325 60111) also offers an inclusive ticket for dinner in their restaurant and a top-price seat at the theatre plus programme and non-alcoholic interval refreshment.

Derby

PLAYHOUSE
Derby Playhouse, Sacheverel Street, Derby.
Box office: 0332 47929.

Built in 1953, the Playhouse under its present joint directors, John Williams and Peter C. Jackson, operates a policy of 3-weekly repertory presenting many new plays in their programme. The auditorium seats 396 on 2 levels fronting on to a proscenium stage. A 50-seat studio theatre attached has an adaptable staging area. The Playhouse is closed during July and August. There is a licensed bar and a coffee bar. A car park is nearby, and on-street parking is also available.

Derby is 130 miles by road from London. Trains take about 2 hours from St Pancras to Derby Midland station, 10 minutes away. Recommended hotels: The Midland (0332 45894); The Pennine (0332 41741); Gables (0332 40633).

Dundee

REPERTORY THEATRE

Dundee Repertory Theatre, Lochee Road, Dundee, Angus, Scotland.
Box office: 0382 23530.

Housed in a Victorian church, "temporarily" converted into a theatre in 1963 and still working successfully, the Dundee Rep has a 3-weekly system of straight runs. Among new work presented here recently has been Michael Barry's documentary, **The Tay Bridge Disaster** which is of special local interest. The proscenium stage fronts a 298-seat auditorium on one level. There is a licensed bar and a coffee bar but no restaurant. Price concessions are offered to Theatre Club members, students, schoolchildren and pensioners. A travel subsidy scheme also operates here for parties travelling from outlying areas. Parking space is available in surrounding streets. There is easy access for wheelchairs into the auditorium, which is at street level with no steps.

Dundee is 430 miles by road from London. Trains take 9 hours from King's Cross to Dundee Tay Bridge station, 10 minutes' taxi-ride away. Recommended hotels: Queen's (0382 22515); Angus (0382 26874); Tay Centre (0382 21641).

Eastbourne

CONGRESS (touring date)

Congress Theatre, Compton Street, Eastbourne, Sussex.
Box office: 0323 36363.

This touring-date theatre houses a wide range of entertainment presented by visiting companies. The auditorium seats 1,701 before a proscenium stage. There are two bars and a restaurant seating up to 200 (0323 25252 for reservations). A park for 200 cars adjoins the theatre. Wheelchair accommodation is available for 5 chairs in the auditorium, and there is a lift to all levels, and sloping floors.

DEVONSHIRE PARK

Devonshire Park Theatre, Compton Street, Eastbourne, Sussex.
Box office: 0323 21121.

This 955-seat Victorian theatre has a weekly repertory programme, with pantomime each Christmas. There is a party booking scheme and concessions for pensioners. A licensed bar is at dress circle level, and a coffee and tea-tray service is available. Arrangements can be made for the accommodation of wheelchairs in the auditorium. A car park is in the theatre forecourt.

ROYAL HIPPODROME

The Royal Hippodrome, Seaside Road, Eastbourne, Sussex. 0323 24336.

This Victorian theatre, built in 1890 and renovated in 1970, is open only from May to October each year, when a summer show—**Golden Years of Music-Hall**—is presented. It has a seating capacity of 668 before a proscenium stage. There is a licensed bar but no restaurant, and no car park but easy street parking.

Eastbourne is 64 miles by road from London. Trains take 1 hour 40 minutes from Victoria to Eastbourne station, 10 minutes away from each of the theatres. Recommended hotels: Farrars (0323 23737); Travancore (0323 23770); Queen's (0323 22822).

East Grinstead

ADELINE GENEE

Adeline Genée Theatre, Lingfield Road, East Grinstead, Sussex.
Box office: 034 287 532.

This little proscenium-stage theatre, named after the ballerina, was opened by Princess Margaret in 1967 and has undergone a number of policy changes since that time. Its present director, Myles Byrne, is operating a mixed-policy programme of visits by touring companies and a ballet festival each June, plus the theatre's own repertoire productions, cinema, pantomime, and Sunday concerts. The 330-seat auditorium is air-conditioned. There is a fully-licensed bar as well as the Genée Carvery for reasonably-priced 3-course meals with wine. There is accommodation for 4 wheelchairs in the auditorium. Two large car parks adjoin the theatre.

East Grinstead is 35 miles by road from London. Trains take 45 minutes from Victoria to East Grinstead station, some 15 minutes away. Gatwick airport is itself only 5 miles from the theatre, which has a most attractive countryside setting.

Edinburgh

KING'S (touring date)

King's Theatre, 2 Leven Street, Edinburgh EH3 9LQ.
Box office: 031 229 1201.

This touring-date theatre, owned and run by Edinburgh Corporation, was built in 1906 and had its most recent major renovation in 1972. The fare which visiting companies appearing here present ranges from straight plays to opera, ballet, summer revue, pantomime, and seasons of the Black and White Minstrels. The proscenium stage faces a 1,472-seat auditorium on 4 levels with boxes. There are 4 licensed bars. Parking is on-street only.

ROYAL LYCEUM
Royal Lyceum Theatre, Grindlay Street, Edinburgh EH3 9AX.
Box office: 031 229 4353.

This Victorian theatre under its Artistic Director, Clive Perry, presents an international repertoire of classical and modern plays, and has a number of premieres to its credit in the past few years. There is a proscenium stage with forestage, and a seating capacity of 1,292 divided between 4 levels. A 60-seat studio theatre with a variable stage houses performances by the Young Lyceum Company who also tour schools in the area as well as smaller theatres and community centres on the Scottish East coast. The theatre is closed for a few weeks in the early summer. Price concessions are offered to students, schools and pensioners. There is a licensed restaurant (box office number for reservations) which opens for lunches and cold pre-performance evening meals. There are bars on each level, including one which serves morning coffee. A few wheelchairs can be accommodated in the auditorium. A multi-storey public car park is adjacent to the theatre.

TRAVERSE THEATRE CLUB
Traverse Theatre Club, 112 West Bow, Grassmarket, Edinburgh EH1 2PD.
Box office: 031 226 2633.

Founded in 1963, the Traverse company originally occupied premises in Lawnmarket, and moved to the present building in 1969. The theatre has no permanent company but produces straight runs of new plays and invites visits from other experimental groups. The accent here is on avant-garde work, and in the past 5 years the Traverse has staged the British or world premieres of 55 plays, notably by writers like Stanley Eveling, Howard Brenton, Megan Terry, David Benedictus, C P Taylor, Olwen Wymark, John Spurling, David Hare, David Halliwell and many others. A completely adaptable studio-type theatre, the Traverse has a flexible arrangement for seating audiences, and the capacity is

around 100. Exhibitions of contemporary art are given in the restaurant and foyer. The theatre is closed for 2 to 3 weeks each autumn following the Edinburgh Festival. Day membership of the Club is available to visitors outside Scotland, and reduced for students. Special combined tickets can be bought for early and late-night shows on the same evening. A licensed restaurant (031 225 4396 for reservations) serves Continental dishes and caters for parties, and there is a bar open at lunchtime and in the evening. Parking space is available in the Grassmarket. No wheelchair facilities.

Edinburgh is 373 miles by road from London. Trains take 6 hours from King's Cross to Edinburgh Waverley Station, which is 10 minutes away from each of the theatres. Flights from Heathrow or Gatwick to Turnhouse airport (7 miles away) take 90 minutes. Recommended hotels: The Caledonian (031 225 2433); Rutland (031 229 3402); The Roxburgh (031 229 3921).

Exeter

NORTHCOTT
Northcott Theatre, Stocker Road, Exeter EX4 4QB, Devon.
Box office: 0392 54853.

The Northcott stands on the green of Exeter University. It opened in November, 1967, and under its present director, Jane Howell, there is a policy of repertoire with substantial touring in the South West. In the past few years, the Company has to its credit the presentation of 14 world premieres including a new version of Measure for Measure by Howard Brenton directed by William Gaskill, and Ronald Millar's Abelard and Heloise. The Northcott also runs a Youth Theatre in conjunction with Exeter City Council, as well as a Theatre-in-Education group. The proscenium stage faces a one-level steeply-raked auditorium seating 433, which is air-conditioned. Price concessions are offered to parties, club members, pensioners and students for most performances. There is no restaurant but a Buttery Bar and a licensed bar open at lunchtime and in the evening. Very good free parking facilities. Two wheelchairs can be accommodated in the auditorium.

Exeter is 180 miles by road from London. Trains take about 2½ hours from Paddington to Exeter St David's station, 5 minutes away. Recommended hotels: The Imperial (0392 72750); The Rougemont (0392 54982).

Farnham

CASTLE

Castle Theatre, Castle Street, Farnham, Surrey.

Box office: 02513 5301.

This part-17th and part-19th century theatre seats 167, making it the smallest professional repertory theatre in the country. In the autumn of 1973 it is hoped building will be completed on the nearby new **Redgrave Theatre**, when the Farnham Repertory Company will move, taking with them the same artistic policy of 3-weekly straight runs with occasional seasons of repertoire. The Castle has no studio theatre, but their Theatreaction troupe takes plays to schools as well as bringing schools to the theatre, and organising experimental shows and other activities. The Castle has a proscenium stage and a fan ventilation system. Price concessions are made to parties of 15 and over at certain performances, and also to pensioners and students. It is a club theatre, but membership is only 50p annually, and members may bring as many guests as they please. There is no theatre restaurant, but under the Playdine scheme theatregoers may buy a special ticket covering a theatre seat and a meal at a nearby restaurant before or after the performance. The Castle has a coffee bar which also serves confectionery, ices and soft drinks, but has no licensed bar. Up to 2 wheelchairs can be accommodated in the auditorium. Ample parking space in Castle Street in the evening, but on matinee days a car park 5 minutes away is recommended.

Farnham is 40 miles by road from London; trains take 1 hour from Waterloo to Farnham station, 10 minutes' walk away. Last trains back to London are the 10.32 pm or the 11.02 pm changing at Woking. Recommended hotels: The Bush (02513 5237); Bishop's Table (02513 5545).

Glasgow

CITIZENS'

Citizens' Theatre, Gorbals Street, Glasgow, Scotland.

Box office: 041-429 0022.

The Citizens' Theatre Company, founded in 1943 by the Scottish dramatist, James Bridie, occupies a theatre built in 1886. One of Britain's leading repertory companies, it presents plays (generally four) in repertoire for autumn and spring seasons. In 1972 it began a system of exchanging productions with Edinburgh's Royal Lyceum Theatre. There is a proscenium stage and a 900-seat auditorium divided between 3 levels, the large upper circle not always being used. The Citizens' has no studio theatre as such, but the **Close Theatre Club** which opened in 1965 and was housed in adjacent converted buildings, fulfilled this function until it was destroyed by fire in May 1973. Mixed policy—mainly experimental—of Scottish plays, revue, theatre workshop, discotheques and many other activities. Attached to the Citizens' is also the Theatre for Youth company, which takes productions to schools and colleges in the area. The whole organisation usually closes during June, July and August. The Citizens' has a bar and a tea room. There is space for wheelchairs at the back of the stalls at the Citizens'. Price concessions are offered for some performances to pensioners, students and parties. Car park 50 yards away.

KING'S (touring date)

King's Theatre, Bath Street, Glasgow G3 4JN.

Box office: 041-248 5125.

This touring-date theatre, built in 1904, is run by the Corporation of Glasgow for the presentation of a wide range of entertainment by visiting companies. It has a proscenium stage, a seating capacity of 1,792, and a system of ventilating fans. There are no restaurant facilities, but bars on all levels, and space for 5 wheelchairs at the back of the stalls. A multi-storey car park has just been built adjacent to the theatre.

Glasgow is 400 miles by road from London. Trains take 6½ hours from Euston to Glasgow Central station, which is 10 minutes away from both theatres. Flights from Heathrow to Abbotsinch airport (9 miles away) take about 1 hour. Recommended hotels: Central (041-221 9680); North British (041-332 6711); Duncan's (041-221 4580).

Grays

THAMESIDE

Thameside Theatre, Orsett Road, Grays, Essex.

Box office: 0375 77982.

Under the control of the Thurrock Urban District Council, this 327-seat theatre opened in October, 1971. Its principal function is to act as host to a wide range of visiting companies presenting straight plays, ballet, opera, films, variety, jazz, recitals and one-night stands. It is housed within a 7-storey Arts Centre complex which also contains a book and record library, local history museum and various meeting and lecture rooms. A large proscenium stage faces a steeply-raked auditorium on one level. Accommodation for 4 wheelchairs is available at the back, and access to the theatre is by lift from the ground floor. There is a coffee lounge which serves snacks, and a licensed bar. Air-conditioning is installed. There is a large car park at the rear of the building.

Grays is 22 miles by road from London. Trains take 35 minutes from Fenchurch Street to Grays station, 3 minutes away. The last train back to London leaves at 11.08 pm.

addition of an apron stage or an orchestra pit. Air-conditioning is installed. There are the usual price reductions offered to parties, pensioners and students. An Arts Council-subsidised travel voucher scheme operates here for most productions. There is a riverside restaurant (0483 69334 for reservations) serving lunch and early and late dinners. Also a coffee bar open from 10.30 am. Millbrook municipal car park is adjacent to the theatre (parking is strictly not permitted in the theatre forecourt) and there is a multi-storey car park in Castle Street, 5 minutes' walk away.

Guildford is 35 miles by road from London. Trains take 40 minutes from Waterloo to Guildford station, 10 minutes away. Last direct trains from Guildford back to Waterloo at night are at 10.30 and 11 pm. The 11.10 and 11.22 pm entail changing at Woking and Surbiton respectively.

Guildford

YVONNE ARNAUD
Yvonne Arnaud Theatre, Millbrook, Guildford, Surrey.
Box office: 0483 60191.

Named after the much-loved actress who lived in the town for many years, the Yvonne Arnaud opened in the summer of 1965. It is built on a site by the River Wey donated by Guildford Corporation. The Director, Laurier Lister, describes his policy of 3-weekly straight runs as "total theatre—entertainment of every kind provided it is first class." There is no permanent company and productions from farce to thrillers, classics, avant-garde work, musicals, revues and Christmas shows are individually cast and directed. The theatre also plays host to visiting ballet companies. In the past 5 years, the Yvonne Arnaud has given the world or national premieres of Marguerite Duras' The Viaduct and Suzanna Andler; N C Hunter's last play The Adventures of Tom Random, Robin Maugham's Enemy and, in 1972, The Effect of Gamma Rays on Man in the Moon Marigolds by Paul Zindel. The Young People's Theatre Company, a permanent group of 5 actors, has recently been formed to present plays for children of all age groups and also to tour specially devised productions to local schools and colleges. The auditorium seats 570 on 2 levels with boxes, and the fairly flexible proscenium-type stage can be adapted with the

Harlow

PLAYHOUSE (touring date)
The Playhouse Theatre and Arts Centre, The High, Harlow, Essex.
Box office: 027 96 31945.

This new theatre, financed by the local Urban District Council and part of an arts complex, opened in November 1971. It is principally a touring-date theatre but also presents films, orchestral concerts, local operatic and drama groups and other events. It has a seating capacity of 500 with an acting area adaptable to proscenium, thrust or apron staging. Air-conditioning is installed. Price reductions are offered to children, students and pensioners. An "in the round" studio theatre seating 128 has "flying" seats so that it can be converted into an open space for rehearsals. It is used for minority and experimental work. The Playhouse also houses a professional Visual Arts Gallery. There is a restaurant (027 96 31947 for reservations) and 2 licensed buffets—the Gilbey Bar and the Club Bar. A large car park is in front of the theatre. There are 6 special spaces for wheelchairs in the auditorium as well as WC facilities for the disabled.

Harlow is 25 miles by road from London. Trains take 45 minutes from Liverpool Street to Harlow Town station, 10 minutes away. Last train back to London leaves Harlow at 11.47 pm.

Harrogate

HARROGATE THEATRE
Harrogate Theatre, Oxford Street, Harrogate, Yorkshire.
Box office: 0423 2116.

The Harrogate (White Rose) Theatre Company present autumn and spring seasons of repertory with a resident company, plus a Christmas musical. Visits by companies presenting opera, ballet and drama occupy the theatre for the rest of the year, with the exception of a period in June and July when the theatre is closed. The resident company has recently presented the first performance of Joyce Rayburn's comedy **Don't Start Without Me,** and Brian Oulton's **Mr Sidney Smith Coming Upstairs,** and the Harrogate programme generally ranges from Shakespeare and the classics to established new plays. Built in 1900, the building was completely restored and renovated in 1972. It has a seating capacity of 476, and now has a proscenium stage with forestage extension over the orchestra pit. Air-conditioning has been installed. A small adaptable studio theatre seating between 50 and 60 is used for young people's theatre activities. Price concessions are made for pensioners, and parties are offered a free seat in every 10 booked. A Buttery Bar is open daily from 10.30 am for coffee, drinks and snacks, and the Green Room Club is available to members and to visitors on a temporary membership basis. A multi-storey car park is 3 minutes' walk away, and there is disc parking in the streets. Two wheelchairs can be accommodated in the auditorium.

Harrogate is 200 miles by road from London. Trains take 4 hours from King's Cross to Harrogate station, 4 minutes' walk away. Flights from Heathrow to Leeds/Bradford airport (approximately 10 miles away) take 1 hour. Recommended hotels: The Old Swan (0423 4051); The Crown (0423 67755); The Prospect (0423 5071).

Hull

ARTS CENTRE
Hull Arts Centre, Spring Street, Hull, East Yorkshire.
Box office: 0482 23638.

Built in 1970, the Arts Centre is open all day for its wide range of activities, which include 3-weekly runs of plays on 4 nights a week, informal workshop sessions (involving all the arts, but based on drama) concerts and poetry programmes. Exhibitions are staged regularly in the Gallery Bar. In recent years, the Arts Centre has presented the premieres of new work by David Mercer and Alan Plater, among others. The Centre is closed during August. Seating capacity is 151 around an open stage. Air-conditioning is installed. Price reductions are made for students and pensioners. Light midday meals are available at the fully-licensed bar. Wheelchairs can be accommodated in the main auditorium. Plenty of parking space around the Centre.

NEW (touring date)
New Theatre, Kingston Square, Hull, East Yorkshire.
Box office: 0482 20463.

Built in 1939, this touring-date playhouse seats 1,179 fronting a proscenium stage. The auditorium is air-conditioned. Entertainments ranging from opera, ballet, drama and pantomime are presented by visiting companies here, and the occasional repertory season is also given. The usual price concessions are offered to pensioners, students and parties. There are 2 licensed bars, a coffee bar and a members' club. Wheelchairs can be accommodated in the auditorium. Ample parking space in Kingston Square, adjacent to the theatre.

Hull is 205 miles by road from London. Trains take 3½ to 4 hours from King's Cross to Hull Paragon station, 2 minutes from the Arts Centre and 10 minutes from the New. Recommended hotels: The Centre (0482 26462); Royal Station (0482 25087); Dorchester House (0482 43276).

Ipswich

ARTS
Arts Theatre, Tower Street, Ipswich IP1 3BE, Suffolk.
Box office: 0473 53725.

The Ipswich Arts Theatre Trust celebrated its 25th anniversary at the end of 1972, although the theatre itself opened around 1850, on the site of an earlier playhouse where Garrick made his first public appearance in 1741. The theatre's Director, John Southworth, is leading the company into new premises by the autumn of 1975 when an adaptable theatre-in-the-round is completed on a nearby site. Meanwhile, in Tower Street there is a policy of 3-weekly repertory with occasional regional tours by the company. Their programme ranges from a good proportion of new work—some of it with a strong local bias—to new translations of work by Marivaux and Claudel, and productions of Peter Nichols, David Storey, Eliot, Shaw and Shakespeare. Throughout each season special one-night performances on Mondays and the occasional lunchtime performances are also given. The **Drama Centre** in Turret Lane (box office: 0473 57208) is the company's Young People's Theatre Centre, with workshops and drama sessions for schools. The Arts Theatre is usually closed in June and July. The 345-seat auditorium on 2 levels faces a proscenium stage. There is a licensed bar open during performance time and also for light snacks at lunchtime. Price concessions are offered to theatre club members and also to parties of 20 and over, to schoolchildren, pensioners, students and the disabled. The Eastern Arts Association subsidises a transport voucher scheme for parties from outlying areas. Overall cheap rates are also available for all preview performances. Wheelchairs can be accommodated at stalls level, with direct access from the pavement. There is a car park at the top of the road.

Ipswich is 72 miles by road from London. Trains take 1¼ hours from Liverpool Street to Ipswich station, 10 minutes away. Recommended hotels: Great White Horse (0473 56558); Golden Lion (0473 52523); Crown & Anchor (0473 53547).

Lancaster

DUKE'S PLAYHOUSE
The Duke's Playhouse, Moor Lane, Lancaster.
Box office: 0524 66645.

The Duke's, opened in November 1971, is a transformation of the former Georgian church of St Anne's into a comfortable twin-auditorium theatre. There is a policy of 3-weekly straight runs presented by the Playhouse company and occasional visiting groups such as Portable Theatre, with a week of films in between. Nine new works have been given their first performance here in the past few years, including Roy Fuller's version of **Ulysses** for children. The main auditorium seats 332 on one level, facing a proscenium stage. The studio theatre, extensively used by the Young People's Theatre Company for their own productions as well as for jazz and blues sessions, is completely flexible and has no defined acting area. Other activities at the Playhouse include late-night poetry readings in the Coffee Bar, lunchtime concerts in the main auditorium and exhibitions by local art groups in the Mezzanine Gallery. The Playhouse is closed during July and August. Price concessions are offered to students, children, pensioners and parties of 10 or more for the main auditorium, but there is an all-over cheap rate for the studio with no concessions. The Coffee Bar serves light meals, and there is a licensed bar. Wheelchair space for up to 12 in the auditorium. Plenty of parking space in nearby streets.

Lancaster is 233 miles by road from London. Trains take 4 hours from Euston to Lancaster station, 10 minutes away. Flights from Gatwick to Blackpool airport (24 miles away) take 45 minutes. Recommended hotel: Royal King's Arms (0524 2451).

Leatherhead

THORNDIKE
Thorndike Theatre, Church Street, Leatherhead, Surrey.
Box office: 537 5461.

This new theatre, which opened in 1969, has the same management under the direction of Hazel Vincent Wallace as ran the old Leatherhead Theatre which immediately preceded it. It is named in honour of Dame Sybil Thorndike- and the attached studio theatre, the **Casson**, is named after her husband, Sir Lewis Casson. There is no resident company, and each new production is mounted for a run of 3 weeks for a period from August to May each year. Visiting companies take over in June, and a film festival in July. On Sundays there are programmes of concerts and films, and art exhibitions are permanently on display in the spacious foyers. The auditorium has a proscenium stage with an adjustable forestage, and seats 526 in one steeply-raked tier. There is a leaning towards the lighter theatre, with comedies and thrillers comprising a substantial part of the regular programme, but among the new plays given at the Thorndike in recent years has been the British premiere of James Goldman's **The Lion in Winter**. The Casson Room seats 100 and is used by the company's Young Stagers group. A theatre and coffee bar are situated off the main foyer, and there is a Green Room self-service restaurant for club members only. For the disabled, there is a lift to each floor, and special WC facilities. Price concessions offered to parties of 10 and over, and to pensioners and Young

Stagers. A car park is 200 yards away in Leatherhead High Street.

Leatherhead is 20 miles by road from London. Trains take 40 minutes from Waterloo or Victoria to Leatherhead station, 10 minutes away. Last train back to London at night is the 11.19 to Waterloo.

Leeds

GRAND (touring date)

The Grand Theatre & Opera House, New Briggate, Leeds LS1 6NZ, Yorkshire.
Box office: 0532 20891.

This large Victorian opera house, which seats 1,552 divided between stalls, dress circle, upper circle, balcony, upper balcony and 21 boxes, has a proscenium stage and houses pre-London and weekly touring companies presenting ballet, opera, musicals, pantomime and drama. Sometimes closed during August. Price concessions of 1 free seat in 10 are offered, as well as 2 for the price of 1 on Monday nights. There are 6 bars which also serve coffee and confectionery. Ample parking space is guaranteed by the management, and details are sent with your tickets. Wheelchairs can be accommodated in the back stalls.

PLAYHOUSE

The Playhouse, Calverley Street, Leeds LS2 3AJ, Yorkshire.
Box office: 0532 42111.

Opened in September, 1970 in the city centre, the Playhouse under its present Artistic Director, John Harrison, operates a system of repertoire presented by a permanent company. In the past few years, much interesting new work has been produced here, including plays by John Spurling, Alan Plater and Clifford Hanley; Colin Wilson's play about Strindberg: **Pictures in a Bath of Acid**; and some local-interest documentaries. Plans for 1973 included a new translation by David Carson of Lorca's **Blood Wedding**. The Playhouse has a Theatre-in-Education company taking theatre to schools in the area, and there is a Playhouse Club and a Young Playhouse Club. Leeds Film Theatre have the use of the Playhouse for late-night films at weekends. Price concessions are offered to parties of 20 and over, as well as to students, children and pensioners. The auditorium, which is air-conditioned, seats 750 before an open thrust stage. There is a theatre restaurant with its own buffet counter (0532 42141 for reservations) and this remains open all day from 9.30 am until after the performance. The 2 licensed bars are open during pub hours, and there are also 2 coffee bars. Wheelchairs can be accommodated in the auditorium. A large car park is close to the theatre. Leeds Playhouse has the distinction of appearing in the Guinness Book of Records as the owner of the largest neon sign in Great Britain.

Leeds, which is on the outskirts of the Yorkshire Dales, is 190 miles by road from London. Trains take between 2½ to 3 hours from King's Cross to Leeds City station, which is 5 minutes away from the Grand and 10 from the Playhouse. Flights from Heathrow to the Leeds/Bradford airport at Yeadon (12 miles away) take 1 hour. Recommended station (0532 31323); Faversham (0532 28615); Merrion (0532 39191).

Lincoln

THEATRE ROYAL

Theatre Royal, Clasketgate, Lincoln.
Box office: 0522 25555.

This small, beautifully-preserved Victorian horseshoe theatre is the home of the Lincoln Theatre Company. It has a policy of fortnightly repertory with a permanent company. Their work concentrates on new plays created by and for the company, although a wide range of other work is also presented. There is no studio theatre, but the Theatre Royal's youth work includes visits to rural areas as well as tours to Rotherham, Scunthorpe and Darlington. The proscenium stage with a large apron faces a 550-seat auditorium on 3 levels, although the gallery is not always used, thus bringing down the capacity to 400. The theatre is often closed during July and August. Price concessions are made to pensioners, students and parties of 10 or more. There is a licensed bar and coffee bar open before, during and after performances, as well as a bar and lunch bar open from midday to 2 pm on weekdays. A public car park is close by.

Lincoln is 132 miles by road from London. Trains take 2½ hours from King's Cross to Lincoln St Mark's station, 5 minutes away. Recommended hotels: Eastgate (0522 20341); White Hart (0522 26222).

Liverpool

EMPIRE (touring date)
Empire Theatre, Lime Street, Liverpool.
Box office: 051 709 1555.

This touring-date theatre, owned by Moss Empires, houses leading touring companies as well as concerts, pantomime and the occasional straight run of a play. It is closed for 3 months in the summer. The Empire has a seating capacity of 2,550 before a proscenium stage. There are 3 bars, facilities for wheelchairs, and a car park.

EVERYMAN
Everyman Theatre, Hope Street, Liverpool 1.
Box office: 051 709 4776.

Housed in a 140-year old chapel adapted to a theatre by the Everyman Company in 1964, the Everyman has a policy of 3-weekly repertory presented by a permanent ensemble under the artistic direction of Alan Dossor. In the past few years they have presented new work by such writers as John McGrath, C G Bond and Charles Wood, and their programme is geared mainly to the work of new writers and to plays of local and contemporary relevance. As well as the Everyman Company, the theatre also has a Youth Theatre group which includes in its activities the setting up of teachers' workshops. The Everyman is closed each year during July and August. The open thrust stage faces a 450-seat auditorium on 2 levels. The usual price concessions are made to students, pensioners and parties at weekday performances. There is a licensed restaurant (box office number and ask for ext. 1 for reservations) which is open until 11.30 pm. Wheelchairs can be accommodated on advance notice to the General Manager. There is space for street parking around the theatre.

PLAYHOUSE
Liverpool Playhouse, Williamson Square, Liverpool L1 1EL.
Box office: 051 709 8363.

Antony Tuckey, Director of the Playhouse Company, runs a policy of mainly 3-weekly straight runs, and the Company have 9 premieres to their credit in the last few years, including specially-written local documentaries. The Playhouse was built in 1911 and renovated in 1968. It has a proscenium stage and a seating capacity of 762 on 3 levels. The theatre is closed during July and August. A studio theatre,

Playhouse Upstairs, seats 90. Catering facilities include a 76-seat restaurant (no table reservations) and 2 bars. Wheelchair space for 3 in the stalls. There are 2 car parks close by.

ROYAL COURT (touring date)
Royal Court Theatre, Roe Street, Liverpool 1.
Box office: 051 709 5163.

This is a Howard & Wyndham touring date theatre, built in 1938. Visiting companies present a wide variety of entertainment from opera and ballet to straight plays, variety, concerts and revue. There are also occasional cinema shows. The theatre has a seating capacity of 1,526 before a proscenium stage, and air-conditioning is installed. There are 3 licensed bars and catering by arrangement. Two large car parks adjoin the theatre.

Liverpool is 198 miles by road from London. Trains take 2¾ hours from Euston to Liverpool Lime Street, which is 10 minutes' walk away from the Everyman, 3 minutes from the Empire and the Playhouse, and almost next door to the Royal Court. Flights from Heathrow to Liverpool's Speke airport (6 miles away) take 45 minutes. Recommended hotels: Adelphi (051 709 7200); St George's (051 709 7090); Shaftesbury (051 709 4421).

Manchester

LIBRARY
Library Theatre, St Peter's Square, Manchester M2 5PD.
Box office: 061 236 7406.

This unique theatre, supported solely by Manchester Corporation and housed in the basement of its Central Library, opened in 1934. Under the present director, David Scase, the Library Theatre Company also runs the new Forum Theatre in Wythenshawe, on the outskirts of Manchester. Two repertory companies alternate between both theatres, playing 3 weeks in each. New plays to their credit in the past 2 years include John Hale's **Lorna and Ted** and Colin Welland's **Say Goodnight to Your Grandma**. The Library has a 308-seat auditorium facing a proscenium stage. As well as its regular activities, free lunchtime theatre is presented on occasional Tuesdays. The theatre is closed during July and August. Price concessions are offered to pensioners and students. Catering facilities are limited to a coffee bar. A National Car Park is 100 yards away, and street parking is also available.

OPERA HOUSE (touring date)
The Opera House, Quay Street, Manchester M3 3HP.
Box office: 061 834 1787.

This is a Howard & Wyndham touring date theatre presenting the usual varied programme of opera, ballet, straight plays and music-hall. Built in 1912, it has a seating capacity of 2,072 before a proscenium stage. The Opera House is usually closed for 2 to 3 months in the summer. There are 5 theatre bars open during performance-time. Ample parking facilities, including a National Car Park in nearby Corporation Street.

PALACE (touring date)
Palace Theatre, Manchester.
Box office: 061 236 0184.

A Moss Empires touring date theatre showing opera, ballet, musicals, pantomime, concerts as well as straight plays. It has a seating capacity of 2,185 facing a proscenium stage. Bars and coffee bars available at each level. There is a car park close by, as well as easy street parking at night.

Manchester is 190 miles by road from London. Trains take 2½ hours from Euston to Manchester Piccadilly station, which is 15 minutes' walk from the Library Theatre, and 5 from the Opera House and the Palace. Flights from Heathrow to Manchester Ringway airport (8 miles away) take 45 minutes. Recommended hotels: Midland (061 236 3333); Piccadilly (061 236 8414); Grand (061 236 9559).

Newcastle

THEATRE ROYAL (touring date)
Theatre Royal, Grey Street, Newcastle-upon-Tyne, NE1 6BR.
Box office: 0632 22061.

This touring-date theatre was originally built in 1837, but after being extensively damaged by fire it was rebuilt in 1901. Both the National Theatre and the Royal Shakespeare Company play here as part of their regional tours, and included in the Theatre Royal's programme of opera ballet, pantomime, straight drama and musicals was a pre-London visit by Godspell. The theatre is closed for about 6 to 8 weeks each summer. The auditorium, which seats 1,691 divided between stalls, grand circle, upper circle, gallery and boxes, fronts a proscenium stage. The usual price concessions are offered for most productions. There are licensed bars in the stalls, upper circle and gallery. There is no official theatre catering but a restaurant (0632 27244 for reservations) is available in a next-door pub called The Royal. A multi-storey car park is close by, with concessions to theatregoers.

UNIVERSITY
Tyneside Theatre Company, University Theatre, Haymarket, Newcastle-upon-Tyne, NE1 7RH.
Box office: 0632 23421.

The University Theatre opened in 1970, and the Tyneside Company under their Artistic Director, Gareth Morgan, have since then been presenting a high proportion of important new work, produced in straight runs of 2½ to 3½ weeks. During their first 2 years, they have given 6 British premieres. The **Gulbenkian Studio Theatre** is occupied by The Stagecoach Company, formed out of the main Tyneside Company, and they present experimental work as well as taking productions to local schools, pubs and factories. The Studio also acts as host to visiting experimental groups. Other features of the Tyneside Company's activities are exhibitions, regular lunchtime and late-night events and Sunday concerts. The main theatre has an open thrust stage with a seating capacity of 449 on one steep rake, and an air-conditioned auditorium. Price concessions are made to students and pensioners, and there is a Northern Arts Association voucher scheme for young people. Bars include a main theatre bar, wine and sherry bar, coffee bar, and substantial snacks are available at lunchtime and in the evening. There are spaces for 4 wheelchairs in the auditorium, and a WC for disabled patrons as well as an exit at ground level without steps. The theatre is closed during August. Parking at the theatre is strictly limited and only available in the evening. A public car park 3 minutes' walk away is recommended.

Newcastle is 274 miles by road from London. Trains take about 4 hours from King's Cross to Newcastle Central station, 10 minutes away from both theatres. Flights from Heathrow to Newcastle airport (8 miles away) take 50 minutes. Recommended hotels: The Royal Turk's Head (0632 26111); The Swallow (0632 25025); The Royal Station (0632 20781).

Norwich

THEATRE ROYAL (touring date)
Theatre Royal, Theatre Street,
Norwich NOR 62E, Norfolk.
Box office: 0603 28205.

This touring-date theatre presents a wide variety of entertainment ranging from pantomime, music hall and local amateur productions to straight plays, opera and ballet. The theatre is closed for 4 weeks each summer. The 1,273-seat auditorium divided between stalls and circle faces on to a proscenium stage. The usual price concessions are offered to pensioners, students and children. There are no bar or restaurant facilities. Space for 2 wheelchairs is available in the auditorium. A large public car park is within 50 yards of the theatre. Norwich's other theatre, the Maddermarket, a replica of an Elizabethan playhouse, is the home of one of the best-known amateur groups in the country; it was founded in 1921 by Nugent Monck for the presentation of plays by Shakespeare and his contemporaries.

Norwich is 111 miles by road from London. Trains take 2 hours from Liverpool Street to Norwich station, 1½ miles away. Recommended hotels: The Nelson (0603 28612); The Castle (0603 24283).

Nottingham

PLAYHOUSE
Nottingham Playhouse, Wellington Circus, Nottingham NG1 5AF.
Box office: 0602 45671.

The 719-seat theatre opened in 1963, and the Playhouse company, considered one of the leading repertory companies in the country, moved here from their former cramped premises. Productions are presented in repertoire, with the occasional visit by a guest company. In the past few years, under the present director, Stuart Burge, they have presented the premieres of Peter Barnes' **The Ruling Class** and his adaptation of Wedekind's **Lulu**; David Caute's **The Demonstration** and Christopher Fry's **A Yard of Sun**. The Company operates a schools touring scheme each spring and autumn, and the Playhouse becomes the centre of the Nottingham Festival every summer when the building is used for jazz and poetry sessions, art exhibitions, visiting experimental groups as well as the usual theatre performances. There is a permanent theatre bookstall in the foyer. The theatre has a proscenium stage with two forestages, and air-conditioning is installed. Price concessions are made for certain performances to parties of 10 and over, who are also eligible for half-price travel subsidy schemes if they come from outlying areas. There is also a gift voucher for an inclusive ticket-and-dinner service. The restaurant (0602 48467 for reservations) is open for dinner before and after the performance. A buttery bar and a wine bar adjoin the auditorium, and there are 2 bars and a coffee bar at stalls and balcony levels. A car park is attached to the theatre.

THEATRE ROYAL (touring date)
Theatre Royal, Theatre Square,
Nottingham.
Box office: 0602 42328.

This Moss Empires touring date theatre was built in 1865. Attractions vary between visits from the Royal Ballet, Brian Rix farces and Ken Dodd. There is a 1,474-seat auditorium facing on to a proscenium stage. No catering facilities, but 3 licensed bars. No parking or wheelchair accommodation.

Nottingham is 123 miles by road from London. Trains take 2 hours from St Pancras to Nottingham Midland station, 10 minutes away from the Playhouse and 15 from the Theatre Royal. Recommended hotels: The Albany (0602 40131); Strathdon (0602 48501); County (0602 46321).

Oldham

REPERTORY THEATRE CLUB
Oldham Repertory Theatre Club,
Coliseum Theatre, Fairbottom Street,
Oldham, Lancashire.
Box office: 061 624 2829.

This old-established company presents a fortnightly repertory programme. The theatre has a proscenium stage facing a 580-seat auditorium on 3 levels. It is closed for the whole of June. Price concessions offered to pensioners and schools. There is a cafe-lounge (box office number for reservations) and a bar. Space for 4 wheelchairs in the auditorium. A car park is at the back of the theatre.

Oldham is 185 miles by road from London. Trains take 2½ hours from Euston to Manchester Piccadilly station, 20 minutes away by road. Flights from Heathrow to Manchester Ringway airport (20 miles away) take 45 minutes. Recommended hotels: The Grapes (061 624 1115); The Greaves Arms (061 624 2759); The Artisans (061 624 5480).

Oxford

NEW (touring date)
New Theatre, George Street, Oxford
OX1 2AG.
Box office: 0865 44544.

The New is one of the larger and newer of the principal touring-date theatres, and is on the Howard & Wyndham circuit. It was built in 1933 and its programme ranges from straight plays to pantomime, musicals and revue. The air-conditioned auditorium seats 1,692 on 3 levels before a proscenium stage. There are 4 licensed bars as well as a snack bar. Wheelchairs can be accommodated in the auditorium. A municipal car park is close by.

PLAYHOUSE

Oxford Playhouse, Beaumont Street, Oxford.
Box office: 0865 47133.

The Playhouse presents seasonal repertory, interspersed with visits by University and other student groups, and professional drama, opera and ballet companies. In the past 3 years, 14 new plays have been given here, including the Dumas/Sartre **Kean** which went on to have a successful London run; Beckett's **Breath** and an adaptation of **Hard Times**. There is also an Exhibition Room where shows by local and other artists are held. The Playhouse is closed for a short period in the early summer. Built in 1938, the theatre went through a bad period immediately after the last war, eventually closing in 1956 to reopen later the same year when Frank Hauser brought in his Meadow Players and gave new life to the theatre. The building was enlarged and completely redecorated in 1964. It now has a 700-seat auditorium on 2 levels and an adaptable proscenium stage with a forestage. Air-conditioning has been installed. There is a licensed bar and a snack bar, which also serves morning coffee and light lunch. Wheelchairs can be accommodated in the stalls, which are at street level. A City car park is close by.

Oxford is 57 miles by road from London. Trains take 1¼ hours from Paddington to Oxford station, 10 minutes away from both theatres. Recommended hotels: The Randolph (0865 47481); Eastgate (0865 48244); Isis (0865 48894).

Perth

REPERTORY THEATRE
Perth Repertory Theatre, High Street,
Perth, Scotland.
Box office: 0738 21031

This old-established repertory company occupies a Victorian building which was extensively renovated and redecorated in 1972. It has a fortnightly straight-run policy with a summer show each year. The theatre is closed from April to June. Under its present director, Joan Knight, a number of premieres have been presented, including N C Hunter's **Henry of Navarre**. For young people there is a Saturday Theatre Club, open to all schools. The proscenium stage fronts a 606-seat auditorium. There are 2 bars and a coffee bar. Wheelchairs can be accommodated. Price concessions are offered to pensioners and members of the Playgoers' Club, as well as to parties of 10 or over. The Scottish Arts Council subsidises a half-price transport scheme for parties travelling from outlying areas. There is a car park behind the theatre.

Perth is 420 miles by road from London. Trains take about 8 hours from Euston to Perth station, 10 minutes away. Flights from Heathrow to Edinburgh airport (35 miles away) take 1 hour. Recommended hotels: The George (0738 24456); The Isle of Skye (0738 22962); The Station (0738 24141).

Richmond, Yorkshire

THE GEORGIAN
The Georgian Theatre, Fryars Wynd, Richmond, Yorkshire.
Box office: Richmond 3021 (dial 100 and ask operator for number).

One of the oldest theatres in this country, the Georgian was built in 1788 by Samuel Butler; the structure and design of the auditorium and backstage areas have been lovingly and skilfully preserved and refurbished, and some of the original bench seating still remains. A Quaker meeting-house adjoining the back of the theatre was some years ago acquired and incorporated into the building to provide greater storage space. A major redecoration was carried out early in 1973. The Georgian is used by touring companies presenting plays, opera and ballet, and for special concerts and recitals as well as being open as a museum (volunteer guides give conducted tours) from May to September each year. It is closed usually between November and February. An unusual feature here is the fact that although the theatre is used by professional artists, all the staff, from electricians and stage hands to usherettes and box office clerks, are amateurs—local people whose hobby it is to work in this historic building. The proscenium stage faces an auditorium seating 238 divided between pit, boxes and gallery. A new ventilation and heating system has just been installed. There is a licensed bar. The Fleece Hotel next door serves as the theatre's restaurant. Substantial price concessions are offered to pensioners and school parties at some mid-week performances. For disabled people, one entrance has been ramped for easy access to the ground floor, although occupants of wheelchairs must be transferred to theatre seating in the auditorium. There are two or three car parks close by, the nearest being in the Market Square, two minutes' walk away.

Richmond is 234 miles by road from London. Trains take approximately 3½ hours from King's Cross to Darlington station, where a half-hourly bus service continues the journey to Richmond, 12 miles away. Flights from Heathrow to Teesside airport, 20 miles from Richmond, take just over an hour. Recommended hotels: The Fleece (Richmond 3381) which is next door to the theatre; The King's Head (Richmond 2311) in Market Square; and the Frenchgate (Richmond 2087).

St Andrews

THE BYRE
The Byre Theatre, Abbey Street, St Andrews, Fife, Scotland.
Box office: St Andrews (dial 100 and ask for the number) 2388.

The original theatre, converted from the Abbey Street dairy farm cowshed, came into existence in 1933. That building was demolished in 1970 to make way for the present new theatre. The Byre Theatre Company presents a season each year from April to December with a small permanent group who undertake all the work connected with running a theatre. Their programme ranges from established modern plays to the classics, and a special feature of the Byre's policy has been regularly to present local plays set in St Andrews and Fife, most of them written by A B Paterson. Two subsidiary groups, Byre Theatre for Youth (which caters for schools and youth clubs in the area) and Byre Theatre Workshop (for interested young people) are run by the main company. From January to March the

theatre is taken over by touring companies. There is an open stage, an auditorium seating 145, and an air-conditioning system. Ramps into the building allow wheelchairs to be accommodated. Concessions are made for parties of 20 and over. There is a licensed bar and a coffee bar. Parking facilities available in surrounding streets.

St Andrews is 430 miles by road from London. Trains take 10 hours from King's Cross to Leuchars station, 5 miles away. Planes from Heathrow to Edinburgh (40 miles away) take 1 hour. Recommended hotels: The Star (St Andrews 3139); The Station & Windsor (St Andrews 2385); Cross Keys (St Andrews 3646).

Salisbury

PLAYHOUSE
Salisbury Playhouse, Fisherton Street, Salisbury, Wiltshire.
Box office: 0722 22104.

A 3-weekly repertory system operates in this Edwardian playhouse which was converted into a theatre in 1945. It is soon to be replaced by a new building. In recent years, the Playhouse has staged a number of British premieres, including a play by William Douglas Home and a Terence Brady-David Wood-John Gould revue. The Playhouse has no studio theatre, but studio-type productions are given on Monday evenings, and there is a touring company called Theatrescope, catering for both adult and young audiences. The theatre is closed from early June to mid-July each year. There is a proscenium stage and a seating capacity of 406. A bar and a buffet provide refreshments, and an adjacent car park accommodates 1,000 cars. Up to 4 wheelchairs can be fitted into the auditorium.

Salisbury is 84 miles by road from London. Trains take 1½ hours from Waterloo to Salisbury station, 3 minutes' walk away. Recommended hotels: The Red Lion (0722 22788); Clovelly (0722 22055); The Cathedral (0722 22993).

Scarborough

FLORAL HALL
Floral Hall, Peasholm Road, Scarborough, Yorkshire.
Box office: 0723 2185.

The Floral Hall, which is owned by Scarborough Corporation, is open only during the summer months, when a

Summer Show is presented. The proscenium stage faces a one-tier auditorium seating 1,620. There is a licensed bar and also a cafe.

LIBRARY
Library Theatre, Vernon Road, Scarborough, Yorkshire YO11 2NN.
Box office: 0723 4279.

Housed, as in Manchester, in the City's main Public Library building, this theatre was founded in the early 1960s by the late Stephen Joseph, who turned it into Britain's first theatre-in-the-round. Playwright Alan Ayckbourn is the current director, and four of his plays—How the Other Half Loves, Time and Time Again, The Story So Far ... and Absurd Person Singular—have had their first performances here. Other work presented in the past few years has included new plays by David Campton and Peter Blythe, as well as established modern plays and some classics; but the emphasis is on new work. The Library is open for a summer season only, from June to September each year, when 5 plays are presented in repertoire. During the rest of the year the auditorium is occasionally used as a concert hall. It has a seating capacity of 254 around the central acting area. The theatre is not licensed, but a coffee bar is open during the interval. A car park adjoins the building. Price concessions are offered to pensioners, students and parties of 8 or more people.

SPA
Spa Theatre, The Spa, Scarborough, Yorkshire.
Box office: 0723 65068.

Like the Floral Hall, the Spa is also open during the summer months only, for the presentation of a Summer Show. There is a proscenium stage and a 641-seat auditorium divided between stalls and circle. Refreshments provided by a licensed bar and a cafe.

Scarborough is 230 miles by road from London. Trains take 4½ hours from King's Cross to Scarborough station, 5 minutes away from the Library and 15 minutes away from the Floral Hall and the Spa. Recommended hotels: The Clifton (0723 64159); Gibson's (0723 60511); The Grand (0723 5371).

Sheffield

CRUCIBLE
The Crucible Theatre, 55 Norfolk Street, Sheffield S1 1DA.
Box office: 0742 79922.

Opened in November, 1971, this £1½ million building, designed from ideas conceived by Tyrone Guthrie, has been acclaimed as one of the finest thrust-stage theatres in Europe. A repertoire system of modern and classical work is presented by a semi-permanent company from October to April each year, with visits from touring companies, opera and ballet and other attractions for the rest of the year, except for a 6-week closed period in July and August. The single-rake auditorium seats 1,000 on 3 sides of the stage, plus boxes. It is air-conditioned. The studio theatre, which has its own permanent group, seats from 80 to 250 using moveable rostra and seats. The young people's company, called Theatre Vanguard, takes performances to local schools. The studio also houses visiting experimental companies. There is a licensed restaurant in the main theatre (0742 70621 for reservations) with a foyer bar open during pub hours, a cold-luncheon restaurant, a coffee shop and a studio coffee stall. For the disabled, there are ramps into the theatre for wheelchairs, 3 of which can be accommodated in the auditorium, reached by lift. Also special WC facilities. Price concessions offered to pensioners, students and children and to parties. A large car park is connected by a tunnel to the theatre, and there are several municipal car parks nearby as well as limited street parking.

Sheffield is 160 miles by road from London. Trains take 3 hours from St Pancras to Sheffield Midland station, 5 minutes away. Recommended hotels: Kenwood (0742 53347); Rutland (0742 65215); Falcon (0742 52280).

Stirling

MACROBERT CENTRE
MacRobert Centre, University of Stirling, Stirling, Scotland.
Box office: 0789 61081.

The MacRobert Centre opened in September, 1971, expressly designed to be the focal point of the University's central area; it is beautifully situated beside Airthrey Loch with views across the Ochil Hills. As well as the main theatre, the Centre has a studio theatre and an art gallery. The main auditorium is used for visits by the leading Scottish repertory companies, Prospect Theatre, Scottish Opera, ballet companies, and for the presentation of concerts and films, and productions by the University's own drama group. The auditorium, which seats 499 in a single tier fan-shaped raked auditorium, is traditional in concept with a permanent proscenium and forestage, although it has adjustable seating to allow for an orchestra pit and other alternatives. The studio theatre has its own small resident company, Theatremakers, who give regular performances here and lead University and other local young people in workshop sessions and special drama projects as well as performing in schools. This smaller auditorium is also host to visiting groups like Portable Theatre, Ken Campbell's Road Show and the Barrow Poets. It is octagonal in shape with seating on tiered cushioned rostra which can be arranged to give a variety of performing areas. Price concessions at the Centre operate for schoolchildren, students, pensioners, and for parties of 10 and over. Books of vouchers can be bought at a discount rate for regular theatregoers, and a transport subsidy scheme is also in operation. There is a restaurant in the University where before-performance food (high-class buffet or self-service) is available. Tables are bookable through the box office. A licensed bar is in the foyer, and is normally open until 11 pm. Two wheelchairs can be accommodated in either auditorium, with entry through a ramped foyer. There is also a paraplegic WC in the foyer. The Centre's own car park is 80 yards away. The Centre is closed for a few weeks in the summer, and occasionally in the New Year.

Stirling is 410 miles by road from London. Trains take 8 hours from Euston to Stirling station, 10 minutes' drive away. Flights from Heathrow and Gatwick to Glasgow airport (35 miles away) or to Edinburgh airport (40 miles away) take about 1 hour. Recommended hotels: The Royal, Bridge of Allan (078 683 2284); The Old Manor, Bridge of Allan (078 683 2169); The Royal in Stirling (0786 5137).

Stoke-on-Trent

VICTORIA
Victoria Theatre, Hartshill Road, Hartshill, Stoke-on-Trent ST4 6AE, Staffordshire.
Box office: 0782 615962.

The Victoria, since its opening in 1962, has been under the direction of Peter Cheeseman, who sees its function as an integral part of the community which it serves. His policy is principally the presentation of a permanent acting company in plays in repertoire, with the occasional straight run. In the past 5 years, over 30 new plays have been produced here, including 6 local musical documentaries (outstanding among them being The Knotty), 4 adaptations of novels by Arnold Bennett, who came from Stoke, and a large amount of work by their prolific former resident dramatist, Peter Terson. There is no studio theatre, but the Victoria's dependent activities in the area include extensive work in schools, talks and demonstrations to adult groups, and a travelling roadshow. The theatre is closed for 3 weeks each year from mid-June to early July. The building, which dates back to 1914, was converted into a theatre in 1962; it is the only permanent professional theatre-in-the-round in this country, and seats 389. Price concessions are offered to parties of 10 and over, and to pensioners and students. There is no licensed bar, but a coffee bar serves snacks, home-made cakes, soft drinks and confectionery. Parking space is available in a nearby parking-area, and also in adjacent side streets.

Stoke-on-Trent is 150 miles by road from London. Trains take 2 hours from Euston to Stoke-on-Trent station, 1½ miles away. Flights from Heathrow to Manchester Ringway airport (38 miles away) take 45 minutes. Recommended hotels: The Grand (0782 22361); North Stafford (0782 48501); The Borough Arms (0782 616117).

Sunderland

EMPIRE (touring date)
Empire Theatre, High Street, Sunderland, County Durham.
Box office: 0783 73274.

This early Edwardian theatre, seating 1,579, was given a major face-lift in 1961, and another in 1972. It is a touring-date theatre presenting entertainment ranging from opera, ballet, musicals and pantomime to straight drama. Price concessions of up to a third are offered to pensioners and children, as well as to party bookings. There is a restaurant (box office number for reservations) and a coffee bar as well as the usual theatre bars. Wheelchair facilities are available in the stalls only. A car park for 700 cars is behind the theatre.

Sunderland is 270 miles by road from London. Trains take 4½ hours from

King's Cross to Sunderland station, 3 minutes away. Flights from Heathrow to Newcastle airport (15 miles away) take about 50 minutes. Recommended hotels: Mowbray Park (0783 78221); The Roker (0783 71786); The Seaburn in neighbouring Whitburn (078 329 2041).

Swansea

GRAND
Grand Theatre, Singleton Street, Swansea SA1 3QJ, Glamorgan.
Box office: 0792 55141.

Built in 1897, the Grand is a perfect Victorian horseshoe-shaped theatre. Major renovation and modernisation in 1969 included the installation of central heating and extraction ventilation. The theatre's present policy consists of a 6-month summer repertory season of 2-week runs, followed by a 3-month pantomime season, and 3 months of touring dates. The repertory season comprises the production of a mixture of classics, modern established work and specially-commissioned local documentaries. The theatre is closed for a fortnight before Christmas each year. There is a proscenium stage and seating for 1,122 on 3 levels. There is a licensed bar at circle level. Generous price concessions are offered to school-children and students. Wheelchairs can be accommodated, and there is direct access from street level. No car park, but adequate space in adjacent streets. Swansea is on the edge of the famous Gower Peninsula, a coastline of outstanding natural beauty.

Swansea is 200 miles by road from London. Trains take 3 hours from Paddington to Swansea station, 10 minutes' walk away. Recommended hotels: The Dragon (0792 51074); The Dolphin (0792 50011); The Osborne, 5 miles away overlooking beach (0792 66274).

Swindon

WYVERN
Wyvern Theatre & Arts Centre, Civic Centre, Swindon, Wiltshire.
Box office: 0793 24481.

This 615-seat theatre in the new Arts Centre was opened in 1971. It presents a mixed programme of touring companies, concerts and films in the main auditorium, which is horseshoe shaped and on 2 levels. There is also a small 94-seat studio theatre, Studio One, with an adaptable stage where experimental drama, poetry sessions and other activities are held. Both theatres are closed during July and August. Price concessions are made to pensioners and students for matinee performances. There is a licensed bar and a snack bar, and ramp access to the boxes for wheelchairs. There is a multi-storey car park in Fleming Way, a short walk away along Islington Street.

Swindon is 79 miles by road from London. Trains take 1½ hours from Paddington to Swindon station, 10 minutes away. Recommended hotels: The Post House (0793 24601); The Goddard Arms (0793 27198); Blunsdon House (079 372 471).

Weston-super-Mare

PLAYHOUSE
The Playhouse, High Street, Weston-super-Mare, Somerset.
Box office: 0934 23521.

This Corporation-run theatre opened in 1969, and its policy is a mixed one of presenting touring companies, concerts, amateur productions, films, pantomime and a summer season of plays. There is a proscenium stage with an adaptable forestage/pit facing on to a 686-seat auditorium which is air-conditioned. There is a licensed bar. A public car park is 20 yards away.

Weston-super-Mare is 138 miles by road from London. Trains take 2½ hours from Paddington to Weston-super-Mare station, 10 minutes away. Recommended hotels: Grand Atlantic (0934 26543); Royal (0934 23601); Salisbury (0934 21321).

Windsor

THEATRE ROYAL
Theatre Royal, 32 Thames Street, Windsor, Berkshire.
Box office: 95 61107.

This attractive Edwardian theatre, under the direction for many years of John Counsell, underwent a major redecoration and renovation scheme in 1965. Its policy is the presentation of 3-weekly repertory, with 6 weeks of home-produced pantomime each Christmas. The Theatre Royal has presented the premieres of a number of light comedy successes and thrillers, including Who Killed Santa Claus and Suddenly at Home. Seating capacity is 644 divided between stalls, balcony stalls, circle and 4 boxes. Air-conditioning has been installed. There are 2 licensed bars, and a snack bar serves coffee and sandwiches. Wheelchairs have access to the stalls, bars and WCs which are all without steps. Price concessions are available for parties of 10 and over at certain performances. A public car park is only a minute's walk away.

Windsor is 30 miles by road from London. Trains take 50 minutes from Waterloo to Windsor Riverside station, or 40 minutes from Paddington to Windsor Central station, both 5 minutes away from the theatre. Heathrow Airport is itself only 20 minutes' drive from the theatre.

Worcester

SWAN

Swan Theatre, The Moors, Worcester.
Box office: 0905 27322.

The Swan was built in 1965, and the Worcester Repertory Company under its present director, John Hole, presents straight runs of between 10 days and 3 weeks. In the past few years it has had a number of premieres to its credit, most notably the children's plays The Owl and the Pussycat Went to See and The Plotters of Cabbage Patch Corner by David Wood and Sheila Ruskin. The Swan Young Theatre and the Society of Artists are two offshoots from the main Company, which in fact shares the theatre with the local resident amateur group, The Swan Theatre Company. The adaptable proscenium stage faces a 353-seat auditorium in one steeply-raked level. Air-conditioning is installed. Price concessions are offered to parties of 10 and over and to students and pensioners. A West Midlands subsidised travel voucher scheme operates here. There is no restaurant but a midday buffèt only, and a bar open during performance times. Wheelchairs can be accommodated in the auditorium, which is on ground level. A large free car park is adjacent to the theatre.

Worcester is 115 miles by road from London. Trains take 2½ hours from Paddington to Worcester Shrub Hill station, 15 minutes away. Recommended hotels: The Gifford (0905 27155); The Star (0905 24308); The Crown (0905 23938).

Worthing

CONNAUGHT

Connaught Theatre, Union Place, Worthing, Sussex.
Box office: 0903 35333.

This repertory company operates from a 1930s building which underwent a major renovation in 1973. The programme here concentrates on the lighter side of established modern work, interspersed with the occasional new play and the revival of a classic. The Connaught has a seating capacity of 1,040 divided between stalls, dress circle and 4 boxes, facing a proscenium stage. There is a 40-seat studio theatre attached for more avant-garde work, and the Connaught company also organises Theatre-in-Education tours to the surrounding area. Price concessions are made to pensioners for all Monday performances, and there is an inclusive ticket-coach-meal voucher for parties. A restaurant (0903 39770 ext. 3 for reservations) serves coffee, lunch, dinner and supper. There are 2 bars. For the disabled, 3 special seats are reserved in the auditorium. The theatre has no car park of its own, but there are several in the vicinity.

Worthing is 58 miles by road from London. Trains take 1 hour 20 minutes from Victoria to Worthing Central station, a few minutes away. Recommended hotels: The Egremont (0903 201541); The Beach (0903 34001).

Wythenshawe

FORUM

Forum Theatre, Wythenshawe Civic Centre, near Manchester.
Box office: 061 437 9663.

Built in 1971, the Forum is part of a £2 million integrated entertainment complex and is run in conjunction with the Library Theatre Company in Manchester, under the direction of David Scase. Two repertory companies alternate between both theatres, playing for 3 weeks in each. New plays to their credit in the past two years include John Hale's Lorna and Ted and Say Goodnight to your Grandma by Colin Welland. There is a proscenium stage, an air-conditioned auditorium and a seating capacity of 483. The theatre is closed during July and August. Price concessions are made to students and pensioners. There is a restaurant (061 437 9770 for reservations) open for lunch and dinner, a coffee bar open until 8.30 pm and a licensed bar operating pub hours. Wheelchairs can be accommodated in the auditorium. Parking space for 380 cars by the theatre.

Wythenshawe is 192 miles by road from London. Trains take 2 hours 40 minutes from Euston to Manchester Piccadilly station, 20 minutes away by road. The last train back to London from Manchester at night leaves at 12.25 am. Flights from Heathrow to Manchester Ringway airport (3 miles away) take 45 minutes. Recommended hotels: The Excelsior at the Airport (061 437 5811), Tatton Arms (061 998 4750); The Belfry (061 437 4321).

York

THEATRE ROYAL
Theatre Royal, St Leonard's Place, York YO1 2HD.
Box office: 0904 23568.

This 18th century theatre, given a £200,000 renovation in 1967, operates a repertoire system in the summer, and straight 2 to 3-week runs for the rest of the year. Under Richard Digby Day's direction, there is a resident company augmented by guest appearances, and the programme ranges from John Gielgud's new version of **The Cherry Orchard** to the best of the established contemporary drama via a number of new plays, including Henry Livings' **Grup** and Charles Dyer's **Mother Adam**. The Theatre Royal has a proscenium stage with an apron, and a seating capacity of 950; air-conditioning has been installed. At York Arts Centre (the De Grey Rooms next door) the Company presents the occasional late-night show and experimental studio work. For young people there is Theatre Activists, an association for theatregoers from 14 to 25, and a Young People's Theatre taking specially-mounted productions to schools. Price concessions operate for members of the Theatre Club at certain performances and for pensioners. There is a restaurant (telephone 0904 55099 for reservations) as well as a coffee and snack bar and 2 licensed bars. Parking for cars opposite the theatre and by the Minster nearby. Accommodation for 3 wheelchairs in the auditorium.

York is 200 miles by road from London Trains take 2½ to 3 hours from King's Cross to York station, 10 minutes away. Recommended hotels: The Viking (0904 59822); The Royal Station (0904 53681); Young's (0904 24229).

Theatre Companies

The following are theatre companies whose aim is principally to tour their productions around the towns and cities of this country, and for that reason have no permanent theatre of their own.

CAMBRIDGE THEATRE COMPANY

Formed in February, 1970, the Cambridge Theatre Company has its roots in the older-established Prospect Theatre Company, and is carrying on that group's traditions in Cambridge. Richard Cottrell, the Cambridge Company's Artistic Director, is also Associate Director of Prospect. Based in Cambridge, they present regular seasons at the Arts Theatre, and in their first 3 years have given 18 new productions there, all of which have then undertaken national tours. The work they present ranges from the classics to the premieres of new plays. A musical version of a Ben Travers farce, re-named **Popkiss**, transferred to the West End after its Cambridge run. The Company have no permanent group of actors and this flexibility has enabled them to cast at various times such artists as Derek Godfrey, Wendy Hiller, Ian McKellen, Virginia McKenna, Daniel Massey and Prunella Scales. They were responsible for presenting the newly-formed **Actors' Company** at the Edinburgh Festival in 1972, as well as on tour and at the Arts Theatre, where their repertoire included the first performance of Iris Murdoch's **The Three Arrows.**

CENTURY THEATRE

The aim of Century Theatre is to present good drama to communities without any facilities of their own. To this end, their unique mobile theatre—the brainchild of John Ridley and Wilfred Harrison—has for the past 20 years been giving performances of the classics and some new plays to audiences in conditions far better than are normally found in their own local hall. Apart from their annual summer season at Keswick, in the Lake District of Cumberland, which is presented in association with John Ridley's West Scotland Theatre Company, the Century stays on the road for its bread and butter. Densely-populated Lancashire is particularly short of theatres, and it is in this area, with excursions into Yorkshire, Cumberland and Westmorland, that Century's work is focused.

The "theatre-on-wheels," re-equipped and modernised 5 years ago with an Arts Council grant, consists of 4 trailers each 33 ft. long (the width of the auditorium) which are lined up on each site; long hinged panels forming the sides of these trailers fold upwards to provide a continuous aluminium roof, and other panels inside fold downwards forming a continuous sloping floor to the auditorium. The 225 tip-up seats are permanently fixed to the floor. The proscenium arch is the side of one trailer and behind it is a stage large enough for most productions. The lighting switchboard and sound controls are on raised bridges at either side of the stage. Dressing rooms are in the 4th trailer which also forms the back of the stage. In good conditions with an experienced team of 8 men, the whole job of setting up can be done in a day.

Local authorities and arts associations in whose districts the mobile theatre plays make donations towards the high running costs of touring.

PROSPECT THEATRE COMPANY

The Prospect Theatre Company exists to tour. It has no theatre of its own, and although since its formation in 1961 it has had 5 West End seasons to its credit, as well as visits to Australia, India, Pakistan, Ceylon and Europe, its primary purpose is to take a high standard of theatre to Scotland, Wales and the regions of England. It has now firmly established itself as a national touring company. Outstanding among its productions in recent years have been Ian McKellen's success in the title roles of Shakespeare's **Richard II** and Marlowe's **Edward II** presented together in repertoire, and also as Hamlet; Lila Kedrova and Patrick

Wymark in **The Cherry Orchard**; Timothy West in a production based on Boswell's **Life of Johnson**, and **King Lear**; and Richard Briers in **Richard III**. The acting company, although not a permanent one, tends to be composed of artists who have worked for Prospect before. The Company's annual appearance at the Assembly Hall as part of the Edinburgh International Festival has become a drama highlight of the Festival.

Toby Robertson has been Director of Prospect since 1964. Richard Cottrell, Director of the Cambridge Theatre Company (founded in association with Prospect and carrying on that Company's traditions in Cambridge, where Prospect was based in its early years) has been Associate Director since 1966. Both men have been responsible for directing the bulk of Prospect's productions.

69 THEATRE COMPANY

For the 4 years until 1972, the 69 Theatre Company made its home in the University Theatre, Ardwick, near Manchester. By 1974 they hope to be installed in a permanent home—literally a new theatre built within Manchester's historical Royal Exchange. Meanwhile the Company, left without a permanent base, is touring, and during the 1973 Manchester Festival from May 17 to June 2 played in a tent on the floor of the Royal Exchange.

The 69 Company grew out of the activities of the 59 Company formed in 1959 by Michael Elliott and Casper Wrede and launched with a highly-praised season in London at the Lyric, Hammersmith. The 69 Theatre Company, in addition to its two original directors, has Richard Pilbrow, Jack Good and Braham Murray as co-Artistic Directors. In the Company's 4 years in Manchester they have presented some 19 productions at the University Theatre and introduced to the North West such international artists as Vanessa Redgrave (in a dramatisation of George Eliot's **Daniel Deronda**), Tom Courtenay (in **Hamlet** and **Charley's Aunt**), Mia Farrow (in **Mary Rose**), Wendy Hiller (in Ibsen's **When We Dead Awaken**) and Juliet Mills (with Tom Courtenay in **She Stoops to Conquer**). Some of its more distinguished productions have transferred to London, among them **She Stoops to Conquer**, Trevor Peacock's musical **Erb**, Jack Good's rock **Othello** called **Catch My Soul**, **Charley's Aunt**, **Mary Rose** and Eric Thompson's production of **Journey's End**.

The new £400,000 building within the Royal Exchange Cotton Hall, mainly being financed by Manchester City Corporation and the Arts Council, will seat 700 plus space for restaurants, bars, exhibition areas, club rooms, dressing rooms, etc.

Ballet & Opera Companies

For those wishing to know more about the current programmes and activities of the principal ballet and opera companies, a list of their addresses is given here.

BALLET

Royal Ballet
Royal Opera House
Covent Garden
London WC2E 7QA
Tel. 01 240 1200

London Festival Ballet
48 Welbeck Street
London W1M 7HE
Tel. 01 486 3337

Ballet Rambert
Mercury Theatre Trust Ltd
94 Chiswick High Road
London W4 1SH
Tel. 01 995 4246

Scottish Theatre Ballet
18 Woodwise Terrace
Glasgow G3 7YL

Contemporary Dance Theatre
The Place
17 Duke's Road
London WC1H 9AB

Northern Dance Theatre
11 Zion Crescent
Hulme Walk
Manchester M15 5BY
Tel. 061 226 3309

Ballet for All
Royal Opera House
Covent Garden
London WC2E 7QA
Tel. 01 240 1200

OPERA

Royal Opera House
Covent Garden Ltd
Covent Garden
London WC2E 7QA
Tel. 01 240 1200

Sadler's Wells Opera
Coliseum Theatre
St Martin's Lane
London WC2N 4ES
Tel. 01 836 0111

Scottish Opera
39 Elmbank Crescent
Glasgow G2 4PT
Tel. 041 248 4567

Welsh National Opera
Welsh National Opera Company Ltd
John Street
Cardiff, CF1 4SP
Tel. 0222 40541/6

Glyndebourne Festival Opera
Glyndebourne
Lewes
Sussex
Tel. 321 0273

Index